TREATING
THE TREATMENT FAILURES

TREATING
THE TREATMENT FAILURES

The Challenge of Chronic Schizophrenia

WITHDRAWN

ARNOLD M. LUDWIG, M.D.

Professor and Chairman, Department of Psychiatry
University of Kentucky College of Medicine
Lexington, Kentucky

GRUNE & STRATTON *New York and London*

Grune & Stratton, Inc.
757 Third Avenue
New York, New York 10017

Library of Congress Catalog Card Number 75-155998
International Standard Book Number 0-8089-0707-7
Printed in the United States of America (PC-B)

This book is dedicated with affection and appreciation
to the staff of the Special Treatment Unit,
also known as "Building 2"

Contents

Acknowledgments

The conduct of these studies and, therefore, the writing of this book could not have taken place without the help and participation of many people. I owe a great debt to Leroy A. Ecklund, M.D., who not only was administratively responsible for the creation of the Special Treatment Unit, but who also continued throughout the years to give active moral support for our various treatment ventures.

Several colleagues must be singled out for special mention. Frank Farrelly, A.C.S.W., and, especially Arnold J. Marx, M.D., participated in most of the treatment studies and were coauthors for many of the prior published articles. In fact, several portions of this book have been adapted from these articles. I am also indebted to them for our many delightful and productive interchanges at coffee breaks and luncheons during which we covered a wide range of topics relevant to the treatment of mental patients. I am certain that many of their views have helped shape my own.

Barbara Lontz, our ward social worker, is another person to whom I am grateful, both professionally and personally. Professionally, she taught me a good deal about the aftercare treatment of these patients. Personally, her warmth, humor, and charm served the entire treatment staff as an antidote for the occasional lulls in morale and the numerous frustrations encountered while working in such a setting.

Philip A. Hill, our research analyst, made a substantial contribution to our various studies by keeping the evaluation machinery running smoothly and constantly harassing staff to fill out the endless streams of data forms. Acknowledgment must also be given to Mrs. Inda Henneger, my former secretary, for typing up the numerous revisions of this book and to Miss Lela Denman, my current administrative secretary, for the careful proofing and editing of the manuscript.

Although their list of names is too long to enumerate, the lion's share of the credit for the ideas contained in this book must go to the entire aide and nursing staff of the STU. It should go without saying that none of the treatment studies could have been conducted adequately without their full cooperation, support, and, most important, dedication to the welfare and rehabilitation of patients. Although occasionally discouraged, they never really accepted the "hopeless" prognosis of patients and were always enthusiastic to implement any new treatment program or approach that might prove of potential benefit. With patients hell bent on staying hospitalized and staff hell bent on getting them well, a clash of wills was bound to occur. In the final analysis, the continuing treatment struggle between staff and patients is what this book is all about.

Introduction

Before these studies began, I could not anticipate having to confront and resolve the many clinical and ethical dilemmas that arose. Nor, for that matter, could I fully predict the radical revision in my conceptualization of the nature of chronic schizophrenia and its consequent implications for treatment.

During the course of these studies, we were soon to tread on a number of controversial and sensitive clinical areas. I was forced not only to reject many conventional theories and textbook facts concerning chronic schizophrenia, but also to deal with such touchy ethical issues as the rights of patients, the manipulation and control of human behavior, the therapeutic efficacy of reward and punishment, the extent of patients' responsibility for their actions, and the obligations and prerogatives of treatment staff.

My personal solution to many of these issues evolved only after much soul-searching, thought, and discussion. Perhaps the very nature of institutional or involuntary treatment creates a situation of moral uneasiness, especially when the techniques employed cause patients some discomfort or deprivation. It is a great responsibility to play god with other people by defining what is best for them, often despite their protests and resistance, and to make decisions that may have far-reaching effects on their immediate and future lives. It is especially difficult to remain firmly convinced at all times of the rightness of one's decisions and procedures, based on a particular treatment philosophy, when this very philosophy runs counter to many traditional views.

Regardless of any personal moral qualms, the nature of the problem is such that some stance has to be taken, even though it be operational, about the appropriateness of certain treatment goals and procedures for these patients. The treatment of chronic schizophrenia cannot be postponed until learned men discover its etiological basis, debate what should be done, or indulge in leisurely harangues about ethics. For the current population of hospitalized chronic schizophrenics, new treatment procedures must be explored to dispel the aura of hopelessness surrounding these patients and to offer them some hope for eventual recovery. Because of the magnitude of the therapeutic problem, it would not be surprising should many of these innovative procedures prove clinically unconventional or ethically controversial.

Much of the material for this book has been gathered over a period of four years from treatment studies with chronic schizophrenics. Most of these studies have been conducted on a special treatment unit (STU) at Mendota State Hospital, Madison, Wisconsin. During this period of time, I spent three years as clinical chief of the STU and was primarily responsible for the design and conduct of the various treatment programs. The last year was spent in a somewhat more removed but nevertheless involved administrative position. Although many of my observations and speculations are directly related to these experiences, the scope of the book is meant to be much broader than a simple description of our therapeutic activities and results. I have taken the liberty of making many generalizations concerning the treatment of these patients since I have had ample opportunity to observe chronic schizophrenics on other wards and to make consultation visits to other mental hospitals throughout the country. From these varied experiences, as well as an extensive review of the relevant literature in the field, I have tried to cull out both what is known and what is not known about treating these patients.

Because so many of our treatment studies took place on the STU, some brief description of this facility seems necessary. The STU was a thirty-bed building capable of accommodating both male and female patients. From the outside, the white brick and wood building, with its sloping green-trimmcd, red-shingled roof, had a rural flavor, looking like a sprawling cottage. It was located in a partially wooded area relatively isolated from most other hospital treatment facilities and commanded a view of beautiful Lake Mendota. The inside of the building, however, stood in contrast to its external appearance.

Although adequate, the lighting was dim, and living space was rather cramped, and the facilities for offices, staff conferences, and general ward meetings were poor. These inconveniences, however, did not influence the conduct of the experimental treatment programs or dampen the morale and enthusiam of the staff.

Not only did patients eat, sleep, and live in this building, but all therapeutic activities took place there as well. Aside from a six-bed dormitory area, there were twelve additional rooms, each capable of accommodating two patients. The large dayroom, located in the center of the building, was used for general ward meetings as well as for more informal patient recreational activities. There was also a small television room with a pool table downstairs and a sewing room upstairs. A long corridor extended from the dormitory and nursing station at one end of the dining room and kitchen at the other end. Patients' rooms were situated on both sides of this corridor.

The treatment mission of the STU was unique compared to the conduct of therapeutic programs in other treatment settings. This was largely because of the changing, evolutionary nature of our studies. Well aware that neither we nor anyone else knew all the answers to the treatment of chronic schizophrenia, we decided to evaluate a number of different psychosocial treatment possibilities rather than commit ourselves to one stable, ongoing program, no matter how promising it might seem. Through this systematic exploration of different psychosocial treatment approaches we hoped to accumulate valuable information relevant to what presently could be done, what could not be done, and what needed to be done for these patients. The experimental treatment programs, then, were conducted on a phase basis, with specific time periods (about four to five months) allotted to the conduct and evaluation of each successive program.

The interim periods (about two to three months) between these treatment studies phases were used to assess impromptu, informal procedures with individual patients. Because no patients could be discharged during a formal treatment program, these interim periods also served as a time for discharging all suitable patients and integrating newly referred patients onto the ward.

Another aspect of the treatment mission of the STU should be mentioned. The STU was originally established for the express purpose of providing a program-oriented rather than individual-oriented approach to treatment, mainly because this would prove most practical and economically feasible in a state hospital setting where the number of patients requiring treatment was large, and financial support for research was scarce. The commitment to a program approach, however, was not without some potential drawbacks. It might fail to meet the individual needs of certain patients. Also, the therapeutic levers used would have to represent the lowest common denominators among patients because it would not be feasible to use idiosyncratic levers specific for only one or several patients. Therefore, the program emphasis on standardized procedures and treatment levers, although designed to reach the general treatment population, might not prove maximally effective for any given patient. Aware of these disadvantages, we tried to compensate for them somewhat during the informal interim periods and through some modifications in the later formal treatment programs themselves.

Rather than confine ourselves to the superficial study of a large group of patients or the intensive study of a small number of patients, we felt that more could be gained by striking a compromise between these extremes. The experimental programs were structured to allow both scrupulous process observations of all patients on a day-to-day basis and the collection and evaluation of data pertaining to treatment outcome. Although the advantages of such an approach were apparent, they were, however, offset by two major disadvantages: (1) The smaller the group of patients studied, the larger and more dramatic the treatment outcome differences would have to be to prove statistically significant. (2) When more than a few patients were studied at any one time by a limited number of staff, many crucial observations were bound to be overlooked or missed.

In order to gain the most clinical mileage from our studies, it seemed essential that we not only concern ourselves with the hard research data but also try to record unanticipated happenings and pertinent, naturalistic clinical observations. Research findings would provide the skeleton, whereas astute clinical observation and speculation would provide the flesh and contribute to the final form this body of knowledge would take. Therefore, whenever possible, our studies attempted to integrate both these important dimensions; we believed that together they would portray a much more accurate picture of our findings than either alone.

Initially, it must be recognized that the chronic schizophrenics referred for special treatment from other wards within the hospital could not be regarded as typical of those backward patients inhabiting the usual state hospitals where, I suspect, the introduction of any new intensive treatment program might meet with impressive results. Mendota State Hospital could not fit the popular stereotype of a large, overcrowded, deteriorated, inadequately staffed mental hospital. Its resident patient population was relatively small (ca. 700), its buildings were tastefully designed, its grounds were lovely, and it was rich both in the quantity and quality of professional staff. To a large extent, the high caliber of its staff could be attributed to its attractive pay scale, its location within Madison, and its close training affiliation with the Department of Psychiatry of the University of Wisconsin Medical School. It was unlikely, therefore, that patients suffered either from a lack of therapeutic attention or the professional incompetence of staff. In fact, during their lengthy hospitaliza-tions, all these patients had been subjected to almost every known popular therapy. Numerous tranquilizing and sedative drugs, electroconvulsive treatments, group and individual psychotherapy, therapeutic community programs, as well as occupational and recreational therapy were prescribed for them on a trial-and-error basis but with little or transient success. Rather than invoke the currently fashionable whipping boys of "therapeutic neglect" or "institutionalism" to account for the chronic nature of their illness, it would be much fairer and presumably more accurate simply to claim that the referred patients represented the hard-core chronic schizophrenics who did not respond well to the commonly used procedures of modern psychiatry.

Table I-1 contains certain general demographic and clinical characteristics of the seventy-four patients who participated in the various treatment studies. All these patients, twenty-one to fifty years of age, had been hospitalized continuosly for at least one year, the range being from one to twenty years. The subdiagnoses (i.e., paranoid, hebephrenic, undifferentiated, etc.) of these patients are not indicated since they are regarded as unreliable. An analysis of patient charts reveals that many of these subdiagnoses change over the years and seem more influenced by the diagnostic styles of the ward psychiatrists than by valid clinical characteristics.

Of these patients, more than 60 percent were discharged from the hospital with a certain proportion of these followed up for longer than a three-year period. It was largely from our experiences with these discharged patients that our special predischarge and aftercare programs were to evolve.

Table I-1. DEMOGRAPHIC CHARACTERISTICS OF PATIENT POPULATION

		Age	No. Hospital Admissions	Total Years Hospitalized	Grade Level at School
Males (40)	$\bar{x}$	34.7	4.1	7.3	11.0
	s.d.	7.0	2.6	5.0	3.0
Females (34)	$\bar{x}$	35.9	3.5	5.5	11.6
	s.d.	7.9	3.0	4.4	2.1
Total (74)	$\bar{x}$	35.2	3.8	6.4	11.3
	s.d.	7.6	2.8	4.9	2.5

Key: $\bar{x}$ = mean; s.d. = standard deviation

It is not my intent to compare the results obtained from our various treatment programs with those obtained by other investigators or clinicians. Nor, for that matter, do I plan to present any detailed descriptions of the methodologies and statistical procedures employed or the actual quantitative data and results obtained. Extensive descriptions of the findings of most of our studies have been published elsewhere and repetition of them seems unnecessary. Rather, I propose to take a broader perspective than the reporting of individual studies. I envision this book as an attempt to pull together and make sense of the myriad of clinical observations, experiences, and results accumulated over time and related to my involvement in a variety of treatment programs for chronic schizophrenics. These programs have been both formal and informal in nature, as well as group- or individually oriented. I am not so much interested in advocating a specific type of treatment program as in indicating what generalizations or treatment principles may be derived from our different studies and those of others. In a sense, the programs that failed to benefit patients proved fortunate. It is often possible to learn more from failure than from success because failure challenges all the clinician's cherished hypotheses and forces him to take a hard look at why things go wrong whereas success reinforces the clinician's notions and provides no incentive for critical appraisal. If an overview of treatment is to have any clinical validity, it must not only isolate and describe the elements responsible for the successful outcome of treatment programs but must also account for the shortcomings and limitations of these programs. Only in this manner can therapeutic advances occur.

I must also point out that this book has been written primarily for clinicians charged with the care and treatment of these patients. Because they are obliged to act, to do something in the present, and cannot put these patients "on ice" indefinitely until researchers come up with definitive answers to the etiology and therapy of chronic schizophrenia, clinicians require some practical guidelines and principles, at least as an operational basis, for therapeutic action. For this reason, I have emphasized common denominators and generalities whenever possible rather than dwelling on the countless qualifications and exceptions which could be given for almost any statement made in this field. The main orientation of this book is practical, here and now, and action oriented.

TREATING
THE TREATMENT FAILURES

part one

A Philosophy of Treatment

chapter 1

Some Basic Clinical Assumptions and Speculations

The stereotyped image of the hospitalized, chronic schizophrenic is that of an older person with head bowed, vacuous expression, stooped shoulders, shuffling gait, and outfitted in loose, drab, institutional garments. He is docile, compliant, and lacks a sense of spontaneity, initiative, and animation. He socializes poorly, is apathetic to his surroundings, and displays a resigned acceptance to a monotonous, sessile existence characterized by a meaningless present, a dead past, and bleak future. In short, he appears to be a person utterly alone, devoid of hope, and abandoned by spirit.

There is some merit to this stereotype, but, as with any generalization, it is greatly oversimplified. Missing from this stereotype are patients who are extremely withdrawn and regressed (e.g., those who exhibit urinary incontinence, smear or eat feces, refuse to eat, etc.) and those who remain agitated and troublesome (e.g., those who exhibit assaultive or self-destructive behavior, sexual acting out, bizarre and florid symptomatology, etc.) throughout the entire course of their hospitalization, thereby representing major management

3

problems for institutional staff. Between these extremes can be found all varieties of patient psychopathology which not only vary in kind and degree but also show different patterns of stability and fluctuation.

In an effort to bring order to this menagerie of psychopathology, various classifications and categories have been proposed. Miller (1961), for example, describes five main clinical patterns found within chronic schizophrenia: (1) paranoid—constantly suspicious and at war with the environment; (2) depressive—diminished activity level with an inadequate environmental response; (3) catatonic—profound psychological and physical withdrawal with intermittent bursts of aggressivity; (4) psychopathic—constant manipulation of the external environment to obtain self-gratification; and (5) passive-neurotic—compliant, infantilizing behavior in accord with institutional pressures. This classification differs considerably from that proposed by the American Psychiatric Association (1968), in which both acute and chronic schizophrenics may be subtyped as simple, hebephrenic, catatonic, paranoid, schizo-affective, and undifferentiated.

More colorful than the above is the classification proposed by Kantor and Gelineau (1969) in which three types of chronic schizophrenics are described— the stormy rebel, the quiet conformist, and the autistic recluse. The stormy rebel is one whose behavior is characterized by constant or frequent displays of anger, complaints, insults, and destructive activity. The quiet conformist, who may be likened to the "key worker," voluntarily submits to all ward expectations, but only to the extent that he is permitted to avoid any human relations regarded as threatening. The autistic recluse, like the stormy rebel, is deviant even from the norms of his deviant ward environment. Although he occasionally responds to social stimulation, he mostly displays no response whatever or actively repulses any attempt to draw him into social participation on the ward.

Aside from these types of clinical classifications, several others have been proposed and found useful for research purposes. One of the more popular of these classifications attempts to differentiate patients on the basis of prognosis, those with poor treatment outcomes labeled "nuclear" or "process" and those with better outcomes "reactive." Generally, process schizophrenics are presumed to show gradual onset of illness, a schizoid premorbid adjustment, and a lack of florid symptomatology at the time of the psychotic breakdown. These patients also tend to show Bleuler's fundamental symptoms. In contrast, the reactive schizophrenics show a rapid onset of illness, may have a relatively good premorbid adjustment, and show confusion and florid, psychotic psychopathology (accessory symptoms) at the time of their mental breakdown. The characteristics associated with process schizophrenia are comparable to those of *classical schizophrenia* and roughly similar to what is now referred to as *chronic schizophrenia*. Reactive or acute features, on the other hand, have been considered by some investigators to be more characteristic of acute confusional states or schizophrenic-like illness than of real schizophrenia.

Another major distinction among patient types is that represented by Venables and O'Connor (1959), who have devised a scale that differentiates patients along the two relatively independent dimensions of paranoid-nonparanoid and active-withdrawn. Still other approaches to classification have been based on empirical, factor analytic techniques. Katz (1965), for example, employing this methodology, describes six main types of schizophrenics: (1) the agitated, belligerent, suspicious, (2) the withdrawn, periodically agitated, (3) the acutely panicked, (4) the withdrawn, helpless, suspicious, (5) the agitated, helpless, and (6) the agitated, expansive, bizarre, suspicious types.

It is not my intention to give a critique of the relative strengths and weaknesses of these or other classificatory systems. Nor, for that matter, do I wish to deal with the objection voiced by many clinicians that the diagnosis of chronic schizophrenia represents a wastebasket term much too gross and inclusive to be of any scientific value. Instead, for present purposes, it is sufficient to recognize that the term *chronic schizophrenia* is a general one and embodies a variety of patient subtypes who display many forms of psychopathology to varying degrees.

Although there can be no question about the wide range of symptoms subsumed under the diagnosis of chronic schizophrenia, it would be clinically naïve not to be even more impressed by the many similarities and common features, both attitudinal and behavioral, shared by all these patients, regardless of diagnostic subtype. In fact, it is the very existence of these common features that, I believe, makes this general diagnosis convenient, practical, and even clinically valid. For example, when these common features are specified (as I shall attempt to do in this and subsequent chapters), it not only becomes possible to formulate assumptions about the nature of this disorder but also to develop and conduct treatment programs based on these assumptions. Moreover, after these assumptions are adequately evaluated and either substantiated or refuted, it may then become feasible to advance broad treatment principles concerning the care, treatment, and rehabilitation of these patients.

For both theoretical and practical purposes, therefore, I shall employ the term *chronic schizophrenia* throughout this text to refer to all patients who share certain general, common clinical characteristics. These characteristics are twofold: (1) the presence of overt schizophrenic symptomatology, such as loose associations, flattened or inappropriate affect, and autism, at least sometime preceding and/or during hospitalization; (2) the element of chronicity, i.e., the necessity for protracted and/or multiple hospitalizations because of this symptomatology or because of certain peculiar socially maladaptive values and behaviors developed secondary to hospitalization. It is the admixture of this "core of craziness" with this peculiar institutional value system that distinguishes the chronic schizophrenic from the ambulatory schizophrenic and the chronic hospitalized patient. The ambulatory schizophrenic displays psychotic symptomatology but tends to remain outside the hospital both because of his strong desire to do so and because his psychopathology tends to be relatively consonant with general social values and/or is not sufficiently socially abrasive as to cause confinement to a mental institution. In contrast, the chronic hospitalized patient, who may harbor a variety of diagnoses (e.g., personality disorder, sociopathic personality, alcoholism), has developed an institutional value system but has never demonstrated episodes of schizophrenic symptomatology.

The Determinants of Chronicity

With most medical illnesses, conceptions of etiology tend to determine the specific types of treatment administered. This situation also holds for chronic schizophrenia. For example, physicians viewing this disorder as resulting from disturbances in brain function are apt to use somatic procedures to treat it, whereas those who explain it as an end product of a certain constellation of familial forces maintain that the patient must be treated within the context of family therapy. Although there have been countless etiologic theories advanced to account for the initial onset and recurrence of schizophrenia, our present concern is less with how these patients become sick in the first place than with why some of them continue to remain so and thereby require extensive hospitalization. We are less interested in what causes schizophrenia than in what causes chronicity among schizophrenics. At present, because of our scientific ignorance about the etiology of schizophrenia, we are not in a position to prevent its occurrence. However, it is my contention that we do possess sufficient knowledge about many of the factors that sustain this disorder to permit substantial modification of its otherwise malignant course. For this reason, we shall confine discussion to conceptualizations more specifically relevant to elucidating the factors involved in pertetuating chronicity, regardless of the nature of the basic disturbance.

With some theoretical outlooks, the influence responsible for causing the more chronic, malignant forms of schizophrenia are believed to be the same as those causing the initial or more acute manifestation of this disorder, the only difference being that with the remitting forms there is an abatement of these influences. With other theoretical outlooks, the factors fostering chronicity are regarded as distinct from those responsible for the basic schizophrenic process. Inasmuch as it would prove unwieldy to consider each of these theories separately, we may simplify matters by assigning them to three general categories, namely, theories that account for this disorder on the basis of (1) underlying cerebral, organic disturbances, (2) insitutional influences, and (3) willful actions on the part of the patient. Each of these categories reflects a different attitude toward the patient's responsibility for his plight. These respective attitudes can be depicted as follows: (1) "The patient can't help himself since he is sick." (2) "The patient can't help himself since others have done it to him." and (3) "The patient can help himself."

There is another category of theories pertaining to the influence of early life experiences on the development and perpetuation of schizophrenia. Included among these theories are the dynamic ones which focus on intrapsychic conflicts (e.g., overwhelming oral needs, murderous impulses, denial of homosexuality), and the communication ones, which stress faulty patterns of communication between parents and child (e.g., double bind, pseudomutuality, schizophrenogenic mother, family scapegoating). Because these theories pertain primarily to past influences that can neither be observed in operation nor undone, I regard them as possessing little operational, clinical value and, therefore, have chosen not to deal with them separately, especially because their implications for patient responsibility overlap with those associated with the other major categories of theories.

A brief review of each of these divergent conceptualizations now seems in order if for no other reason than to fix our bearings and to determine whether a reconciliation among them is possible and in accord with the clinical facts. Should these seemingly discrepant conceptualizations mesh, a more clinically salient picture of this disorder may emerge. This, in turn, may generate some hypotheses about the necessary ingredients for effective therapy.

A Malignant Process

One of the oldest and still widely held views of chronic schizophrenia is that it represents an organic mental disorder characterized by progressive, irreversible intellectual and emotional deterioration. In earlier psychiatric parlance, this disorder is referred to as *dementia praecox*—an insidious, dementing process that tends to afflict young adults. Implicit in these views is the notion that the psychopathology shown by patients must be regarded more as manifestations of the basic underlying disease process or toxic brain disturbance than of either motivational or external situational factors.

Such a view has spurred countless research ventures aimed at discovering the "twisted molecule," toxin, or "X factor" responsible for producing the aberrations in thought, emotion, and behavior evinced by these patients. During more recent times, abnormal metabolites, metabolic or hormonal imbalances, vitamin deficiencies, neurophysiological dysfunctions, genetic factors, and a host of other possibilities have all been implicated as causes for this disorder. That none of these speculations or investigations has yet borne fruit does not invalidate the basic etiologic assumption underlying these efforts.

It is not surprising to find that adherents of the X factor hypothesis of schizophrenia are apt to view these patients as afflicted with a "disease" over which they have little or no control. This view basically represents the medical model of illness whereby noxious influences or agents, either of an internal or external nature, produce a disruption of biological and/or neurophysiological homeostasis. This disruption then leads to certain characteristic symptom or behavior patterns that presumably will vanish only when homeostasis is restored. With this view, there is the strong implication that the patient cannot be regarded as responsible for the display of deviant behavior. Just as a patient suffering from pneumonia or tuberculosis cannot be held accountable for his symptoms, this is likewise assumed to be the case for the schizophrenic. He thinks, feels, and behaves as he does only becasue of his toxic condition. Can a person be blamed for his thoughts while he dreams, his behavior while undergoing a psychomotor seizure, his emotions while under the influence of powerful psychotoxic chemicals, such as LSD, or during delerium tremens? With all these conditions, as with schizophrenia, the individual supposedly behaves as he does only because he must.

In regard to therapy, this etiological view further implies that the ultimate cure for schizophrenia and its more malignant chronic forms will only come about through discovering the identity of the underlying metabolic culprits and then finding ways to render them impotent. Until this amibitious goal can be realized, somatic procedures, such as tranquilizer medication and electroconvulsive or insulin coma therapy, represent the major but inefficient means of "restoring normal brain functioning." In addition, adequate nutrition, rest periods, and activity programs are advocated for their nonspecific salubrious effects. The necessity for simultaneously exposing their patients to an active psychotherapeutic and rehabilitation program is also consistent with this view.

The Institution or Society as the Culprit

Another conceptualization of the nature of chronic schizophrenia currently popular among professionals is the view that the institution is largely responsible for producing the clinical characteristics associated with chronicity. The proponents of this conceptualization lay great emphasis on certain features common to all "total institutions," such as prisons, convents, military schools, POW camps, and mental hospitals. According to Erving Goffman (1961), who has given a brilliant exposition of this viewpoint, institutional inmates are exposed to countless mortifying pressures which supposedly shape their subsequent attitudes and behaviors. Regimentation in dress and conduct, forced scheduled activities, especially in the company of other patients, the abdication of unnecessary possessions, prohibitions against individualistic means of emotional expression and gratification, confinement to a limited physical space (i.e., dayroom, ward, grounds), the invasion of psychological and bodily privacy (i.e., forced mental and physical examinations), privilege and punishment systems, rigid ward regulations and procedures, the deemphasis on autonomous decision-making in favor of the collective scheduling of daily activities, and a host of other degrading practices all contribute to the eventual deterioration in the personal habits, morale, and morals of the inmates.

This thesis, as applied to chronic patients, has had much amplification in the writing of others. Russell Barton (1966), for example, believes that mental hospitals bear the blame for producing the condition known as *institutional neurosis* through permitting loss of contact with the outside world, including friends, family, and personal possessions; enforced idleness and unnecessary use of drugs; a sterile, drab ward atmosphere; and a pervasive pessimism concerning the patient's prospects for rehabilitation. Were it not for these dehumanizing practices (Vail, 1966), chronic patients supposedly would not behave as they do. Rather than representing a necessary manifestation of the basic disturbance that brought the patient to the hospital, this artifactual constellation of chronic behaviors may be regarded, at least by Barton, as a type of mental bedsore.

Further dimensions to this view are offered by John K. Wing (1962) who postulates that institutionalism is caused by the interaction of three types of variables: (1) social pressures within the institution, including those associated with hospital routines and special treatment practices; (2) the susceptibility to these pressures that an individual possesses when he is admitted; and (3) the length of time the individual is exposed to these influences. Greunberg and Zusman (1964), who likewise regard chronicity as the result of an interaction between the susceptible person and a particular kind of environment, list successive states in the genesis of this syndrome. In brief, these progressive stages include the patient's susceptibility, owing to a deficiency in self-concept and a resulting dependence on current stimuli regarding appropriate behavior; the social labeling of the person as incompetent, crazy, or dangerous; the patient's induction into and subsequent learning of the sick role; an atrophy of work habits and social skills while hospitalized; and a final identification with the chronically sick patient community.

Regarding the potential molding and shaping influence of an institution on expressed psychopathology, Zarlock (1966) performed an interesting study in which he exposed a group of thirty schizophrenics to four different environmental conditions, namely, recreational, occupational, social, and medical. An attempt was made to have the trappings for all these conditions as authentic as possible. For example, in the medical setting the attendant wore a white jacket, the nurse, a uniform, and the psychologist, a long white coat. From observations made on these patients, there was a significantly greater number of both pathological verbal responses (i.e., references to their illness, symptoms, etc.) and bizarre behavior in the medical setting compared to any of the other three settings. The author concluded that schizophrenic patients showed an adaptability to different environmental conditions and expressed role behavior appropriate to a particular environment, thereby indicating that language and role pathology might to some extent represent artifacts of a social milieu.

Although the institution has borne the major brunt of blame, several authors extend culpability to other agencies, such as society or the very family of the patient, for working in league with the mental hospital to keep the patient within its confines. Scheff (1966) even goes so far as to claim that society makes the individual schizophrenic and that social labeling of the patient as "crazy" combined with institutional influences consolidate the process. Others hold that society's intolerance of deviant behavior and unwillingness to accept eccentricity is largely responsible for maintaining patients within an institution either through direct legal commitment proceedings or the lack of rehabilitative facilities or job opportunities within the community. The institution, therefore, becomes an agent of society rather than of the individuals confined to its care.

On another tack, there appears to be some evidence that whatever influence the patient's family has had in producing the original illness may be extended toward sustaining it within the institution. Marx and Lontz (n.d.) and Marx and I (1969), in a series of clinical studies, have accumulated considerable anecdotal evidence to indicate that the families of chronic schizophrenics have not only resigned themselves to the life-long institutionalization of their relatives but often actually resist any efforts to rehabilitate these patients. Metaphorically, the open wound caused by the initial hospitalization of the family member has now healed and families become loathe to reopen the wound either through involving themselves in discharge planning or lending a helping hand to the patient once he is discharged. There seems to be some justification for this stance of families for they are reluctant to reexperience the same aggravations and emotional turmoil as during the patient's first or numerous hospital admissions. Despite their protestations of interest in the rehabilitation of their patient kin, these families clearly convey the message of rejection to their institutionalized · relative and provide him with little incentive to change his status. In addition to this message, the family may transmit numerous others, all of which are exquisitely designed to maintain the patient within the hospital or at least to make him fearful of leaving.

In general, then, all these conceptualizations share two implications in common: (1) The patient is regarded as a relatively ineffectual person who cannot withstand the debilitating pressures of institutional life or control the type of adaptation he makes to it. As a result, he soon relinquishes any vestiges of individuality and assumes the role defined for him. (2) The hospital is regarded as the principal determinant of the patient's behavior, his subsequent status, the nature of his psychopathology, or, at best, the deterioration of his personal habits.

With the institution or mental hospital indicted as the chief *agent provocateur* of the patient's chronicity, certain treatment implications must necessarily follow. Theoretically, if the noxious or pernicious policies and philosophies of the mental hospital can be reduced or eliminated and supplanted by healthy ones, then patients should stand a much better chance for recovery and rehabilitation. Moreover, where society is likewise held at fault, the public must be educated to show a greater tolerance and acceptance of the mentally ill.

Games and Tactics

Another view of the nature of chronic schizophrenia deserves mention. Whereas the first conceptualization lays greater emphasis on the deficit and disabling aspects of this disorder and the second incriminates the institution, this particular view denies the deficit and stresses the purposive role of the patient himself in contributing to his own continued hospitalization. Institutional influences may still be considerable, but they are regarded as far less important than the tactics of the patients, which the latter willfully employ to gain certain ends.

One of the major assumptions of this viewpoint is that patients remain hospitalized for lengthy periods of time because, at some level of consciousness, they choose to do so. Factors that may contribute to this choice are exaggerated dependency needs, escape from external demands and responsibilities, or, most simply, a decision that hospital life is much better than extrahospital life. This choice need not be a conscious one, but may be reflected continually in the negative attitudes and responses of patients toward efforts to treat and rehabilitate them. They behave as they do not because they are crazy or are forced to conform to institutional expectations but rather because their behavior pays off for them in a number of ways, one of which is the guarantee of remaining hospitalized and thereby avoiding the stresses associated with social responsibility and productivity.

In earlier publications, I and Frank Farrelly (1966, 1967) presented numerous clinical examples of attitudes and manipulative tactics of chronic schizophrenics that seem countertherapeutic and specifically directed toward the goal of staying hospitalized. These attitudes and tactics, unwittingly reinforced by complementary ones on the part of the hospital staff, tend to create a vicious circle, the end product of which is the perpetuation of chronicity. Inasmuch as these particular attitudes and behaviors are directly relevant to the treatment of these patients, they will be elaborated on more fully in the following chapters.

To some extent, these views are portrayed almost in caricature by Jay Haley (1965). In a delightful article, "The Art of Being Schizophrenic," he argues that the hospitalized schizophrenic uses his craziness to control both people and situations. Within the hospital, his manipulations with staff may prove even more effective than those with family. The patient, in the process, comes to derive much pleasure in his power and ability to frustrate or anger others or get them to respond in some predictable way. Because the patient can get his needs so readily met within the hospital, there is little incentive for him to leave.

The notion that patients may play an important role in determining their destinies is not without some experimental confirmation, albeit inconclusive. Gordon and Groth (1961), in a questionnaire study with stayer and goer schizophrenic patients, showed clear-cut differences in patients' attitudes concerning the attractiveness of life outside the hospital. Stayers regarded the outside world as much less desirable than did goers. In another experiment, Braginsky, Gross, and Ring (1966) found support for the hypothesis that "staying or leaving is directly related to patient motives and manipulative strategies rather than being solely a product of hospital decision-making processes." Essentially, these investigators presented the same specially constructed questionnaire to two groups of old-timer and short-timer patients. These groups were then informed that answering the questions one way indicated either a healthy response or a sick response (with the associated implication of continued hospitalization). The results of this study, in brief, demonstrated that old-timer patients had a greater need to present themselves as mentally ill, thereby requiring hospitalization, than did short-timers. Employing Goffman's concept of "impression management" (i.e., the ability of a person to control the impressions others form of him), the authors conclude that "wishing to remain in the hospital . . . is not necessarily an expression of helplessness, but rather one of a different set of values and goals."

Operating on a similar premise that "a very substantial amount of psychopathological behavior is maintained and elicited in accordance with the characteristics of the person's current social situation in relation to his goal of creating a sick, incompetent impression on others," Fontana and co-workers (n.d.) have engaged in a series of neat experiments to support this premise. By separating patients into healthy presenters and sick presenters on the basis of certain questionnaire criteria, they were able to demonstrate significant differences between groups not only in their attitudes toward their illness but also in task performance as well. These shifts in attitudes and performances were dependent on whether patients had a need to present themselves in either a good or bad light in accord with the set of instructions given by the experimenters.

The treatment implications of these various studies, as well as clinical observations of the purposive nature of much of chronic schizophrenic behavior, seem relatively clear. If the patient can be regarded as the prime mover in his own long-term hospitalization, then treatment efforts must be directed toward attacking his need to do so and undermining the effectiveness of his methods. Rather than being a helpless, impotent victim of oppressive or benign institutional influences, the patient may be viewed instead as both responsible and accountable for his actions.

A Reconciliation of Viewpoints

Where conceptualizations of chronic schizophrenic behavior are so divergent as to regard it either as a symptomatic expression of an underlying disease process, an artifactual adaptation to institutional influences, or goal-directed, willful activity, it seems reasonable to presume that certain qualities about the very behaviors of patients can account for this disparity of view. It is my thesis that these three different conceptualizations are more complementary than mutually contradictory, each defining a different aspect of the nature of chronic schizophrenia. To view chronic schizophrenia solely through the lens of one theoretical framework presents a far too biased and distorted image. Only through an integration of viewpoints can we account for the diversity of clinical observations and interpretations made about the behavior of these patients. However, as the basis for this integration, certain assumptions about patient behavior must be made.

An Alteration in Consciousness

The first assumption is that the active schizophrenic condition is marked by the presence of an altered state of consciousness which may vary both in depth and frequency of appearance among patients or in the same patient over time. Presumably, this altered state of consciousness represents a subtle cerebral toxic condition caused by some abnormality in cerebral metabolism or neuronal synaptic transmission. Some general characteristics of this altered state of consciousness are alterations in thinking in which more archaic modes of thought predominate—impaired reality testing to various degrees, changes in emotional expression either in terms of greater lability, inappropriateness or flattening, body image change, perceptual distortions, and greater preoccupation than usual with internal thoughts and perceptions. As elaborated on elsewhere (Ludwig, 1966a), these characteristics also represent common denominators of alterations in consciousness produced by a variety of other means, such as psychedelic drugs, dreaming, sensory deprivation, hypnosis, and even mystical states.

I cannot regard this particular assumption of the presence of an altered state of consciousness as too unreasonable in that, as we shall see, it parsimoniously accounts for much of the subjective experiences, communications, and cognitive functioning of patients. Whether the specific cause of this alteration in consciousness results from an underlying organic disturbance makes little difference for a phenomenological understanding of the clinical manifestations of this alteration. Nor, for that matter, is the present concern with whether the altered state of consciousness originally arises in response to psychological or physical stresses or through no apparent precipitating cause. What is pertinent is the simple recognition that, because of some unknown and at present unspecifiable brain dysfunction the patient comes to experience and perceive reality differently than he ordinarily would if this dysfunction did not exist.

Once we admit to the concept of a subtle cerebral dysfunction producing an alteration in consciousness, we are further bound to the notion that this alteration may vary in depth or level of awareness along a continuum of consciousness. This quantitative variation in depth can be observed in almost any altered state of consciousness and affects the resultant experience. Drowsiness may pass into deep sleep; elation may give way to to ecstasy; mild depression may lead to stuporous depression; hypnosis may produce either a light or profound somnambulistic trance; and various drugs may alter consciousness in direct proportion to the dosage given. Likewise, for the chronic schizophrenic, the depth in alteration of consciousness may vary from no apparent disturbance to mild or even severe deviations from normal, waking consciousness.

The conceptualization of this depth continuum has several practical applications. From the vantage point of categorization, we must note that the degree of altered consciousness not only may vacillate over time within given patients but may be relatively stable over long years of hospitalization. For these latter patients, a psychic equilibrium becomes established and is very difficult to disrupt. This state can account for the model patient whose alteration in consciousness is mild or even absent, the actively delusional and hallucinating patient whose alteration is moderate, and the profoundly withdrawn, stuporous, and periodically assaultive patient whose alteration is severe—all of whom can be categorized as chronic schizophrenics.

Moreover, in working with these patients over a number of years, I have been struck by the dramatic metamorphoses in psychopathology occurring within the same individual over time. Paranoid patients may become catatonic; passive, compliant patients may suddenly become agressive and assaultive; relatively intact patients may become floridly psychotic; hebephrenic patients may become catatonic or paranoid; etc. To my mind, these temporal clinical manifestations argue more for a unitary concept of chronic schizophrenia than for viewing this disorder or diagnosis as a composite of numerous, discrete clinical types. The continuum concept of altered consciousness takes these clinical findings into account because its emphasis is mainly on degree rather than on kind. For example, as the depth of alteration becomes more profound, we should expect a progressive disturbance in attention span, thought processes, purposeful behavior, reality testing, responsiveness to social stimulation, as well as the appearance of more varied and bizarre forms of psychopathology. The changing clinical patterns in patients, therefore, may partially be accounted for by fluctuations in their levels of consciousness.

Concerning the factors responsible for altering the depth of consciousness either in patients with more fluid or stable states, we may presume that stress, either internal or external, represents one of the chief causes for increasing alteration. For example, a minimal or even absent disturbance in cerebral function in patients may become moderate or severe whenever their psychic equilibrium becomes threatened through a perceived homosexual advance, emotional upset, curtailment of privileges, or prospect of hospital discharge and active therapeutic intervention. Conversely, it is much more difficult to define the factors conducive to a lessening of this alteration. Some factors that seem to ameliorate this alteration include the imposition of external controls and structure through psychosocial, pharmacological (i.e., tranquilizer medication), or electrical (i.e., electroconvulsive shock) means, increased therapeutic attention, and emotional support.

A Mutual Venture

The second assumption is that there is a dovetailing of the schizophrenic's needs for structure, direction, and control with institutional influences. It is unlikely that these institutional influences would be so powerful were it not for the susceptibility of patients to them. Aside from the premorbid dependency needs of patients or their desires for escaping reality and responsibility, the very presence of the cerebral dysfunction enhances these predispositions even further. When reality props begin to dissolve, when rational thought becomes difficult, when emotional controls weaken, and when ambiguity and anxiety arise, patients are much more prone to cling to some external authority structure. In this respect, many mental hospitals—through regimentation, monotonous routine, and diminished social stimulation—admirably fit the emotional requirements of these patients for a more controlled, organized, and unstressful existence.

Because the patient himself seeks structure and guidance from the institution cannot be taken to mean that the institution is free of any guilt for what subsequently happens to the patient. The institution may be giving the patient what he wants, but what he wants is not always what is therapeutically best for him. If its influences are dehumanizing, custodial, or even misguided, the institution becomes an unwitting conspirator to the patient's chronicity—a result that would probably not happen if the patient were not so psychologically receptive. The process of chronicity, therefore, may be regarded as a joint enterprise between patient and hospital.

Regarding the role of institutional influences in molding patient behavior, another point deserves mention. Just as institutions can exert adverse influences, so, too, can they exert healthy ones in terms of a salubrious ward milieu in which active therapy and rehabilitation programs take place. The problem, however, with many active treatment programs is that their demands and pressures are often in direct conflict with the needs of these patients for an unstressful environment, thereby causing further intellectual deterioration or disorganization in some patients. Often, it is possible to provide a structure or environment that fosters more responsible behavior in patients and encourages individuality and decision-making, but this very structure may subject the patient to considerable anxiety and stress because it encourages him to engage in the very same behaviors his illness enabled him to avoid. Whereas the chronic schizophrenic patient may be a willing partner to a custodial type of program, he is apt to become a stubborn antagonist to a more intensively therapeutic one aimed at discharging him into the unhappy environment that contributed to his initial illness. In other words, we assume that the patient tends to be compliant with institutional rules and regulations largely to the extent that these meet his needs.

Method in Madness

The third assumption is that the behavior of these patients, even while under the influence of an alteration of consciousness, is for the most part purposive and goal directed. What often makes this behavior and its underlying motivation seem crazy and inexplicable is that it does not conform to patterns of behavior or values regarded as socially appropriate and acceptable. For example, it is difficult for many middle-class clinicians to accept the fact that anyone in his right mind would choose to remain hospitalized rather than to lead an independent, responsible life. This attitude is simply a variant of the commonly held myths that anybody who commits suicide or chooses to reject society or experiment with mind-altering drugs must, almost by definition, be mentally ill. In other words, it represents a value judgment rather than a statement of fact.

In the topsy-turvy world of schizophrenia, social standards and expectations not only may lose most of their original importance but may become completely reversed. Unless the clinician is willing to go "through the looking glass," he may be at a complete loss in understanding the method behind a patient's madness. Although being institutionalized may represent one of the worst horrors to a clinician imbued with the Protestant work ethic, he may fail to recognize that the values of patients often do not conform to his and that the very behavior of patients is fully consonant with their particular value systems. For many patients, life within an institution holds many distinct advantages that cannot be negated by others simply by claiming that "this should not be so." Also, because a patient behaves in a deviant or crazy manner cannot automatically be considered to mean that he does not know what he is doing and therefore cannot help himself. I shall say more about these matters in later chapters, but these brief remarks seem sufficient for present purposes.

If we can accept these three assumptions, at least on an operational basis, the seeming contradictions of the three major etiologic conceptualizations of chronicity now seem capable of reconciliation. All three conceptualizations must be viewed as complementary rather than mutually contradictory. Only by adopting such a multidimensional view of the process of chronicity can clinicians begin to organize and account for the seemingly discrepant and contradictory behaviors of these patients. Let us pursue this further to determine how well it accords with clinical observations.

Adaptation to Cerebral Dysfunction

It is common to find that the first mental break for chronic schizophrenics tends to be much more frightening and shattering to them than consequent ones. With the initial disruptions in psychological functioning the patient may complain about or be aware of his disability (assuming the sick role), but as time elapses he no longer regards these psychotic experiences as alien. After repeated occurrences or the continued existence of this alteration in consciousness, the scary feelings or terror associated with its presence slowly diminish as a psychological adaptation begins to take place. In fact, patients soon come to learn that the presence of this state is not entirely disadvantageous, for it confers on them many unanticipated benefits. Not only does it provide a convenient vehicle and ready-made excuse for the expression of otherwise taboo feelings, thoughts, and behaviors but it also guarantees them a kind of attention and concerned care that they would not receive while behaving sanely.

As with alterations in consciousness produced by the repeated administration of alcohol, marihuana or LSD, or trance-inducing procedures, a type of psychic desensitization seems to occur whereby volitional control over the manifestations of these states increases. Through long practice, patients become much more adept at controlling both the subjective content and outward symptoms of this altered state, as well as becoming better able to turn it off and on. Aside from indulging in wish-fulfillment fantasies, patients also come to use these altered states of consciousness as a type of mental belly ache—a way of avoiding problems, satisfying dependency wishes, gaining attention, and securing power through manipulation of other persons. What originally started out as a type of mental handicap may become transformed eventually into a useful skill or coping mechanism.

Just as a person with a long experience can succumb easier to the effects of a moderate amount of alcohol or marihuana or else keep himself relatively sober and controlled, the schizophrenic patient has the option of letting go and drifting off into the nether regions of his mind or remaining intact. The selection of one or the other of these options will be dictated by the motivation of the patient and external circumstances. Naturally, the greater the psychic disruption, the less the patient's ability to resist its effects. However, with milder alterations, the patient has some choice in deciding whether he will succumb.

Another interesting feature associated with the development of control over these states is that patients seem also to learn how to nurse, or sustain, their altered states of consciousness as long as possible. This behavior seems similar to that shown by someone awakening from a deep sleep to answer a phone or momentarily sobering up when drunk to attend to some necessary task, such as going to the bathroom. During these activities, the person may arouse himself only enough to do what he has to do, provided of course that full waking consciousness is not required for this activity. By nursing this semiconscious state throughout the perfunctory or automatic activity, the person can then return easily to his slumber or stupor. Such an analogy seems to hold for chronic schizophrenics who, at staff prodding or because of physiological necessity (i.e., eating, urinating, etc.), will rouse themselves sufficiently to attend to their chores or needs, often in the manner of automatons, only to drift back into their mental oblivion once the annoying external or internal stimulus is removed.

Another dimension to the alteration in consciousness has to do with certain intrinsic features of most altered states. Aside from the patient's role in controlling the manifestations of this state, the altered state of consciousness may be presumed to possess an innate resistance of its own to influences that threaten it. Once established, especially for some lengthy period of time, the cerebral dysfunction exhibits an inertial quality, tending to persist simply because it exists or because of the mental equilibrium attained.

Should this supposition prove correct, it would partially account for the great resistance shown by patients when attempts are made to rouse them from their apathy or stupor or to modify their bizarre behavior. Just as a person may become irritable or belligerent at being awakened from a sound sleep or hypnotic trance or aroused to full consciousness while mildy anesthetized or under the influence of psychedelic drugs, the schizophrenic often behaves similarly when pressed to emerge from his mental confusion, oblivion, or fantasy life and attend to reality-oriented tasks. It is a common clinical finding that chronic schizophrenics may become extremely stubborn or even assaultive when pressed to do anything stressful or substantially different from their usual perfunctory chores and routines—activities that they are often able to carry out with their eyes half-closed. In this respect, their behavior is comparable to patients with organic brain syndromes who display catastrophic crises (i.e., becoming confused, annoyed, agitated, belligerent) under varying conditions of mental stress, such as being forced to abstract, perform difficult tasks, or marshal their thoughts in an organized, logical manner (K. Goldstein, 1939). This organic-like behavior has led many clinicians to presume the existence of a progressive intellectual deterioration in chronic schizophrenics. To my mind, however, this particular type of behavior seems more related to psychological protection than to psychological deficit. By narrowing the range of their mental faculties, thereby achieving a type of psychostenosis, patients become better able to shield themselves against frustration, stress, and the resulting anxiety which will arise with a shakeup of their delicate mental equilibrium.

Another feature associated with mental inertia also must be considered. Just as quiescent or steady systems tend to preserve themselves, so, too, do moving systems. In this regard, we have encountered numerous instances where relatively intact chronic schizophrenic patients, in the fact of the adversity, stress, or desire for attention, seem to turn on their craziness either to avoid or control the situation. Once their mental ignition switch is turned on, a psychological momentum results, rapidly carrying the patient into the depths of psychological chaos. It is as though the patients' mental brakes have failed or their psychic flywheels have gone awry, and activity that may have started out as purposeful and volitional may end as fragmented, disorganized, uncontrolled, random behavior. To analogize further, once the patient opens the flood gates of his mind, he cannot predict with certainty whether a trickle or flood of craziness will come through. The situation becomes comparable to that of a tail wagging the dog in that patients are no longer in control of the very process they set in motion. Purportedly, this was also the plight of Celius who found that "What may not man with care and art obtain./ He feigned the gout, and now has ceased to feign."

Although we have observed this uncontrolled, mental flywheel effect in many patients, it also happens frequently that the alteration in consciousness does not progress to its more severe forms. Instead, patients may take quantum jumps from one level of altered awareness to another, each level representing a relatively stable, mental plateau. Fears and anxieties may be responsible for disrupting the existing equilibrium, thereby inducing the patient to regroup his psychic forces and retreat to a safer, more remote level of consciousness. The further along the continuum of altered consciousness the patient progresses, the more immune he becomes to therapeutic intervention as well as disturbing, outside influences.

In addition to these characteristic features of the postulated cerebral dysfunction in both acute and chronic schizophrenic patients, the influences of prolonged hospitalization likewise seem to color the manifestations of these states. For the chronic patient, the very presence of an alteration in consciousness with its consequent bizarre psychopathology serves as a badge for automatic admission and care in the hospital, acceptance by fellow patients, and continued attention from staff. Whether the altered state of consciousness is authentic or put on becomes almost beside the point after a while, because patients, through long experience and practice, begin to add to their repertoire of effective tactics and symptoms through observing fellow patients or through their own trial-and-error activities. In their dealings with patients and institutional staff, they soon learn to employ those behaviors that lead to the immediate gratification of their wishes or that seem most effective in eliciting the desired response in others. Unfortunately, as mentioned previously, much of this behavior is reinforced unintentionally by certain hospital philosophies and practices which fit hand in glove with certain patient attitudes.

Another complicating feature of prolonged hospitalization is the development of maladaptive habits. Instead of the alteration in consciousness representing a unique happening in the life of the patient, after a period of time it tends to become a way of life. With long exposure to this psychic malfunction, the chronic patient tends to forget former healthy, adaptive behaviors and supplants them with socially maladaptive attitudes and behaviors acquired during his initial illness and sustained during long hospitalization. Many of these behaviors continue and show a refractoriness to modification, mainly because they have become incorporated into the life style of the patient and have acquired all the self-perpetuating power of bad habits.

Even when there is no apparent disturbance in cognition or subjective experience, the patient continues to act crazy in an automatic, perfunctory manner that conveys as much conviction as a "good morning" or "how are you" salutation in normal social discourse. He continues to indulge in conversation with imaginary people when he is not hallucinating or makes grandiose claims and persecutory remarks when he is not delusional simply because he has become used to communicating in this style. He is quite capable of behaving sanely, but either has gotten out of the habit of doing so or is unwilling to expend the effort to break those patterns of behavior that have served him so well over his extended hospital convalescence.

General Treatment Issues

From the discussion so far, we may hypothesize that any potentially effective treatment approach must deal with and modify the three major dimensions of chronicity: (1) the potential presence of an altered state of consciousness of varying depths, (2) the socially maladaptive attitudes and tactics of patients, (3) and noxious institutional influences. Certain treatment implications follow from such a hypothesis.

Lessening the Alteration of Consciousness

Of initial importance is the problem of lessening whatever alteration of consciousness may be present in these patients. Although therapists may experience little difficulty in influencing or communicating with patients displaying milder forms of cerebral dysfunction, the value and potency of ordinary motivational levers and verbal communications become progressively reduced as the dysfunction worsens. Therefore, if relevant, potentially therapeutic communications are to take place, the therapist must employ some means of diminishing this dysfunction and increasing responsiveness to external reality through psychopharmacological, somatic, or psychosocial techniques. The therapeutic approach, whatever its nature, must address itself to four facets of this problem.

1. How does one get the patient's attention? It seems almost unnecessary to state that before any effective therapeutic intervention can occur the patient must be attentive and receptive to the communication. This brings up the related problem of just how to transmit the message. Should it be predominantly of a verbal, emotional, physical, or pharmacological nature? From our experience with these patients, it appears that the potency or magnitude of the stimulus or communication, either having a positive or negative emotional valence for the patient, must increase proportionately to the depth of alteration in consciousness. Also, the greater the depth, the more concrete, specific, immediate, and tangible must be the transmitted message or reinforcement for the appropriate response. In other words, different types of communication must be used depending on the extent of the patient's psychological disturbance.

2. How can one sustain attention once it is obtained? Although the patient's attention may be gained momentarily through the application of certain motivational levers or stimuli, these levers tend to lose their arousal potency over time once psychological adaptation to them takes place. Aside from this adaptation to repeated external stimuli, the intense motivation of the patient to remain in his altered mental state may cause him, in the manner of a dreamer or hypnotized subject, to incorporate the disturbing stimulus into the content of his mental vagaries rather than awaken to this alarm. Unless the patient can be aroused from the oblivion or swirling confusion within his brain, and this arousal sustained, most treatment programs will have little more effect than a fly or mosquito nagging a heavy sleeper. They may cause him to stir momentarily or swat out, but afterwards he will turn over and go back to sleep.

3. How does one get the patient to internalize these external alarms or arousal stimuli so that he can remain alert and attentive without the continual prodding of others? In other words, there must come a point at which the patient provides his own self-arousal stimulation. Without this transformation from external to internal prods it is likely that the patient will drift back into his former condition once the external stimuli are withdrawn. The underlying assumption of all these issues relating to attention is that if the patient can be "sobered up" long enough to become more accessible to more ordinary forms of therapeutic intervention and communication, he will gain some incentive to shake out his mental cobwebs and sustain his sobriety.

4. What can be done with the sober or intact mental state once it is attained and sustained? Many of these patients' disturbance in consciousness seems minimal or nonexistent but their attitudes and behaviors are antagonistic toward treatment and rehabilitation planning. Even if the patient no longer displays any psychotic phenomena, the therapist may now have to confront all the problems involved in treating a sociopathic personality, character disorder,

or lazy rather than crazy person. For example, it is not so unusual to encounter many patients who are far more likeable when they are crazy than when sane.

Of further interest is my clinical impression that it requires far more powerful stimuli to diminish the depth of the altered state of consciousness in these patients than to increase it, especially in those patients with milder cerebral dysfunctions. With these patients, it is difficult to budge them in the direction of normal psychic functioning even with the use of a psychological sledgehammer, whereas an emotional straw may trip the balance toward more severe mental disorganization. At best, when these patients appear relatively well, there is a certain fragility or instability to the established mental equilibrium and exacerbations of craziness can occur at the slightest stress, frustration, emotional upset, or provocation. Whether this is primarily due to a learned pattern of behavior for handling stress and avoiding responsibility or to the unstable nature of their psychological adjustment cannot be determined with certainty. Nevertheless, it does represent a major treatment problem in that these patients will require continual or periodic interventions on the part of therapists to keep them from "falling apart."

Modifying Socially Maladaptive Attitudes and Tactics

Let us turn now to the second dimension, namely, problems related to the modification of the willful, countertherapeutic tactics of patients. Although we will deal with these problems at length in subsequent chapters, at this point we need only mention two preconditions for therapeutic intervention: (1) These behaviors cannot be changed unless they can be conceptualized and categorized as tactics. This is not so easy to do; the motives of patients are often obscure and the gratifications or ends achieved are not always apparent. This is an especially difficult task for clinicians who view this disorder solely within the framework of a medical model of illness. (2) It seems almost axiomatic that the deviant or undesirable behavior will not change unless it no longer continues to pay off. Therefore, procedures have to be developed and employed that not only discourage the use of these deviant behaviors but encourage the use of healthy, responsible ones in patients, regardless of the severity of the illness.

Eliminating Noxious Institutional Influences

As to the matter of restructuring hospital influences so that they operate to promote healthy, constructive, and socially responsible behavior in patients, there are a number of crucial philosophical dilemmas or issues that must first be resolved. The very nature of the general ward milieu will be dependent on the answers postulated. For example, will these patients be regarded as sick and not responsible for their actions or as competent and responsible? If viewed as responsible, will this designation change in relation to how far out in mental orbit they appear? Also, does responsibility imply accountability for the social impact of behavior? Other issues of utmost importance pertain to the development of a treatment philosophy regarding the basic rights of these patients, the rights of the hospital and its staff to demand some modicum of conformity and cooperation from them, and just how far therapists are obliged or permitted to go in their efforts to treat and rehabilitate patients who are either unmotivated or even resistant to therapy.

Most of my comments have been addressed primarily to the problems involved in the hospital treatment of these patients. I have deliberately ignored the equally formidable problems associated with rehabilitating and maintaining the discharged, chronic patient in the community. Even with the most ideal treatment response from hospitalized patients, what must be remembered is that they have been out of social commission for a long time and handicapped by a "Rip Van Winkle effect." Also, through their many relapses and long hospitalization they have become conditioned to failure, thereby developing an attitude of "Why try?" Undoubtedly, these, as well as many other important rehabilitation problems, will have to be worked out before any therapeutic programs can prove completely successful. I shall have more to say about these matters later.

chapter 2

Ethical Axioms and Clinical Corollaries

From a strictly scientific viewpoint, if there is good reason to suspect that a new treatment procedure will prove more effective than existing ones, it seems incumbent on therapists to fully evaluate its potentialities. From a practical, clinical viewpoint, it may prove impossible to do so because of the influence of factors, other than those concerned with the usefulness and effectiveness of the procedure, that may prevent or modify its clinical application. These factors primarily involve a variety of ethical issues pertaining to the manipulation of human behavior, especially against a person's will or consent.

These ethical issues are not simply matters for idle speculation, pleasant academic discussion, or casual curiosity; the direction and nature of their resolution will determine whether these techniques or procedures can be applied. Often, general professional and social morality or administrative concerns prohibit the development, use, and evaluation of promising techniques and, at the same time, promote the continued application of inefficient or ineffective ones.

Generally, the influence with which clinicians or scientists must contend relate to the standards and expectations imposed on them not only by their particular professional organizations but also by the community at large, including dominant religious, political, economic, or social organizations. These organizations can exercise considerable power over deviant, novel, or nontraditional clinical practices either directly through legal and professional sanctions (malpractice suits, administrative prohibitions, loss of medical license, jail, etc.) or through more subtle but equally effective means, such as ostracism or ridicule.

To illustrate in a very specific way how administrative policy as shaped by public concerns, can curtail the application of new therapeutic procedures, we may cite some excerpts from a regulatory policy statement concerning operant conditioning programs recently issued by high ranking officials in the Minnesota Department of Public Welfare (Lucero, Vail, and Scherber, 1968). The basic contents of this statement are as follows:

Aversive reinforcement is never to be used in a general program for groups of patients . . . .

Deprivation is never to be used. No patient is to be deprived of expected goods and services and ordinary rights, including the free movement of his limbs, that he had before the program started. In addition, deficit rewarding must be avoided; that is, rewards must not consist of the restoration of objects or privileges that were taken away from the patient or that he should have to begin with. The ban against deficit rewarding includes the use of tokens to gain or regain such objects or privileges . . . .

Positive reinforcement is the only conditioning technique to be used . . . .

In defense of such regulations, Lucero and Vail (1968) claim that:

A "treatment" measure used in a public facility that is bizarre or cruel or otherwise impossible to explain to the public—*even if it gets results*—is of its nature against the public interest; the burden of proof is on him who maintains that the results in a case or cases supersede the public interest. And when the public cannot be so convinced, it is usually not the individual therapist of the research department who will take the rap, but the hospital superintendent or the state commissioner, or, in extreme cases, the Governor [italics added].

There is no need to respond to such an arbitrary and clinically short-sighted policy. Rather, this exerpt is presented merely to show that issues other than treatment efficacy may determine whether a given treatment may be employed, regardless of its promising nature. In the above illustration, the authors openly admit that considerations of "public interest" (whatever that means) and the possibility of public reprisal have entered into their decision to formulate such a policy.

This does not mean that these extrascientific moral influences need always be restrictive or bad. There is little question that they may serve many valuable functions, such as defining the ethical implications of certain scientific activities. It is essential to point out the obvious fact that the discipline of science has no intrinsic morality of its own; only the use to which its achievements are put can be subjected to ethical or moral analysis. For example, the development of atomic power has an ethical neutrality; however, the constructive or destructive purposes for which it will be used have profound ethical implications. Given these considerations, it does seem crucial that science be subjected to some type of regulatory, or check-and-balance, system to prevent clinicians from going off half-cocked, infringing on the rights and prerogatives of patients, or employing potentially harmful procedures. A serious problem results, though, when these same regulatory influences become so short-sighted, restrictive, or invested in preserving the status quo that they inhibit the growth of psychotherapy as a science and limit its potential efficacy for helping patients to become well and lead sane, responsible lives.

To understand the nature of ethical judgment, we must first have some appreciation of how ethics—social, professional, or otherwise—come into being. According to Harvey A. Stevens (1964):

> Man, being a rational creature, can usually justify whatever activity he decides to pursue. When the rationalizations become common enough and are accepted as truths, they tend to be established in the mores of the people. When the mores are codified and are accepted by certain professions as "the" way of action, then they become "ethical" principles. As pressure to conform or to avoid problems increases, these ethical codes are then formalized into law.

When we invoke the concepts of ethics or morals, both of which involve judgments of good and evil, it also is essential to recognize that these judgments possess no absolute immutable validity. In fact, ethics may be regarded as relativistic in that they not only vary from culture to culture and over time, but several different systems of ethics may coexist simultaneously within a given society or even within a given profession. In other words, no one person or group of people has a monopoly on virtue.

One of the major practical problems confronting innovative psychotherapists, especially those working in institutions, is that they are exposed to a number of double messages concerning their responsibilities toward patients. The mutually contradictory nature of these messages may require the adoption of mutually contradictory ethical systems. The dilemma, therefore, is that if the clinician responds to one aspect of a message, he may become professionally derelict according to another aspect, thereby making him "damned if he does and damned if he doesn't." For example, in our own work with hospitalized schizophrenics, we continually have had to contend with such ethically incompatible goals as being responsible for the treatment and rehabilitation of patients (= good) but not at the cost of making them uncomfortable (= bad). Moreover, we also have had to find our way through the maze of other ambiguous ethical expectations, as reflected in administrative policies pertaining to placing patients in the community but avoiding complaints from family members or social agencies, activating patients but maintaining a quiet ward, or even designing innovative treatment approaches that do not deviate from traditional, conventional, constitutional practices. Often, it requires more than the wisdom of Solomon to be certain that the course chosen is both correct and moral.

At the present time, the dominant ethical and philosophical themes shaping the nature and goals of psychotherapy emphasize the rights and prerogatives of mental patients, the use of democratic and nondirective treatment procedures, the basic worth of individuals, the understanding of deviant behavior through knowledge of early life history and socio-economic determinants, and the education of communities to promote tolerance and acceptance of the mentally ill. All these liberalizing and humanizing influences have played an important role in the evolution and implementation of such clinical practices within mental hospitals as open door policies, reduction in the use of physical restraints, elimination of punitive practices, provision for adequate medical and psychiatric care, and an emphasis on self-government by patients. There is no doubt that all these humanistic, liberal influences and practices have resulted in the better understanding and care of the mentally ill; however, they also seem to have created a number of unforeseen difficulties for the treatment of special groups of patients, such as chronic schizophrenics.

It is one matter to espouse a philosophy of ethics concerning treatment and to formulate administrative policies based on this philosophy and another matter to expect that this philosophy is always clinically effective for all patients and for all circumstances. A philosophy of ethics that does not permit exceptions is divorced from clinical reality. The luxury of liberality accorded to administrators and theoreticians who view all forms of mental illness at a safe distance and whose outlook is often shaped by issues other than effective therapy may have little relevance to the clinical, nitty-gritty problems encountered by staff who are charged to work with and treat these patients "on the firing line." In fact, as I hope to document later, such a liberal outlook may inadvertently complicate the treatment of chronic schizophrenics by reinforcing the very conditions or factors contributing to the perpetuation of their illness.

Naturally, when clinicians buck or challenge the current morality or interpret it differently than they are supposed to, they are likely to feel great pressures to modify their views and techniques to conform to ill-defined, conventional standards. These pressures may take the form of administrative sanctions, social or legal reprisals, or even fear of professional disapproval. Fortunately, there are at present enough loopholes, inconsistencies, and contradictions in the present, traditional therapeutic morality to permit substantial elbow room for innovations in the treatment of chronic schizophrenics. However, before these innovations can be applied, the clinician must formulate a system of ethics that not only is consonant with his scientific and therapeutic procedures but that also concerns itself with the ultimate welfare and care of these patients. Such a system must be consistent with both clinical and social reality.

Ethical Issues

⌒The formulation of any treatment program for chronic schizophrenics must start with an attempt to answer the age-old and generally insoluble problem of whether the end justifies the means. Translating this problem into clinical terms, we must be prepared to define to what lengths we will go to implement or ensure the success of the treatment goals. Should the goal be to maintain a chronic schizophrenic comfortably in the hospital or to undertake the more ambitious task of helping him become a more socially responsible member of society, even though he may feel occasionally unhappy or experience some discomfort in the process? If we choose the former goal, the task is relatively easy. We simply continue to minister to and satisfy all his basic needs of food, clothing, shelter, and entertainment while, at the same time, attempting to alleviate all his immediate psychological frustrations. If we choose the latter goal, many formidable difficulties, of both an ethical and clinical nature, lie ahead. ⌐)

It would prove redundant and hackneyed to cite statistics on the incidence of schizophrenia, the relapse rates, the amount of hospital beds these patients occupy, or the relative failure of existing treatment approaches to cure this disorder or prevent rehospitalization. These statistics can be found in most textbooks on psychiatry. Rather, it seems more appropriate simply to remind ourselves just how serious and malignant the problem of chronic schizophrenia is. As the situation now stands, these patients represent serious economic, social, political, and psychological debits not only to society but themselves as well. Many represent the psychological equivalents of terminal cancer patients, devoid of any prospects of a productive existence. Therefore, we have to make the operational value choice of either preparing them for a comfortable psychological demise or using unorthodox or even radical procedures that may measurably increase their chance for responsible, meaningful living.

⌐In any radical or unorthodox procedure there must be a willingness to balance the potential risks against the possible gains⌐ Most professionals working in this area have been reluctant to confront the issue of risk and have chosen instead to play it safe. The most prevalent way of playing it safe has been to settle for more modest treatment goals for these patients and to avoid innovative, nontraditional procedures. In this manner, clinicians can be assured of protecting their psychological and professional skins against censure and criticisms from colleagues and society. Unfortunately for the patients concerned, clinicians seem to have interpreted the generally wise medical dictum of *primum non nocere* 'first, do no harm' to mean 'first, do very little.' As a result, for the most part, they have been employing a variety of perfunctory gumdrop or lukewarm therapies, with a primary emphasis on talk, work, and recreation, for a very malignant problem. If some patients respond, all well and good; if the majority do not, then this is to be expected, especially as these patients are assumed to have a bleak prognosis. The trouble with adopting this kind of approach is that it turns out to be a self-fulfilling prophecy.

Because patients tend to have a poor prognosis in response to conventional psychiatric therapies does not mean that they will have a poor response to any type of therapy. In actual fact, it is impossible to know at this point in time just how hopeless the chronic schizophrenic's prognosis is until numerous systematic treatment studies specifically designed to answer the many treatment issues are undertaken. Even though we possess a relatively primitive knowledge about this disorder, therapists have not even begun to scratch the surface in terms of exploring a wide variety of already available, potentially powerful, psychosocial techniques for the treatment of these patients. Until these are given a fair trial, judgment about the ultimate prognosis of this condition must be held in abeyance.

This type of general ethical problem cannot be resolved by reason or debate. In the final analysis, the decision reached will be based more on conviction than absolute reality; there is no objective yardstick to measure the degree of morality inherent in a particular choice. Personally, I believe it is far more immoral for clinicians to settle for the goal of making patients comfortable rather than well. Unless clinicians are willing to stick their professional necks out and assume the risks associated with employing and evaluating potentially effective therapeutic techniques, especially when traditional procedures seem so inept, they are derelict in their duties toward patients. Even though the new procedures may not work or prove somewhat hazardous, we feel that these patients are entitled to every chance no matter how remote, for responsible living outside an institution.

Currently, there is considerable legal concern about the patient's right to treatment. This concern is one I likewise share. There can be no excuse for providing custodial care or conducting ineffective treatment programs for patients who possess the potentiality for improvement. It is my contention that this potentiality can never be fully assessed until patients are afforded the opportunity of exposure to new treatment approaches. When these new approaches are not readily available, it is incumbent on administrators, clinicians, and researchers to tax their creativity and imagination in a continuing search for more effective procedures.

My position is not too dissimilar to that of Goldstein, Heller, and Sechrest (1966, pp.8-9), who advance the following philosophy:

> Manipulative approaches may be attacked on the grounds that they dehumanize, treat the patient as a machine or object, or more generally, that they reflect a nonhumanitarian orientation to sick or unhappy people. Our position, quite the contrary, is that *current* psychotherapeutic approaches are deficient on a humanitarianism continuum largely because they do not incorporate or reflect research findings regarding the most effective means of altering an individual's behavior—the very reason for the existence of psychotherapy. To know that solid research dealing with attitude change, learning, group dynamics and a score of other domains offering other manipulative means of altering an individual's behavior exists, and to deny in an a priori manner the potential relevance of such research to the psychotherapy patient, is to perform a disservice to both the advance of psychotherapy and to one's psychotherapy patients. Obviously, there will be limits that society will impose upon its psychological practitioners. But to imply that these limits can be imposed without evidence, without research on behavioral control, is to deny the experimental foundation on which science rests. We have an obligation to society and to our psychotherapy patients, and this obligation demands that we publicize and use the best possible scientific findings in our own field. To do less than this, we hold, is a failure to meet our ethical responsibilities.

Such a view must always prove an ethically delicate and uncomfortable one for clinicians and investigators in that it demands a continual appraisal of whether the goal justifies the extremity of the means or whether the means themselves may in fact vitiate the end. There is the additional problem of continually trying to balance the potential risks of the procedures against the possibility of patient harm, either of a psychological or physical nature. Certainly, there are matters for concern, but these cannot serve as excuses for perpetuating ineffective treatment procedures or for not pursuing new possibilities.

Opting Out

One of the most immediate ethical or philosophical questions a clinician must resolve is whether patients have the right to resign from or opt out of living in normal society. For those who find life or responsibility too onerous or stressful, should society provide some haven, sanctuary, or retreat in the form of mental hospitals where people can spend the remainder of their days in relative peace and quiet? This question is not so easy to answer because it has much broader ramifications in society. Chronic schizophrenics are not the only ones who prefer to withdraw from the demands of a highly civilized life; there are many ways to opt out besides resorting to mental illness. Beatniks, drug users, alcoholics, religious fanatics, etc. have found the game of life too arduous or upsetting and have chosen a variety of unproductive, self-destructive ways to escape from its demands and responsibilities. The basic problem centers on whether individuals have the right to give up and, if so, whether society has the right to interfere with this.

For people with a philosophical bent, the ramifications of this issue could be debated endlessly. For those with a clinical bent, some resolution, right or wrong, of this issue must be made as a basis for therapeutic action. If it is decided that patients do have the right of resigning from life, then it would be wrong to force them to relinquish this prerogative. On the other hand, if they do not have this right, then clinicians are justified in trying everything possible to force patients out of their psychological retirement. This issue can be resolved by forming opinions on two aspects of this problem:

1. Individuals may be granted the right to resign from normal living only if they have explored all the constructive alternatives to opting out and have received no satisfaction from them. Also, if they are going to opt out, they must do so in a way that does not impose additional problems on others or society. Once they become a burden to society in terms of the economic drain of continued hospitalization and care or becoming a menace or nuisance, they forfeit their right of giving up. It now becomes society's responsibility to rehabilitate and revivify them.

2. Social and legal ethics dictate that a person does not have the right to commit suicide; clinical ethics should dictate that the chronic schizophrenic does not have the right to commit a psychological form of suicide by opting out through prolonged hospitalization. Just as, when a person attempts suicide, it is incumbent on the physician to employ every possible technique or treatment, no matter how drastic, to revive him, so it is the clinician's responsibility to do likewise with the chronic schizophrenic. It is not sufficient to simply sustain these patients in a perpetual psychological coma.

There are certainly instances when suicide may not only be justified, such as relief from intractable, incurable pain, but also when it may represent a selfless, enlightened act. In these circumstances, the individual certainly seems to have the right to terminate his life—especially as his final act has not been taken at the expense of others. However, for a therapist to accept and even facilitate the chronic schizophrenic's withdrawal from life becomes tantamount to his partaking in a form of psychological euthanasia.

Besides, just as parents need not abide by or honor the decision of a child regarding what is best for him, trained, conscientious therapists are likewise in a position to be much more objective and realistic concerning the ultimate welfare of patients than patients themselves. It would be the height of folly to presume that the patients' original illness and subsequent hospitalization resulted from a process of mature, enlightened deliberation on their part. Although the patient may have opted out through hospitalization because he saw no other options open to him, it is the therapist's job to find and present other options to the patient rather than accept the patient's pessimistic, inevitable view of the situation.

Involuntary Therapy

Related to the question of the patient's right to opt out of life is another problem that involves the right of clinicians to force unwilling patients, who are legally committed to the hospital, to be treated. There is currently much concern and debate within the mental health fields concerning the morality and legality of these practices. It is assumed that unless a patient endangers his or another person's life, it is an infringement on his rights both to hospitalize and treat him. The physician treating such a patient can be regarded as an agent of society rather than a benefactor of the patient.

Although this issue is an ethical rather than scientific one, when applied to the chronic schizophrenic it merely becomes academic or moot. For the most part, the clinical problem is not one of keeping these patients hospitalized or locked up against their will but rather one of encouraging them to leave the hospital and to do so in a way that will ensure their sustained social adjustment. Even those patients who protest their desire to be released from the hospital's jurisdiction make it impossible or difficult for their therapists to comply with their requests. Therapists would feel both inhumane and delinquent in their duties if they released from the hospital confused, paranoid, and grossly delusional patients who have no visible means of support, no desire to attain it, and whose reality testing is poor enough to represent a potential danger to themselves or others in society. The issue, then, is not whether it is unethical to force treatment on these patients but whether it is ethical to withhold treatment from them.

There can be little question that many injustices concerning the involuntary treatment of patients have been perpetrated by mental hospitals. At times, patients committed to institutions are merely scapegoats for family or spouse or else have been put into custody because they represent social nuisances. In these instances, we may presume that the rights of patients as individuals have been infringed on. However, it is my impression that such instances, especially with schizophrenic patients, are far rarer than sociologists and lawyers would have us believe. Generally, the reasons for hospitalization may be regarded both in the best interests of these patients and members of the community. For example, Smith, Pumphrey, and Hall (1963) studied 100 schizophrenic patients in an effort to determine the "last straw" (i.e., the decisive incident) preceding hospital admission. Their results indicated that 53 percent of patients constituted a danger to themselves or others (e.g., threatened to hit spouse, attacked parent with gun, choked a child, cut wrists, etc.), 38 percent showed flagrant violations of social norms (e.g., nude in public park, ate raw chicken, spit on neighbors, etc.), and 9 percent voluntarily sought help for illness complaints (e.g., fear of losing mind, etc.). The authors concluded that

> Because of the serious nature of the final incidents and the strong feelings they evoked, it seemed mandatory that a hospital setting offer protection and support when the family and the community had had all the stress they could tolerate. Present collaborative methods include no other effective techniques for handling extreme fear when the possibility of genuine danger remains, or for relieving extreme emotional and physical exhaustion on the part of the family.

Despite these results, we must acknowledge the findings of several studies indicating that a substantial number of acute schizophrenics can be managed adequately in the community with phenothiazine medication and follow-up care. However, for the therapist assigned the task of treating already hospitalized patients, the issue of an alternative to hospitalization is really academic. In the case of chronic schizophrenics, regardless of the reasons for their initial mental hospital admission, the practical problem is not one of leveling blame at family, society, or institution for their incarceration but one of changing the patients or their circumstances so that they can be released and integrated into the community. What many critics of mental hospitals do not realize is that, for the most part, hospital staff would be delighted to do just this but are hampered in their goal by the recalcitrance or degree of psychopathology of the patients themselves or by the intolerance of society and/or family for the deviancy displayed by patients.

The problem of involuntary incarceration and treatment is not peculiar to psychiatry for there are common parallels in a person refusing a life-saving operation—a Jehovah's Witness refusing a blood transfusion or a Christian Scientist refusing to allow his diabetic child to receive insulin. Without resorting to philosophical harangues, there does seem to be an equitable solution to this problem—at least, on a practical basis. The solution is similar to the one (already practiced by society) that reserves the right to treat people against their will when their disease is such that it may affect others or when these people are either unconscious or incompetent to make an enlightened decision. For example, compulsory vaccinations and inoculations, quarantines for contagious diseases, forced hospitalization and treatment for lepers and tubercular patients all represent instances where society and its physician agents exercise the right to treat people against their will for the purpose of preventing the spread of disease to others and to help the afflicted people themselves.

On a similar basis, it can be held psychiatric clinicians have responsibilities both to society and the patients entrusted to their care. The question of whether the clinician is an agent of society or of the patient is an artificial problem; with the treatment of the chronic schizophrenic, it is often impossible to serve one master without serving the other. However, with the alternative of life-long hospitalization, forcing the patient to become a responsible, contributing member of society can only benefit him—even if the price is to manipulate him against his will. As long as the purpose of these therapeutic maneuvers is to help the patient realize his full personal potential as a social human being rather than to create a socialized automaton or an unobtrusive patient, I regard this ethical stance as sound and humane.

Manipulation and Punishment

Intimately associated with the problem of involuntary hospitalization and treatment is the question of whether it is ethical to manipulate or control patients, especially without their consent. For many clinicians the concept of manipulation conjures up horrible visions of Orwell's *1984* or Huxley's *Brave New World*—utopias in which man is stripped of his individuality, freedom, self-determination, and dignity. The manipulation of human behavior carries with it the connotation of a Machiavellian abuse of power whereby the aspirations and basic rights of man are sacrificed for the nefarious goals of some monolithic organization. The mental hospital has been portrayed by many as just such an organization.

There is no need to wax philosophical about the many moral implications of behavioral control. Such issues as free will versus determinism and the rights of individuals versus the rights of society are part and parcel of the same problem and have been dealt with extensively by many clinical theoreticians. Suffice it to say that no absolute answers to these issues are possible; the conclusions reached will depend on the initial assumptions made and the values on which they are based. My position, therefore, reflects a pragmatic bias—that is, not what ideally should be but what is and must be.

It is essential to point out the obvious, namely, that man, living in a social structure, is the product of countless influences which have shaped and molded him and which continue to shape and mold him. Parents, teachers, supervisors, spouses, advertising agencies, public relations firms, and churches are only some of the innumerable subtle and often blatant forces attempting to influence and control man's thought and behavior. Therefore, to harangue about the evils of any form of human manipulation would be to blind oneself to psychological and social reality. Likewise, the very essence of psychotherapy, whether we like to admit it or not, involves an attempt to alter the behavior and thought of patients in a direction defined as personally and socially constructive. Although therapists may employ an abundance of euphemisms or rationalizations for their procedures, the fact of the matter is that they are trying to manipulate patients through either somatic means (e.g., psychotropic drugs, electroconvulsive therapy, etc.) or psychosocial means (e.g., insight-oriented and relationship-oriented approaches, persuasion, suggestion, reinforcement procedures, etc.).

It is also necessary to realize that the amount of freedom granted patients in the context of therapy depends on the type of patient treated. For bright, introspective, verbal, socially functioning neurotic or character disorder patients, the degree of overt control and guidance necessary to change behavior may be far less than for chronic schizophrenics who show little motivation to seek help or little inclination to take advantage of the help offered them. Moreover, when the kinds of choices chronic schizophrenics make may be regarded as self- or socially maladaptive and destructive, then it obliges the therapist, who is charged with their care, to intervene and assume control.

This brings up one of the most important issues in behavior control concerning the question of who should be in the position to judge what is best for the patient. This question could be debated endlessly among people of different biases without any prospects of an amicable agreement. If we can take this question out of the esoteric realm of philosophy and relate it to the treatment of chronic schizophrenics, there is only one practical answer—that is, if trying to get these patients well is the goal. There is either the possibility that the patient himself decides what is best for him or someone else does it for him. For anyone who has worked intensively with chronic schizophrenics, the first possibility must be regarded as clinically unrealistic. Therefore, someone else must assume responsibility for the patient's psychological and physical welfare. The most qualified person to do this is the therapist charged with his care. This may be morally untenable for some, but it is the only realistic possibility for offering the patient some hope for a socially productive existence outside the hospital. Moreover, if a therapist is to make these decisions, he must find some way of implementing them. This implementation involves the control and manipulation of patient behavior.

This, in turn, leads to a related but somewhat more sensitive ethical issue. In the search for more effective therapeutic levers, the clinician must soon confront the prospects of adopting operant conditioning principles, with an emphasis on rewards and punishments for the modification of deviant behavior. In general, the use of rewards for appropriate behavior presents no ethical problem for most clinicians; everyone is for giving kindness and mothering. However, the use of punishment for inappropriate behavior is bound to cause some moral concern and apprehension. Rewards (i.e., positive reinforcers) are equated with good whereas punishments (i.e., negative reinforcers, aversive stimuli) are equated with evil.

For the purposes of discussion, it is irrelevant to deal with the question of whether punishment represents an effective and efficient therapeutic modality. For the present, we shall assume that it may or may not be. Rather, the real question is one of whether we can talk about punishment openly, objectively, and without fear of automatic censure. Because of the current benevolent and liberal philosophy concerning the rights and privileges of patients, the purposeful employment of punishment (e.g., pain, discomfort, deprivation) as a therapeutic modality has become a sensitive if not taboo issue. Partly in reaction to the popular and somewhat justified image of the old asylum where supposedly sadistic custodians bullied, abused, and mistreated inmates, modern-day clinicians and administrators have found these practices so repugnant that they have attempted to outlaw all forms of punishment for patients. Generally they have tried to handle this problem by either a blanket, automatic condemnation of all forms of punishment of patients, regardless of therapeutic rationale or a studious denial of the existence of these practices, thereby permitting them to continue sub rosa. Unfortunately, this is not a problem that can be avoided by sweeping it under an administrative rug; it will continue to arise under many guises, under different names, in a variety of circumstances, and associated with different issues.

Without exploring all aspects of this issue, we will simply say that the question of whether punishment should or should not be used on mental patients is largely moot, for all psychosocial techniques for instituting human behavioral change employ the very potent influences of both reward and punishment. Any clinician working with chronic schizophrenics for any length of time will be forced to employ some type of punishment system for controlling their behavior, even though he may do so unwittingly, call his procedures by euphemistic names, or rationalize these procedures according to some acceptable, traditional clinical terminology. Even those programs that espouse only benevolent treatment approaches use such punitive or unpleasant procedures as the withholding of privileges, the withdrawal of love or approval, diminished attention, restraints, and seclusion, sticking patients with needles to tranquilize or sedate them, and electroconvulsive therapy for the avowed purpose of controlling patient behavior. The issue, then, is not whether punishments can or should be used; they are and will continue to be since this is simply a fact of all social and clinical life. The real issue is whether punishments will be administered openly, unapologetically, and in a consistent, systematic, goal-oriented manner rather than on a disguised, apologetic, and haphazard basis.

The contradictions in our therapeutic morality concerning punishment are sorely apparent. Unfortunately, these contradictions exert considerable influence on therapeutic practice. Therapists may employ such drastic procedures as lobotomies but be prohibited by administrative or social reaction from using such innocuous procedures as limited food deprivation in order to discourage inappropriate behavior. They may administer electroconvulsive shock treatments with professional impunity but be castigated by colleagues for the use of counterconditioning procedures, such as harmless but painful electric shocks applied to the bodies of assaultive patients. They may use Antabuse therapy on alcoholic patients, even with the danger of severe adverse reactions, but not be permitted to employ similar aversive procedures (e.g., apomorphine or Anectine to countercondition bizarre or destructive behavior) on other types of mental patients. They may place a child in physical restraints and seclusion for assaultive behavior but not be allowed to spank him or slap his hands. All these contradictions emphasize the confusion and hypocrisy that currently reign in the field of institutional psychotherapy and also point up the need for more honesty and consistency in our ethical stance concerning punishment or painful therapeutic procedures.

The fact of the matter is that punishment (euphemistically termed *negative reinforcement* or *aversive conditioning*), along with rewards or approval, represents one of the most potent and useful psychosocial means for modifying the behavior of human beings. We may rail against its use or decry its immorality, but we employ it, nevertheless, whether we admit it or not, in almost every attempt to shape behavior. By claiming to avoid any procedure that smacks of punishment, we may salve our consciences and take pride in our nobility, but we do so at the cost of fooling ourselves, deceiving our patients, and dealing with myths rather than reality.

One point must be made clear. I am not advocating punishment for the sake of punishment nor do I regard myself as an apologist for its use. It would be nice if punishment did not exist and even nicer if therapists could effectively change the behavior of chronic patients while never causing them emotional or physical discomfort. These possibilities, however, are nothing more than fanciful notions. Punishment exists, and it is difficult to modify patient behavior without its occasional use. Therefore, when there is good rationale for its use, it is too valuable a therapeutic tool to disregard—that is, if the commitment of the clinician is toward rehabilitating his patients. To summarily dismiss its use as odious or repugnant without weighing its merits seems a false morality and makes as much sense as a surgeon not performing an essential operation or a dentist not pulling out a diseased tooth because they are against pain. Quite often, some pain or discomfort must be experienced temporarily in order for a person to become well and comfortable over the long run.

There are those who fear that once the use of any form of punishment is openly acknowledged and condoned, it might well serve as a vehicle for sadism. However, the essence of the problem is whether the therapist uses punishment solely for his own emotional gratification or the patient's welfare. If the therapist is basically humane, he will apply the punishment in a judicious and concerned manner, taking pleasure in a healthy or hopeful patient response. If he is sadistic, he will be ingenious enough to find a vehicle for his sadism in any type of therapeutic approach, even in benign nondirective therapies. To put it differently, the beatific smile of the therapist does not guarantee that there are no fangs hidden behind it.

One other problem in the use of punishment must be recognized. In the administration of negative reinforcements or aversive stimuli, it may become difficult to distinguish where therapeutic enthusiasm ends and unnecessary cruelty begins. Many inhumane procedures have been justified in the past on the basis of religious, political, or even therapeutic zeal. Man's ability for rationalization is unlimited when his emotional stake is great enough. This is certainly not an easy problem to resolve. In the final analysis it will depend on the awareness, sensitivity, and objectivity of the clinician, his obtaining consensual validation for his procedures, his weighing the balance of risks against potential benefits, and his continuing appraisal of just how far it is permissible to go to achieve his ends. However, that this problem is so ticklish is no excuse for avoiding it entirely by adopting a safe but nihilistic therapeutic position.

The Keystone Concept of Responsibility

It should be apparent that discussion of all the above ethical issues rests on one basic assumption, namely, that chronic schizophrenics are treatable and capable of social rehabilitation. If this assumption were false, there would be no reason to expose these patients to all the stresses associated with an active therapy program and there would be no reason for therapists to consider all the sensitive ethical issues associated with therapy. An enlightened and humane custodial setting with an emphasis on meeting all the creature comforts of patients would be all that would be required to discharge society's obligation to such presumably hopeless and sick people.

Because, as a clinician, I cannot accept the view that these patients are untreatable and socially irredeemable—that is, until every innovative treatment modality has been explored and discarded as ineffective—and also believe we have not yet taxed the limits of our clinical ingenuity, I feel that the assumption of treatability represents the only tenable one, at least on an operational basis. If, in fact, patients are regarded as potentially curable, especially through the use of psychosocial treatment modalities, another basic assumption must be made, namely, that chronic schizophrenics, no matter how crazy they may seem, are essentially responsible for their actions and can muster up the necessary will power to act sanely and decently if they should choose, or be made to choose, to do so. Without this keystone assumption, there can be little justification for launching any traditional or novel treatment program.

According to William Glasser (1965), many of whose views parallel my own, the concept of responsibility refers to "the ability to fulfill one's needs, and to do so in a way that does not deprive others of the ability to fulfill their needs." This definition, however, is too broad for present purposes. A more useful view of the concept of responsibility has two essential components: (1) The patient is regarded as the perpetrator and initiator of his own behavior. In other words, the notion is rejected that the patient's present behavior is solely mechanistically determined by past influences, present institutional influences, or biochemical abnormalities. (2) If the patient initiates certain actions, he must also be held accountable for them—that is, receiving approval for appropriate behavior and disapproval for inappropriate behavior. Although most clinicians espouse the concept of responsibility for mental patients, they are often reluctant to accept the associated feature of accountability, thereby rendering this concept both hollow and limp.

Moreover, by invoking this concept of responsibility, we must also accept the implication of morality of behavior. Deviant patient behaviors are not only viewed as pathological but as bad, whereas appropriate behaviors are not only viewed as healthy but as good. Such a morality may prove an anathema to deterministic scientists, but, for clinicians, it provides a more simplified, practical philosophical framework for therapeutic intervention and interaction with these patients.

There are other implications associated with the concept of responsibility. Without regarding patients as responsible for their behaviors, we would be relegating them to a subhuman, even animal status where behavior is presumed to be determined more by instinct and drive level than by volition. For patients driven by forces beyond their control, their prognosis must be assumed to be bleak. On the other hand, by making the operational assumption of responsibility, we invest patients with human dignity and hope; their actions, right or wrong, can now be regarded as purposive, goal-directed, and, to a large extent, subservient to their own interests. Therefore, we may further presume that actions that can be initiated by patients can also be stopped or modified either by patients themselves or through outside intervention. This represents a far more hopeful outlook for launching treatment and rehabilitation programs in behalf of patients.

Today's dynamically oriented theoreticians have placed far too much blame for the patient's behavior on such scapegoat devils as mother, society, or mythical biochemical abnormalities rather than on the individual patient himself. With such convenient whipping boys, where everyone is at fault, then nobody is at fault. It is rather paradoxical and contradictory that many clinicians can excuse the pathological behavior of mental patients as due to factors beyond their control but do not invoke similar nebulous explanations for all the appropriate behavior of patients. Logically, it would seem that if patients cannot be blamed and held accountable for their deviant behavior (e.g., hitting out, lack of involvement with others, refusing to work), then it would follow that they cannot receive credit for healthy behavior (e.g., going to meals, appropriate grooming, performing well at work details).

Undoubtedly, this represents a rather naïve and simplistic view of a very complicated problem. In this age of mechanistic or deterministic psychology, it is unsophisticated to maintain that human beings still exert considerable influence on the nature of their current predicaments and future lot by the choices they make. This does not mean that all people are responsible to the same extent or that numerous influences—genetic, physiological, psychological, economic, social, etc.—are not powerful determinants of human behavior and thought. All that is claimed is that there is another motive force, call it *free will* or *will power* for want of a better term, that also must be reckoned with in understanding human nature. Unless the treatment approach is addressed eventually toward helping or even forcing the patient to exert his will in an appropriate manner, it seems unlikely that therapeutic success ever will be attained.

The question naturally arises of just how conscious a person need be to be regarded as responsible. However, with this conception of responsibility, the degree of conscious decision-making underlying behavior—with the exception of comatose, profoundly stuporous, or very toxic patients—is irrelevant. It is possible for a person to be responsible both as a result of careful deliberation or at almost a gut, or reflex level. If a chronic schizophrenic or anyone knows enough to indulge his own needs or desires, such as seeking out food, snacks, cigarettes, or rest, he has sufficient consciousness to be responsible for other areas of his personal and social behavior. No matter how withdrawn or bizarre he appears, if he can display sufficient motivation to gratify his whims, and if there is intent to his actions, regardless of whether he is aware of them or not, he also possesses the necessary psychological resources for engaging in appropriate, socialized behavior—that is, if he wants to or is made to do so.

This does not mean that the matter of responsibility is an either-or proposition; either patients are completely responsible for what they do or they are not. Obviously, many patients are much more aware of reality and able to manipulate it to their satisfaction than others. However, I do maintain that even for seemingly regressed or floridly psychotic patients, there is at least a kernel of will power, lurking somewhere in the nether regions of their minds and amid the maelstrom of thought and emotion, which can be employed constructively to counter and control their deviant impulses. No doubt it may require considerable effort for patients to master and channel these impulses, but this does not exonerate them from making a sustained effort to do so or from being receptive to outside therapeutic help.

Undoubtedly, this unsophisticated view of the concept of responsibility runs counter to much modern forensic, psychiatric thought with its abundant tests of insanity, uncontrollable impulsive behavior, etc. Unfortunately, these distinctions are far too academic and legalistic to be of much practical clinical importance. The practical problem is that psychotherapists, even though they may harbor doubts about the extent of patient responsibility for behavior, must at least operationally accept this view; without it there would be no springboard for therapeutic action, especially with psychosocial techniques. For example, if clinicians view the patient as purely impulse driven and unable to control his behavior, it follows that nothing he talks about or is told or nothing that is done to him in the way of rewarding or punishing him will have any impact on his subsequent behavior. Such a view must lead to a position of therapeutic pessimism and nihilism. Clearly, then, if psychotherapeutic procedures are to be employed, the concept of responsibility must serve as a keystone assumption for all further principles of psychotherapy with these patients.

This simplified view of psychotherapy dictates that the acceptance of responsibility by the patient represents a prerequisite for any further constructive behavioral change. If patients are to be receptive to treatment, their attitude must include the following components: (1) I am responsible and, hence, accountable for my behavior. (2) I want to change my behavior because it dissatisfies me. (3) I need help. (4) I will cooperate with the help offered me. The major problem with the chronic patient is to get him to move from a position where he denies all responsibility for his behavior or excuses it under the banner of insanity to the first of these stages. Once this is done, a major therapeutic barrier is crossed.

In the prior discussion of various ethical issues as well as the concept of responsibility, there has been an attempt to sketch some of the essential ingredients for a general treatment philosophy for chronic schizophrenics. A treatment philosophy, though, represents only an initial step in the formulation of treatment programs and cannot be assumed to be synonymous with treatment itself. If the treatment philosophy is to have any clinical relevance, the therapist must devise ways for implementing this philosophy. This cannot be accomplished simply by armchair extrapolation from this philosophy of what specific and potentially promising treatment procedures will be employed. The treatment procedures involved will have to be subjected to careful clinical and research scrutiny in order to determine which procedures are most effective and efficient in attaining the desired treatment goals. Often, in the assessment of therapeutic procedures it is just as important to learn what does not work as what does work; such knowledge will enable the clinician to discard the irrelevant and focus on the relevant.

Subsequent parts shall deal both with the factors and the techniques that seem to facilitate constructive behavior change and those that do not. However, it is first essential to have at our disposal more knowledge about the nature of the beast to be treated. As shall be seen, this knowledge pertains not only to the patient himself but also to the patient culture in which he lives and the hospital staff involved in his treatment.

part two

The Chronic Culture

chapter 3

The Code of Chronicity

Take a group of male and female chronic schizophrenic patients of mixed diagnostic subtypes, place them in an open or closed ward setting, eliminate the use of psychotropic medications or other somatic therapies, demand a modicum of responsible behavior from them, attempt to treat them primarily with psychosocial techniques, and then expect to encounter a number of unanticipated and formidable obstacles to therapy, no matter how ambitious the treatment program, elegant its experimental design, or brilliant its conceptual basis. These obstacles have little to do with the known, anticipated difficulties involved in treating seriously ill psychiatric patients; rather, they involve superimposed, artifactual factors, which, if unrecognized and unresolved, conspire to undermine any form of psychotherapeutic intervention, perpetuate chronicity, and

Portions of this chapter have been adapted from A. M. Ludwig and F. Farrelly, The code of chronicity. Arch. Gen. Psychiat., *15:561-568, 1966, and The weapons of insanity.* Amer. J. Psychother., *21:737-749, 1967, with permission.*

reduce the prospects of hospital discharge and successful rehabilitation. These factors do not seem directly related to any hypothesized etiological basis for the schizophrenic process but rather pertain to certain schizophrenic subcultural attitudes and behaviors, which are nurtured within a mental institution, enhanced by the presence of other chronic patients, and reinforced by a complementary set of attitudes and behaviors on the part of the hospital staff, as well as the professional community at large. This constellation of factors has been named the *code of chronicity.*

We have derived the construct of a code, referring to a system or body of explicit or implied rules governing behavior, from certain analogous situations in society. This construct, which may or may not be valid, is nevertheless convenient for organizing observations about and interpretations of the behavior of chronic schizophrenics. Moreover, as we shall see later, such a conceptualization leads to certain simple but inescapable conclusions regarding the kinds of therapeutic tactics necessary for disrupting the process of chronicity.

The code of loyalty or honor among delinquents, prison inmates, criminals, and certain oppressed minority groups represents a well-known social phenomenon. This code of behavior pertains not only to the acceptance of socially deviant group values but specifically prohibits a member of the group from consorting with members of other groups, especially those representing authority. A breach of code, resulting in the apprehension or punishment of other group members, is likely to result in social ostracism, ridicule, physical punishment, or death for the transgressor. Such epithets as "stool pigeon," "stoolie," "rat-fink," "teacher's pet," "ass-kisser," and "brown-noser" are reserved for those group members who cooperate with authority figures responsible for controlling or modifying the behavior of the group.

Of interest is the ambivalent attitude of those in authority toward informers. On the one hand they are dependent on these people for vital information; on the other hand they regard informers as traitorous and despicable. In a sense, then, both the deviant subcultural group and the group vested with authority have formed an unwritten, informal pact to withhold sanctuary and solace from people who break the group code.

Although such codes have been commented on widely, little has been written about the existence of similar codes among hospitalized chronic schizophrenic patients. Not only are such codes operative in mental hospitals, but staff attitudes toward patients breaking the code often parallel those of persons in authority toward informers. A situation, therefore, unwittingly is created whereby patients find it difficult to relinquish their identification as chronic patients and to adopt more socialized values and attitudes. It is as though patients and staff form an antitherapeutic pact to preserve each other's identity and status.

Surprisingly, the patients themselves were the ones who informed us of the existence of the code and the exacting demands the code imposed on them. This code would go into operation whenever the staff attempted to set limits, withdraw priviliges, or demand appropriate, responsible behavior from patients. For example, when certain patients were confined to the ward and denied coffee, cigarette, and snack privileges for breaking ward rules, other patients surreptitiously and at times openly rallied to their support by smuggling these items to them. Most often, when patients were caught passing contraband articles, they excused their behavior by saying they did not know the offending patients were on restrictions, claimed that these articles were stolen from them, or defiantly stated that the staff had no right to deprive mentally ill patients (who "couldn't help themselves") from their God-given privileges.

There were even certain patients who functioned as custodians of the code. These patients, under the guise of concern for their fellow patients, would serve as self-appointed guardians of obstructive patients, coming to their defense when the staff or other patients showed anger toward them because of their deviant behaviors. These, so to speak, keepers of the faith would console the offending patients, shield them from the wrath of offended patients, provide them with lots of attention and understanding, keep them well stocked with "goodies," and provide them with further vindictive justifications for their actions.

Still other patients would serve as lookouts for one another when engaging in forbidden sexual perversions or behavior, sneaking smokes, or planning elopements from the ward. When a fellow patient got in trouble by breaking ward regulations, other patients seemed to identify vicariously with him, casting the deviant patient in the role of martyr and the staff in the role of villains.

Even those patients who did not actively help other patients break the rules or who did not smuggle in cigarettes or candy engaged in passive obstructive behavior. When they were witness to other patients' wrongdoings, few of the "withdrawn" patients felt under any obligation to intervene or inform staff what was happening, even though the behavior of the offenders was potentially harmful to themselves or others. By engaging in this conspiracy of silence, these presumably innocent, uninvolved patients might be viewed as accessories after the fact. As one patient stated, a cardinal tenet of the code was to "hear all, see all, say nothing."

Another tactic of patients was their tendency to destroy pertinent paraphernalia or equipment of value to the staff and essential to the conduct of a treatment program. For example, announcements posted on the ward bulletin board enjoyed a short life; they were often ripped up, desecrated, or destroyed by patients. When the tape recorder was used during certain group treatment sessions, it soon became an object of great temptation for several patients, who both threatened and made periodic attempts to break it. As more examples of patients' efforts to prevent the staff from continuing to make demands for responsible behavior from them, patients set at least three fires in the building so that they might be transferred back to their former home wards. These, as well as numerous other harassments, were designed to take their toll of the staff's therapeutic enthusiasm.

Of interest was the fact that when several patients tried to behave responsibly by helping the staff enforce ward regulations, other patients began deriding or ridiculing them for being squealers or brown-nosers. Not only did we note several instances where helpful patients were picked on or provoked into fights by more antagonistic patients, but we were surprised to find other more subtle pressures being exerted, such as epithets being written after their names on the ward sign-out sheets. As an actual example of the tremendous pressures at work to produce conformity to the group code, one of our most responsible patients, after weeks of external peer pressure against cooperating with the staff, deliberately and obviously smuggled in contraband cigarettes for another patient on restriction, informed the staff of his misdeed, and virtually insisted that he likewise be placed on restriction to prove to the other patients that he was really one of them.

From these observations, it became clear that members of the chronic patient group, in order to enforce group solidarity and undermine an active treatment program, could and did reward one another with affection, conversation, money, cigarettes, and companionship. By the same token, they could punish one another by ostracism, threats, physical assaults, and withholding the above-mentioned rewards. Because these rewards and punishments were concrete, meaningful, and immediately contingent on certain deviant behaviors, they were extremely potent in perpetuating the code of chronicity.

It is interesting that other authors familiar with these types of patients have made similar observations but have interpreted them within the context of a different theoretical framework. Goffman, for example, who has so eloquently harangued against the evils of institutions and the mortifying, degrading influences they exert on hapless, helpless patients, weakens his thesis by presenting evidence that mental patients are anything but impotent against the monolithic institution. In fact, it apprears as though patients display considerable initiative in determining the kinds of lives they lead in a mental hospital. In an essay on the underlife of a public institution, Goffman (1961) comments on the special communications existing within a patient culture. Patients on back wards may act mute and withdrawn to frustrate the staff. Other patients may smuggle forbidden liquor and matches on the ward or set up an illegal "kiting" system for communication between wards. Still other ways of frustrating and getting back at the staff (thereby undermining the general treatment program) include smuggling comforts to fellow patients who have "messed up" and therefore been placed in a locked ward, plugging up of sinks or toilets, sabotaging lighting, and listening and agreeing with other patients' exposition of their cases.

H. F. Ellenberger (1960), comparing the mental hospital to a zoological garden, also makes some intriguing comments on the characteristics of a patient subculture. Similar to animals in captivity, patients not only engage in nesting behavior (i.e., marking off territory) but also set up their own pecking order and rules for social conduct.

In describing the patient society within a mental hospital, Talbot and Miller (1966) make a number of obervations paralleling our own pertaining to a mutually reinforcing situation between patients and staff. For example, the staff and patients alike believe that illness and deviancy represent the norm for hospitalized patients. These authors have noted that:

> ... if a patient does something that is productive or is evidence of improvement, such as wanting to get a job or actually getting one, other patients are threatened by it. They often jeer at such a person, tease him or ostracize him, in effect putting pressure on him to return to the "patient" group. ... In order to maintain their membership in the subsociety in which they have to live, they must be careful not to exhibit too much reliability, maturity or consistent activity.

Commenting on another important characteristic of the patient society, the *mutual protective alliance*, Talbot and Miller state that:

> We have observed that patients tend to develop among themselves an informal social pattern in which they say to each other, in effect, "if you let me be sick, I'll let you be sick," or "we can't help what we do because we are patients." When a person is admitted to the hospital, many adult expectations, requirements, and demands no longer are made upon him. In return for being relieved of them, he must make himself keenly aware of his own incapacity, and he must be sure that it is visible to others. It is as if he had a social obligation to exhibit his symptoms and incompetence, or to be just crazy. ... The informal social pressure, which at times comes close to being formalized, is for each person to guard his and the other's deviant behavior, even when it places great stress upon all.

Similar observations about the existence of a discrete patient subculture and its characteristics have been made by other authors. However, in our own treatment endeavors with chronic schizophrenics, we found that this informal antitherapeutic pact and pathological equilibrium between patients and staff extended far beyond the dimensions already noted and seemed to pervade almost all aspects of patient-staff interaction. Not only did this pact define an extensive code of attitudes and behaviors appropriate for chronic patients but also prescribed the specific staff reactions toward them. The staff reactions could be regarded as providing partial reinforcement for this code of chronicity. Therefore, as long as this type of patient-staff interactional pattern was permitted to exist, the task of treating and rehabilitating the chronic schizophrenic would be overwhelming; it created a situation conducive to the perpetuation of crazy behavior, the maintenance of a patient-staff barrier, the inevitability of continued hospitalization, and the reduction of patient incentive for change, improvement, and eventual rehabilitation.

It is interesting to find that most treatment programs for chronic schizophrenics pay little heed to the patients' subculture as a major determinant of chronic behavior. Instead, there is a great emphasis placed on the individual psychopathology of patients, the countertransference feelings and behaviors of the ward staff, adverse institutional influences, and the nature of the treatment techniques themselves. In as much as any treatment program that does not make any provision for offsetting and combatting the powerful destructive influences of the code of chronicity is destined to founder, it seems essential to define the parameters of this code more fully. This, in turn should point up the types of therapeutic procedures necessary to disrupt the unhealthy equilibrium between the deviancy of patient behavior and the predictable staff reactions to it. To treat a chronic schizophrenic without understanding the predominant mores and values of his hospital culture would make as much sense as treating a captured aborigine with classical psychoanalytic methods.

Before describing the components of this code, I must make three qualifications: (1) It would be false to portray the behavior of chronic schizophrenics as always deviant, bizarre, manipulative, or selfish. Many schizophrenic patients at times spontaneously show varying degrees of human warmth, concern, humor, sanity, responsibility, courage, and meaningful interpersonal involvement. Naturally, the frequency of appearance and persistence of these qualities are directly proportional, almost by definition, to the patient's level of functioning. However, the very fact that all these patients have demonstrated that they can behave humanly, if only for brief periods of time, is largely related to much of the staff's frustration in working with them. If these same patients behaved crazily under all circumstances and for all times, staff expectations for treatment and rehabilitation would not be so high. It is much more exasperating and discouraging to find patients continually employing self-destructive behavioral tactics when one knows full well that patients are capable of behaving sanely and responsibly should they choose to do so or allow others to help them to do so. (2) These observations and comments represent generalizations across all subgroups of chronic schizophrenics. In some instances, the features to be described will be more characteristic of one subgroup than another even though they will have differing degrees of relevance for all. (3) The various components of the code should not be regarded as separate and distinct but rather as mutually related and overlapping. The quotes below, which were obtained from the patients and staff, are given to illustrate the attitudes associated with each of these components.

Components of the Code

The Model Patient

PATIENT [*to staff*] : "I just want you to know that when I get to the unit I promise to be a model patient."
PATIENT: "I don't want to get in any trouble. Just tell me the rules."

STAFF: "He's such a good patient. He does whatever you tell him to."
STAFF: "Now don't push her too hard. She does a good job in the laundry."
STAFF: "He's a good worker. Never have any trouble out of him."

Within the context of the mental hospital, there is an informal, loosely structured, patient, social-class hierarchy, ranging from restricted, confined, assaultive patients at one extreme to almost well, predischarge patients at the other. The task of most chronic schizophrenic patients is to find some stable equilibrium between these extremes that assures them the greatest amount of privileges, the least amount of restrictions, and the minimum of demands without having to leave the protective setting of the hospital. Although patients often miscalculate the implications of their behavior by ending up in seclusion or physical restraints for troublesome behavior or being prepared for discharge for prolonged, relatively sane behavior, they come to learn over the years, often by trial and error, a repertoire of behaviors that will preserve their hospitalized status quo. To attain the enviable status of model patient or institutional trustee, patients learn that all they need do is to participate perfunctorily in scheduled therapeutic activities, such as recreational and occupational therapy or ward therapy meetings, perform a minimal work assignment, remain inconspicuous enough to avoid some staff member with therapeutic zeal pushing them out of the hospital, and not threaten or assault the staff.

Unfortunately for many patients, the set of behaviors characterizing the model patient is only learned after much painful, haphazard behavior during acute flareups in their psychoses, with its consequent confinement, restrictions, and loss of privileges. With the resolution of these florid symptoms, patients must be prepared to face the emotional anguish of renewed attempts at rehabilitation. However, with the passage of time, the fluctuations in their behavior tend to lessen until finally many patients reach a relatively imperturbable state, characterized by a narrow range of specifiable behaviors, which safeguards them against the equivalent traumas of seclusion or restraints and hospital discharge.

Once these patients learn to meet the unwritten but specific criteria established for model patients, they come to gain a new recognition and status in the hospital, which, in turn, reinforces the maintenance of their chronic behavior. As "well but hopeless" patients, they are gratefully accepted by hospital staff and administration as key workers who cooperate with ward routine—a source of cheap help essential to the maintenance and repair of the hospital grounds, facilities, and services. Because most mental hospitals are notoriously under-staffed, there are pressures on administrators to retain key workers for such menial tasks as dishwashing, serving food, mowing lawns, collecting refuse, laundering, and related tasks.

This does not mean that these patients are exploited by the hospital. Actually, the pact or contract between patients and hospital staff is fair and equitable. The work demands on patients are minimal (two to six hours per day at the most); the work supervisors have much tolerance for their inefficiency, ineptness, and stubbornness and grant unlimited, extended leaves of absence from work whenever patients do not feel well enough to come, grant ample rest periods, and provide unlimited job security. Such job situations are not easy to secure, even for successful, responsible members in society at large. By meeting these minimal hospital work demands, the patient not only makes himself valuable to the hospital but also earns a small amount of money for use in the canteen or for his brief jaunts into town. In this manner, both the patients and administrative staff develop a mutually beneficial, symbiotic relationship in which the needs and desires of both are met.

The Hospital as Home

PATIENT: "What I'm really worried about is that I might get out of here."

PATIENT X [to Y]: "You want to get out of here, don't you?"
PATIENT Y: "Only as far as the canteen!"

PATIENT: "The hospital is a lot better than outside—at least you get your meals and room here."
PATIENT: "I just feel the hospital is the place to be—a place to sleep."
PATIENT: "I'm not getting out. Shit, I like it better here."

STAFF: "She really has had it rough. Maybe the hospital is the best place for her."
STAFF: "I really feel sorry for some of these patients, I'm not so sure its wrong to give them a home in the hospital. Somebody has to take care of them."

The prevalent conception of mental hospitals as snake pits or horrible asylums from which all patients eagerly long to depart has little truth when applied to the vast majority of chronic schizophrenics. In fact, one of the major problems in rehabilitating these patients is their adamant refusal to be dispossessed from their adopted hospital homeland. For many patients, especially those who feel emotionally and financially deprived, the mental hospital represents a promised land where the whole range of their needs is met. Not only are the basics of food, clothing, and shelter provided within the hospital but also protection from harm and pain, relief from major responsibilities and demands, and exposure to a wide variety of entertainment and recreation activities. The hospital also provides the patient with ready-made companions who, because they share similar experiences, give him understanding and sense of belonging. Among patients who have likewise failed, the patient need not feel so inferior and inept.

One of the major problems in treating chronic schizophrenics pertains not so much to their lack of motivation for help but rather to their stubborn commitment and dedication to remaining hospitalized and employing whatever techniques are necessary to achieve this goal. It has become clinically obvious in working with these patients that, if they could direct only one small fraction of the energy and ingenuity they employ in staying chronic toward sanity and rehabilitation, the task of treating them would be greatly simplified. What many therapists fail to understand about these patients is that they are in fact highly motivated, but in a negative direction, to attain the nihilistic goals of security without responsibility, rewards without effort, and survival without meaningful living.

Similar to Lewis Carroll's *Through the Looking Glass,* patients live in a topsy-turvy world in which all acceptable attitudes and standards of behavior are reversed. Life outside the hospital becomes synonymous with death or punishment, and hospitalization becomes equivalent to survival.

PATIENT: "I'm hopeless. I have nothing tangible. I have no feelings. If I went out into the world I would die."

Also, getting well becomes equated with the prospects of getting sick again.

PATIENT: "I'm afraid if I get well, I'll get sick again."

PATIENT: "I have to sleep—that keeps me from getting crazier."

Therefore, if they are to get sick again (so patients reason), then why should they disrupt their current equanimity and security by trying to get well?

In choosing to remain chronically hospitalized, patients likewise make the choice of discarding most of the values and morals associated with human dignity and socialization. Surprisingly, we have encountered patients who show an open pride in their insanity: "Schizophrenia is the worst mental illness—it takes the worst to beat me!" Their new morality is anything but spiritual or humanistic but pertains to the immediate satisfaction of whims and acquisition of tangible, concrete rewards, such as meals and snacks, watching television, and bedtime. Indeed, it is almost unheard of for patients to question staff about more esoteric and abstract matters as to therapy and the rationale for its use.

To illustrate further this 180° reversal of the middle-class, work-oriented, responsibility-laden value system, I would like to quote the responses of two patients confronted with the possibility of hospital discharge. These responses may be regarded as representative of the attitudes (if not verbalized, then in behavior) shown by the vast majority of chronic schizophrenics. One patient stated "You'll never railroad me out of here!" The other patient, when asked what he would do if he were released the following day, replied "First I'd find out what I did wrong, and then I'd try to correct it!" Surely, these are not the views of people who feel abused by a nefarious institution or who are pounding on the doors to get out.

Aside from the wealth of emotional needs of patients satisfied by the mental hospital, there is another practical, economic reason for the reluctance of patients to leave the hospital. There is little question that after years of hospitalization, hospital discharge paradoxically becomes equivalent with downward mobility both in terms of social status and financial security. To obtain anything nearly equivalent to the services they receive within the hospital, patients would have to make a veritable fortune outside the hospital. Unfortunately, the realities of rehabilitation make the acquisition of such wealth improbable; chronic patients most often must start off with menial, low-paying jobs and at the bottom rung of the social and economic ladder. The sharp contrast between all the security and services that they automatically gain within the mental hospital but may never be earned in society is often great enough to discourage them from ever wanting to leave such a protective setting.

The attitude of the hospital staff, reflecting that of society at large, tends to complement the attitudes and expectations of the patients. Where the hospital comes to represent the idealized, childhood home for the chronic patient, a modern, therapeutically oriented staff does everything possible to make the patient feel at home. Where patients expect to be taken care of in terms of their basic needs of food, clothing, and shelter, the current therapeutic philosophy decrees that all patients are entitled to the satisfaction of these basic needs. Where patients stake their territorial claim within the hospital, the staff are more than willing to uphold the legality of this claim rather than risk uprooting the patient with the prospects of activating his psychosis or getting him upset. Where patients must experience the insecurity, anxiety, and trauma of fending for themselves outside the hospital, the staff are all too willing to intervene by readmitting them to the hospital at the slightest show of discomfort. Undoubtedly, all these attitudes on the part of staff are highly humanitarian and reasonable, but the complicating dilemma is that they may unintentionally reinforce certain unhealthy patient attitudes and behaviors. If patients can get all their material and emotional needs met within the hospital, it seems unlikely that they will ever develop the necessary motivation to leave.

The Prerogatives of Insanity

PATIENT: "You've got to take care of me. That's what you're paid for."

PATIENT A [to B]: "You can't do what you want in a mental hospital."
PATIENT B: "Yes you can. I always do what I want."

PATIENT: You can't treat me that way—I'm mentally ill."
PATIENT: "Don't upset me, I'm too sick."
PATIENT: "Sometimes it's impossible to keep the devil under control. All these temptations are too much."
PATIENT: "I'm a devil all winter and the model patient all summer since I like to go to the recreation hall and down by the lake."
PATIENT: "Give me what I want first if you want me to behave better."
PATIENT: "I'm not responsible for what I do—I'm mentally ill."
PATIENT: "If I don't want to listen to you, I can turn you off anyway."
PATIENT: "I was helping out, so why don't I get credit for it?"

STAFF: "You can't blame someone for something they can't control."
STAFF: "The only reason he does that is because he's sick."

One of the main problems in treating the chronic schizophrenic centers around the reluctance of therapists to regard patients as responsible for their actions. At present, the label of insanity often confers diplomatic immunity or sanctuary for all a patient's deviant behaviors. Patients can gratify almost every impulse or whim without fear of serious retaliation. They have the sanction to indulge their feelings because, by definition, they are presumed not to know any better or are unable to control their impulses and, therefore, cannot be held accountable for what they do. Not only is the patient immune from retaliation by society, but he can also buy protection from his own conscience for repugnant actions by employing the ultimate excuse of craziness. Under the sacrosanct banner of insanity, he can avoid guilt and shame for normally shocking or sickening behavior. If he so desires, he can defecate when or where he chooses, masturbate publicly, lash out aggressively, expose himself, remain inert and unproductive, or violate any social taboo with the assurance that the staff are forced to understand rather than punish his behavior.

Chronic patients seem to harbor certain paradoxical attitudes whereby they expect to receive the prerogatives of both the crazy and the sane—the best of both worlds. If they act crazy, they "couldn't help it"; if they act sane, they deserve rewards. They regard themselves as responsible and capable of handling things they want to do, but regard themselves as helpless and incapable of controlling impulses or conforming to unpleasant staff or group demands. In other words, they expect plus points for sanity and no deductions for insanity.

In many ways, the modern-day patient has prerogatives similar to the medieval absolute monarch with the power and sanction to gratify his every whim. Just as the divine right of kings ensured that "the king can do no wrong," so, too, the mentally ill can do no wrong; they can only engage in "sick" behavior.

The divine right of the mentally ill confers other advantages. Like any monarch with his retinue of servants, chronic patients also have a number of helpers or servants to wait on them. In any well-staffed mental hospital, professional dieticians prepare their meals, and psychiatric aides serve them;

should patients need some assistance in dressing, shaving, or showering, some staff person is always available. Recreational and occupational therapists make detailed plans to amuse and keep them from becoming bored. Should they get upset, some doctor or nurse is always nearby to quell their anxiety or relieve their hurts. Social workers are ready to act as emissaries with their families and diplomatically explain the patients' illnesses to elicit understanding and acceptance. It is not uncommon to hear many patients delusionally refer to the staff as their servants and state that the hospital exists—as in fact it does—to take care of them and minister to their needs.

The State of Suspended Animation

PATIENT: "Over on the other ward I used to sleep all day, but I can't here, so I've been pacing and scared all day."
PATIENT: "I thought we were supposed to stay here and remain calm, cool and collected, and forget our problems."
PATIENT: "I have to sleep—that keeps me from getting crazier."
PATIENT: "Not being on medication makes you have more feeling."
PATIENT: "There's no death. We just live on and on."
PATIENT: "I'm dead already—just leave me alone."
PATIENT: "I feel like shit and I want to die. I've thought of suicide but I probably wouldn't do it. I'm a spook, I can't grasp. My dream machine isn't working. I can't love and I don't think I ever did. My erotica is all goofed up."
PATIENT: "You're supposed to keep the ward quiet. It's too noisy for me to rest."
PATIENT: "If I don't get my meds pretty soon, I'm going to start batting some heads around!"

STAFF: "The patient can't sleep. I think he needs a sedative."
STAFF: "RG's upset. Don't you think we ought to calm him down?"
STAFF: "AB's been pacing around and hollering and keeping the other patients awake. Can't we give her something to quiet her?"

In Bram Stoker's *Dracula,* there is a description of people who turn into huge vampire bats at night after remaining in an unfeeling, nonreacting, trance-like undead state during the day. The behavior and expectations of chronic patients often parallel this description. They will display psychotic equivalents of temper tantrums only if roused from their state of suspended animation. They cannot tolerate emotional stress or discomfort of any kind, be it fear, anxiety, depression, love, or human closeness, and they immediately seek to quell these feelings. They seem to prefer the foggy benumbed calm of tranquilizers, the stuporous feeling of sedatives, or the confused oblivion following electroshock therapy to the unpleasant experience of their own thoughts and feelings. In other words, minimal activity and minimal stimulation by others help preserve the equilibrium of chronicity.

The hospital staff help meet these patient needs. Out of sympathy and concern for the patient's plight, staff members minister the mental healing balm of tranquilizers, sedatives, and antidepressants as soon as the patient seems upset enough to gain attention. Because it is inhumane to allow the patient to continue to suffer, it becomes incumbent on the staff to dull the edge of patient anxiety or allay his fears. Lots of sleep, rest, reassurance, and medication are used to keep patients comfortable and quiescent. The quiet ward, highly valued by administrators and therapists, is considered necessary to good therapeutic practice. As long as patients are not upset; there are no fights, injuries, or fires on the ward; patients do not complain to relatives, lawyers, or reporters about the treatment they are getting; some patients are not bothering the sleep of other patients; and the serious incidents on the ward are minimal—then the physician in charge can pride himself on running a smoothly functioning therapeutic ward.

There are good reasons for maintaining a relatively quiet ward on most acute admission services. It simply leads to less administrative and clinical hassles for all concerned. However, the concepts of the quiet ward, with its reliance on heavily tranquilized, sedated patients may not be appropriate for the care and rehabilitation of chronic patients. The major problem with these patients often is not one of employing techniques to keep them perpetually in a Dracula's coffin but rather of finding ways to rouse them from their torpor and to keep them emotionally and socially responsive.

Not My Brother's Keeper

PATIENT: "What's she ever done for me?"
PATIENT: "It's his problem. Let him take care of it."
PATIENT: "The staff's getting paid to take care of him, not me."

STAFF [patient attempts to intervene in fight between two fellow patients]: "Not now, Sam. You might get hurt."
STAFF: "I don't think a patient should have to assume the responsibility for another patient."

After years of hospitalization, patients begin to lose all sense of social or group responsibility. They regard their own problems as unique or overwhelming, and others be damned. If they observe sexual acting-out in others or aggressively destructive behavior, then it is the staff's job to intervene and reestablish equilibrium and ward peace. They have enough problems of their own to worry about and cannot be bothered taking the responsibility for others. Their attitude is one of me, myself, and I.

This attitude not only holds in instances where some patients are engaged in potentially harmful activities, but it also pertains to their unwillingness to help other patients get dressed, clean up, go to meals, or get prepared for various ward activities. They seldom volunteer their services in behalf of their fellow inmates. They are quite content to sit back and watch disinterestedly as the staff tend to these various chores.

For the most part, the hospital staff tend to perpetuate this attitude by intervening in patient fights, subduing the offender, and not placing the burden of responsibility on the shoulders of the patient group. The staff are reluctant to call on patients to help out in critical ward incidents and thereby imply that these patients in fact are inept and not responsible for the welfare of fellow patients. Even in more minor, mundane ward activities with withdrawn patients, the staff do not capitalize on the potential helpfulness of other patients who might be willing to get involved if they felt needed. Unfortunately, such a staff attitude tends to discourage meaningful patient-patient interaction by protecting patients from one another.

Victims of Society

PATIENT: "You all want to drive me insane."

STAFF: "How about doing your detail?"
PATIENT: "Do it yourself. I've worked enough in Minnesota. I'm gonna rest now."
STAFF: "For the rest of your life?"
PATIENT: "Yes!"

PATIENT: "I'm out to get society—they killed me!"
PATIENT: "I've had enough and seen enough bitterness in my time, and it hurt. I want no more!"
PATIENT: "You and your goddam society are responsible for my being here!"
PATIENT: "Listen. What would you have chosen—sixteen years of your folks bitching at you and slapping you around and accusing you of this guy and that guy or being nuts? I choose this!"
PATIENT: "I just feel like saying the hell with it. Like when I go to communion and pray for milk shakes and tequila, all I ever get is piss and shit!"

STAFF: "The problem is no one really understands her."
STAFF: "God, what a background. It's no wonder he's so aggressive."

PATIENT: "I'm sorry I hit you."
STAFF: "Oh, it's okay. You were just upset."

Although not true of all patients, many regard themselves as social pariahs—outcasts of a disinterested and uncaring society. They come to view society, or certain social agencies or institutions, as vaguely responsible for their present predicament. As a result of their being short-changed, society owes them recompense. After years of hospitalization, they begin to consider themselves entitled to total care. They become chronically and aggressively dependent and begin to feel that everything they receive is coming to them.

Another variation of this all-pervasive attitude may take the form of a personal vendetta against society for its harshness and rejection. Patients feel that they have been dealt a raw deal by life, and their global response is not flight but fight—to strike back, get even, and settle accounts. On the ward, they may implement this attitude by frequent threats or attacks on the staff at the slightest instigation.

In reacting to the deprivations of patients, hospital staff members often do, in fact, appropriately feel sympathy toward patients for their past sufferings. However, through misguided kindness and understanding they may reinforce a patient's attitudes and behaviors by exonerating his present sins on the basis of the horrible circumstances of his past life. Moreover, they may refrain from venting anger or punishing a patient for acts that, under normal circumstances, would be reprehensible simply because they understand the psychological genesis of his behavior. To understand may be to forgive, but to forgive a deviant act without punishing it may be to condone, encourage, and perpetuate it.

The Hospital as Jail

PATIENT: "There are three people I'm going to get even with before I leave this place. . . I'm going to shoot that goddam Dr. L. Who in the hell do they think they are, taking away my privileges?"
PATIENT: "The reason I'm sick is because I'm hospitalized."
PATIENT: "Youse did this to me. You made me crazy. You treat me like an animal."

STAFF: "Keep your eye on JT. If she breaks the rules again we'll put her in seclusion."
STAFF: "She's striking out again. We'll have to put her in restraints until she shows us that she can control herself."

Because many patients have been committed involuntarily to the hospital and seemingly lack insight into their behavior, they feel resentful toward hospital staff for their forced incarceration. The common complaint, especially of the more paranoid patients, is that they would be well if only they were discharged, but all their nonverbal behavior belies any serious intention to be released. They present a ridiculous attitude which places immediate discharge as a prerequisite for sanity. Therefore, as patients view the situation, if they are kept hospitalized, the staff must be prepared to bear the blame and consequences for whatever bizarre, retaliative measures the patients employ.

With such an outlook, it is not surprising that patients eventually come to view the hospital staff more as jailers, custodians, wardens, keepers, or guards than as therapists. From the patient's perspective, the staff, similar to prison authorities, determine length of sentence (hospitalization), grant parole (conditional release), award privileges, and mete out punishments.

Although the staff may view themselves as therapists and regard all their efforts as therapeutic, they (as well as society) seem to reinforce these patient attitudes. Patients accurately perceive that the staff do, in fact, police patient behavior, suppress acting-out, and determine privileges. Although staff may not be permitted to punish patients physically for deviant behavior, under the banner of therapy and the scientific appellation of negative reinforcement they are permitted great latitude in handling this behavior. Restraints, seclusion, electro-convulsive therapy, drugs, and the withholding of privileges are effective ways for keeping patients in line.

Representation Without Taxation

PATIENT [at general ward meeting]: "How 'bout some better food? Let's all vote on it."
PATIENT: "We've got a right to be heard. A mental patient has rights. Why don't you turn the ward over to us?"
PATIENT: "I don't like these goddam rules. I don't see why you can't change them like what they were before."

STAFF: "If you want the coffee pot fixed, why don't you bring this up at the ward meeting and see what the other patients feel?"
STAFF [to patient]: "Your opinion does count. If enough of you feel this way, then we'll have to do something about it."

Patients have been well schooled in the principles of democracy, equality, therapeutic community, and the virtues of teamwork—so much so that they vociferously claim their inalienable right to behave as they choose but speak in whispers, if at all, about their corresponding obligations and duties.

Hospital staffs have provided patients with numerous opportunities and forums to voice their gripes and participate in decisions affecting ward privileges and routine. However, under the banner of self-determination and therapeutic decision-making, patients are frequently granted privileges without corresponding obligations—a situation that has no comparable model in society. In society, a person gains the prerogative of being heard by assuming the obligation of being productive and consistently fulfilling the role of responsible citizen. Where the model breaks down in the mental hospital is precisely at this point: Patients are all too often granted representation without being expected to pay the taxes of appropriate, socialized, responsible behavior.

Social Push Buttons

PATIENT: "I like to make people angry to see how far I can push them."
PATIENT: "If I don't get a cigarette, you wait and see what I do tonight."
PATIENT: "Aren't you afraid I'll kill you? I might, you know."

STAFF: "We better give him an extra portion of food since that will keep him quiet."
STAFF: "It makes me want to throw up to watch him pissing in the water bubbler."

It is interesting that helpless and confused schizophrenics are often much more adept at producing certain reactions on the part of staff, family, and society at large than are the latter of evoking desired patient responses. Because patients have a far better understanding of our social value system with its inherent limitations than we have of theirs, they can employ a repertoire of behaviors that function as push buttons to elicit the desired staff or social response, thereby ensuring the attainment of their goals. These patient behaviors and the reactions they trigger off have an "if . . . then" quality to them. For example, if the patient presents any one of the following behavioral stimuli, it will elicit a specific related staff response with a high degree of probability: (1) nuisance behavior evokes irritation and anger; (2) overt sexual behavior evokes outrage; (3) aggressive-combative behavior evokes fear; (4) self-destructive behavior evokes pity; (5) stubborn withdrawal evokes frustration; and (6) crazy, bizarre behavior evokes confusion and helplessness. When staff, family, or society become irritated and angry, outraged, fearful, pitying, frustrated, or confused and helpless, they are automatically forced to take action in a variety of forms, the end result of which is continued hospitalization or rehospitalization for the patient.

When patients are confronted with or held accountable for these triggering behaviors, they almost always invoke the following ritualistic formulae: (1) "I didn't do it—you did." (2) "If I did do it, you made me do it." (3) Even if I did do it, I'm not to blame—I'm emotionally and mentally disturbed."

Another related tactic used by patients, which is likewise effective at stymieing plans for hospital discharge, is the tyranny of the weak. When confronted with the prospects of discharge, patients may appear completely helpless, lost, downcast, frightened, and inept, thereby arousing the protective instincts of staff who rush to their rescue to shield them from the anxieties and traumas of the outside world.

In other instances, patients who otherwise are functioning well within the hospital may simply refuse to work at the jobs arranged for them during transitional rehabilitation planning. These patients may try to justify their reluctance to work by invoking a variety of excuses, from headaches to hallucinations; failing to convince the staff of the authenticity of their complaints, they simply become tardy, unreliable, and inefficient at their jobs, thereby forcing their employers to fire them. Still other patients may not even go to the trouble of trying to convince staff and potential employers of their difficulties; they just dig in their heels and defy the staff to force them to work.

To illustrate this attitude, here are a couple typical patient remarks: "I don't feel like working—if I can't get what I want I quit!" or "I've worked enough in the past—I'm going to rest now."

Because the staff cannot lead all these patients by the hand or drag them to work each day and then supervise them continually, there is no humanitarian way to make unwilling patients work. The complicating problem is that the staff are apt to feel heartless and antihumanitarian when faced with the prospects of sending patients into the cold, cruel world without their having a job or any visible means of support. As a result, they rationalize their position as follows: (1) The patient must be sicker than we thought. (2) He obviously is not ready for discharge. (3) He had better be kept in the hospital for a while longer, a while longer, a while longer, etc. Undoubtedly, such a position must be regarded as humane; the difficulty is that patients often capitalize on this predictable staff response to their advantage—namely, for continued hospitalization.

Aside from the apparent reason of assuring continued hospitalization, it appears that two other factors keep patients pushing these buttons: (1) They attain power and recognition. By pushing any of these buttons, patients can mobilize social agencies, communities, families, and hospital staff to cope with their behavior. ("I'll *make* you pay attention to me.") This affords them a sense of control which reduces their feelings of helplessness and impotence. (2) They continue to push these buttons simply because they are so effective. People invariably respond to these patient behaviors and thereby continue to reinforce them.

Acts of Contrition

PATIENT A [*to patient B*]: "You're a perfect example of a hypocrite. You're singing hymns and reading the Bible one minute and swearing the next."
PATIENT: "They could at least give us good food!"
PATIENT: "Do you expect a T-bone steak for what you did?"
PATIENT: "But this is a mental hospital. You have to expect patients to do things they can't help!"
PATIENT: "Then they should be punished. Funny, you always act sick just at the time you should be doing something!"
PATIENT: "They all act so cooperative, but right after the meeting they go and do the same thing again!"

STAFF: "I'd feel a lot warmer to him if he'd apologize."
STAFF: "You'll get all your privileges back once you admit you were wrong."

Often patients, after they have engaged in a serious transgression of ward regulations or have physically hurt another patient or staff member, show some remorse. Unfortunately, even when patients do apologize, their confession of wrongdoing seems to be ritualistic without any sustained, firm purpose of making amends. Their usual pattern is to do something bad, contritely confess their wrongdoing, ask for forgiveness, and shortly afterward repeat the same process, sometimes in a different form, which calls into question the credibility of their acts of contrition. Their behavior can be summarized in the formula Slap—"I'm sorry." Slap—"I'm sorry." Slap, etc. An apology lasts only until the next time they repeat the same offense.. When staff find these repetitive acts of contrition unbelievable and convey their disbelief to patients, the typical patient response is to become hurt or furious at staff for not being gullible and naive enough to accept the magic words "I'm sorry."

To a large extent patients cannot be blamed completely for their expectations of instant forgiveness from the staff; the staff do give aperiodic reinforcement for these expectations. Because of the pressures of the current treatment philosophies, the staff are forced to show tolerance and understanding toward deviant behavior. Because, presumably, the mentally ill patient does not know what he is doing, it is not considered appropriate to offer punishments commensurate with the offense. All will be forgiven when the patient provides a token display of sanity and sorrow. It is an interesting phenomenon that the only penance a patient must pay to absolve himself of any guilt for repugnant and destructive actions is to utter certain socially magical words. We have encountered numerous instances where these otherwise penitential words were offered in a perfunctory, automatic manner immediately following the misdeed. That patients are fully aware of the power of penance is illustrated by the following conversation between two patients at a general ward meeting.

PATIENT A: "What do you think they would do to me if I decided to kill one of the staff?"
PATIENT B: "Not much, if you told the staff afterward that you were sorry."

The mentioning of these words, like the ritualistic repetition of "Hail Mary," may or may not be done sincerely. However, even in those instances when the patient does seem sincere, the apology is often only of the moment and has no binding quality or carryover effect in terms of future behavior. The repetitive utilization of these magic words enables patients, (1) to be granted a suspended sentence from any guilt or shame they themselves might experience at their behavior; (2) to placate the staff's animosity through this show of penance; and (3) to secure the restoration of full privileges. Generally, humane staff tend to comply with all three purposes.

All or Nothing

PATIENT: "Fly to the moon or wallow in the mud. Do one or the other but don't stay inbetween."
PATIENT: "If I can't be a vice-president, I prefer to be a patient!"

STAFF: "It's a shame he only got a job as janitor—he's got so much potential."

Ask any patient whether he wants to be rehabilitated and the invariable answer will be "yes." Try to do anything to effectively bring this about and the invariable behavioral response will indicate "no." One reason for this discrepancy between verbalization and behavior is that it requires minimal effort to utter the socially appropriate "yes" and maximal effort to do something about it.

There appear to be four basic components to the patients' view concerning rehabilitation: (1) They sincerely want all the good things, such as status, power, love, material possessions, that come with discharge. (2) They want an iron-clad guarantee that they will get these things. If they are to prepare themselves for leaving the hospital, they want firm assurance that people will accept them, not derogate them for being mental patients, not hold their behavior against them, not reject them, and treat them with dignity and respect. (3) They expect the good things to be given to them free. (4) They are unwilling to expend any persistent effort or expose themselves to undue frustration to acquire the good things.

Almost any therapeutic staff working with these patients will recognize the all-or-nothing principle in most of their behavior. Patients want the whole pie and are often dissatisfied with only one piece of it at a time. If they have to experience any emotional pain or stress in achieving socially appropriate goals, their most common response is to give up or say "to hell with it." This attitude and behavior is reflected in their whimsical work week or their attendance at and participation in any constructive rehabilitation program where they readily throw away all their gains at the slightest frustration or rejection—knowing full well that they can afford to do so because they can always fall back on the good will and beneficence of the hospital.

The essence of such a world view is captured beautifully in the remark of one patient, "If you don't succeed at first, then give up." We have encountered numerous variations of this attitude. Some patients talk about wanting to be corporation executives or highly paid skilled workers when they leave; others have unrealistic expectations about their athletic prowess or artistic abilities. Or, as one patient put it, he preferred to be "a saint or hero rather than an ordinary person." Because they are intelligent and aware enough of social reality to know that their presumed abilities or talents will not be recognized or rewarded immediately after discharge, they develop a "Why try?" attitude. Still others, who at some previous period in their lives demonstrated a high degree of social competence, realize that they can never again take up where they left off. Whatever skills or knowledge they once had would have to be relearned and at a time in their lives when they are much older, less adaptable, and more sensitive to their failings. Rather than settle for second best or start out life anew at the bottom rung of the economic or social ladder, they prefer to play it safe by staying hospitalized or by extinguishing any flicker of therapeutic motivation with the slightest failure or frustration.

Most rehabilitation programs for chronic schizophrenics are bound to experience problems simply because the staff have not come to grips with these patient attitudes and behaviors. The staff may even inadvertently complicate these problems further by invoking such scientific terms as low frustration tolerance, infantile omnipotence of the wish, and poor impulse control to account for these patient attitudes, but these terms are only substitutional euphemisms for saying that patients often want what they want, the way they want it, when they want it, and effortlessly. For those who once functioned adequately, they want what they once had; for those who never functioned adequately, they want what they never had. In other words, it is possible that laziness rather than craziness may account for a large portion of the patient's outlook.

The Shifting Limelight

PATIENT: "If it's not one, then it's another!"
PATIENT: "She's doing just what I'd like to do."

STAFF: "There's never a dull moment."
STAFF: "You just get one patient settled down, and then there is another one you've got to deal with."

Since the inception of our treatment studies, we have noticed an interesting group phenomenon, which seems exquisitely designed to frustrate and confuse the therapeutic efforts of the ward staff. Both in general ward meetings and less-structured ward activities, one or another patient would assume the role of a representative of the insane by waging a single-handed uprising. These uprisings would consist of floridly crazy, bizarre behavior, vociferous threats toward the staff, occasional physical assaults, and impulsive destructive behavior, often lasting for several days to a week or two. This behavior had a "too much" and "too long" quality to it, thereby forcing the staff to intervene and deal with the patient. As soon as the staff succeeded in constraining the patient, another equally difficult patient would step into the clinical limelight. It was as though each patient was serving as an understudy, ready to step in at a moment's notice when the lead performer stepped off the ward stage. Naturally, this phenomenon created an unending series of crises for the staff, who often tired in coping continually with each new bearer of the touch of insanity.

Once a patient came to the center of the stage, he or she would carry on with this disruptive behavior, making it difficult to conduct any type of therapy for any of the remaining patients. During their moments on stage, they would refuse to share the limelight with any other patient—nor would any other patient seriously attempt to compete with them. Only when these performers were dragged off stage, often through the use of medication, would another patient dare venture forth.

This phenomenon has also been witnessed by Michael A. Woodbury (1964) who refers to it as the *mad dictator cycle.* The mad dictator patient

> monopolized all the attention of personnel, who were either fighting her, subduing her, secluding her, taking her to the bathroom, or just waiting for her to do something. When the first "mad dictator" reached a state of exhaustion, usually becoming depressed and self-destructive, a second, and then a third mad dictator took over and continued the cycle.

We soon came to realize that this phenomenon served a number of vital functions for the group as a whole. Because of these functions, there were powerful group influences always operating to sustain this phenomenon. Some speculations about the causes for these behaviors are as follows:

1. The primary and most obvious function of the onstage patient was to serve as a decoy for the remaining patients by diverting staff attention and time away from general therapeutic activities with all patients. For example, the noisy, disruptive behavior of the performer tended to hamper the conduct of many group therapy meetings. In this manner, the patient in the limelight seemed to relieve group pressure; he momentarily took the therapeutic heat off the group and served as a buffer between the remaining patients and staff.

2. The patient performer served as a scapegoat for the group in that he (she) had the opportunity to act out all the group's pent up anger, sexuality, and destructiveness toward one another and the staff. In many instances, it was obvious that patients vicariously identified with the performer, who dramatically portrayed and enacted common group attitudes toward the staff and authority.

3. By engaging in such bizarre behavior, the performer came to represent a standard or control against which other patients could compare themselves and feel relatively sane and emotionally controlled.

4. The preservation of this phenomenon assured for all patients an air of excitement and constructive external stimulation, which tended to relieve the humdrum, monotonous existence of their daily ward life. They could still remain withdrawn and uninvolved as long as something was always happening.

The existence of this phenomenon likewise had a number of drawbacks for patients. Although they often were amused by the behavior of the deviant patient for short periods of time, they tended to weary of this behavior when it became protracted, intense, and continued after hours. They resented it when the noisy, restless behavior of the patient performer began to interfere with their sleep or when his controls became so weakened that he might lash out at them rather than staff. Also, if this behavior continued too long, some patients became annoyed at all the attention the performer received and sought to curtail his show, either by pointing out the attention-gaining aspects of his behavior or requesting staff to intervene.

Despite these drawbacks for the patient group, their behavior toward one another indicated a greater investment in the perpetuation of the shifting limelight phenomenon than in its extinction. The subtle manner in which the patient group reinforced a fellow patient's performance became quite apparent during various group meetings. Although a number of patients might show revulsion or disgust for the performer's behavior, they might rise to his defense if he verbalized resentment toward staff, would show interest in sexually exhibitionistic displays, would laugh at certain inappropriate remarks, and would refuse to intervene during fights initiated by the performer. Because of the differential and varied group response to these bizarre behaviors, the response could be compared to a kind of aperiodic reinforcement—a powerful influence for encouraging the continuation of selected behaviors.

Not all patient performances were solo affairs. There were also frequent occasions when patients seemed to band together as a chorus and wage a spontaneous "nut-in" during general ward meetings. These were occasions in which a number of patients would produce a cacophony of sound by simultaneously shouting, talking, mumbling, singing, or engaging in other meaningless vocalizations, thereby drowning out any serious discussion initiated by staff or other patients. Because it was difficult to focus discussion, quell the source of the disruption, or even muster up enough vocal decibels to outshout patients, the staff would shortly become frustrated, angry, and helpless in these situations. The nut-in, therefore, became a highly effective form of patient protest, enabling them to choke off meaningful group discussion, avoid the anxiety associated with it, and discourage staff in their therapeutic endeavors.

Another aspect of this phenomenon deserving comment pertains to the unwitting role of the staff in perpetuating it. As we began to study the behavior of the staff, it soon became apparent that they also needed some excitement to relieve the boredom associated with working on the ward as well as some scapegoat on whom to vent all their exasperation and frustration arising from working with these patients. In addition, the patient in the limelight often permitted many of the staff to get their minds off their own personal or work problems.

The above, then, represent many of the components of the code of chronicity. Undoubtedly, many clinicians will take exception to a conceptual formulation that interprets deviant behavior within the context of a chronic schizophrenic subculture and that attributes a volitional, manipulative, goal-directed dimension to most crazy behavior. As I have admitted previously, the sole reliance on any one conceptual model to explain patient behavior will prove far too oversimplified and biased from a theoretical standpoint. For example, it is also possible to account for all the clinical phenomena observed on the basis of a model emphasizing an underlying, cerebral dysfunction or a combination of other factors. In all likelihood, a multidimensional interpretation of patient behavior is more valid theoretically than a unidimensional one. However, from a practical treatment standpoint—because at this particular point in time we are not in a position to unravel twisted genes, correct subtle biochemical aberrations, undo the past, or eliminate institutions—it is my contention that the conceptual framework used to organize the attitudes and behaviors of patients and staff alike provides the best operational and prognostically optimistic foundation on which novel psychosocial treatment procedures can be constructed and evaluated. Although some of these psychosocial procedures may prove ineffective, this should not deter the clinician from first exploring the degree and range of their efficacy.

Regardless of the particular manner in which clinicians may choose to interpret the subculture phenomena observed among chronic schizophrenics, there can be little question about the actual existence of these phenomena. For the present, suffice it to say that no therapeutic programs can prove maximally effective for a given schizophrenic patient unless provision is made for neutralizing those countertherapeutic, subcultural influences that sustain and nurture his deviant behavior, as well as the complementary actions of staff that unwittingly reinforce these influences. Therefore, it seems reasonable to assume that the initial step to be taken in breaking this vicious circle of interaction between patients and staff is to change radically the role of the institutional staff (who, presumably, are more mentally flexible and healthy than patients) from protagonists to antagonists of chronicity. As we shall see, this represents a formidable task, requiring far more than signing official memoranda or verbally instructing staff to mend their ways.

chapter 4

The Syndrome of Chronic Staffrenia

Generally a psychiatrist and occasionally a psychologist assume or are delegated the major responsibility for the conduct of treatment programs with chronic schizophrenics. Although these clinicians may be highly knowledgeable, espouse a humane philosophy, and propose ambitious treatment goals, the therapeutic program is destined to falter if the ward staff do not accept the philosophy or work toward the goals. This clinical truism derives from two basic premises: (1) The amount of time the staff spend with patients is inversely proportional to the degree of professional status, clinical training, and salaries. (2) The ward staff spending the greatest amount of time with patients have the greatest opportunity for influencing their behavior. As a result, the ward director or team leader may make momentous therapeutic pronounce-

Portions of this chapter have been adapted from A. M. Ludwig and F. Farrelly, The code of chronicity. Arch. Gen. Psychiat., *15:561-568, 1966, and The weapons of insanity.* Amer. J. Psychother., *21:737-749, 1967, with permission.*

ments from his Olympian professional heights, but these vocalizations will prove fruitless and limp if they are not implemented and translated into action by the personnel on the firing line.

Anyone having conducted treatment programs within a mental hospital must soon become keenly aware of the assortment of ways the ward staff, knowingly or unknowingly, subtly or overtly, actively or passively, can sabotage the program as effectively as the patients who resist its influences. For example, aides may be assigned several patients to talk with but not do so or, if they talk with them, not talk about what they are supposed to. In other instances, if aides disagree with the therapeutic regimen prescribed for given patients, they may decide to instigate their own programs. Or, if they identify with patients whose privileges are being withheld, they may slip them forbidden cigarettes or treats. In extreme cases, when the supervisor is absent they may even choose to rough up troublesome patients. These are some of the more obvious means for undermining a treatment program. Actually, as we shall shortly see, these problems are only minor compared to ones that do not arise at the initiation of lower echelon staff but develop as a result of their working primarily with chronic schizophrenic patients for any extended period of time.

Before turning to these treatment-related problems, we should first note some general characteristics of institutional aides that may affect their functioning within a therapeutic setting. These characteristics are unrelated to the kind of treatment program or kind of patients treated but pertain more to the types of persons filling these jobs and the nature of these jobs. At the outset, let me emphasize that my remarks must not be construed as critical of these personnel. These lower echelon staff must be regarded as just as humane, conscientious, considerate, and responsible as any degreed professionals; they merely do different jobs and see their jobs differently than many higher echelon staff would like them to. However, because their activities represent such a vital aspect of any treatment program, we are obliged to examine the ways in which these activities may facilitate or hamper the total treatment effort.

It is becoming the vogue for enlightened administrators and team leaders to foster open communication among the staff, to blur traditional professional roles, to encourage participation of all members of the treatment team in decision-making activities, and to stress the equality of all staff members as an integral part of the total treatment effort. All these are beautiful and worthwhile sentiments. Unfortunately, because they tend not to be completely credible to lower echelon staff, they are often difficult to translate into practice. Like Orwell's *Animal Farm*, where all pigs are created equal, the staff also fully realize that some pigs are created more equal than others. This discrepancy between professed professional equality and *de facto* inequality may lead to dissension among the staff.

Although career aides generally tend to be people with low aspirations, the economic and professional realities of their job situation do little to enhance motivation and emotional investment in assigned therapeutic activities. Economically, there is marked differential in salaries between aides and hospital professionals, such as doctors, social workers, and nurses. Professionally, the status and prerogatives of aides roughly correspond to the low level of their salaries. Therefore, why should they exert themselves more than necessary or take on additional responsibilities when they receive so little tangible or intangible incentive for doing so? If they cannot share the salary, status, prerogatives, and glory of professionals, why share their headaches, anxieties, expectations, and responsibilities? Obviously, it will take more than token liberal propaganda to convince aides that they are as important as enlightened professionals would like them to believe.

To further complicate matters, most hospital staff work within the context of a civil service system. Although this type of system offers many protections and advantages for personnel (e.g., job security, medical and retirement benefits, sick leave), it may produce the unfortunate by-product of a civil service mentality, which is antithetical to innovative, active treatment programs (it must be added that this type of mentality may pervade all levels of hospital personnel, degreed or not). This mentality places great store in punctuality and the eight to five workday (fostering clock-watching and discouraging voluntary overtime), paperwork and committees, and the perpetuation of tradition—all of which contribute to organizational inertia. Moreover, the seniority system, although ensuring protection against whimsical layoffs, tends to reward length rather than quality of service. In effect, then, personnel can better their lot not by initiative and creativity but by their ability to avoid getting in trouble and thereby jeopardizing their jobs. To do nothing beyond certain minimal job expectations receives as much tangible and intangible reinforcement as performace above these expectations. As a result, mediocrity rather than the pursuit of excellence comes to be the rule rather than the exception.

In such a work setting, other detrimental values tend to develop. Jobs tend to be viewed as work rather than as a source of enjoyment and self-fulfillment. Coffee breaks and goofing off become the highlights of the workday. In addition, a culture develops among lower echelon staff that tends to discourage initiative on their part and that also protects them against criticism from their superiors. Although aides represent the majority of clinical personnel within a mental hospital setting, their reactions are often those of an abused minority. For example, it is common to find that aides will cover up for one another in cases of maltreatment of patients, stealing hospital property, etc. This is not done because aides are less moral than hospital professionals, but because they do not want to be branded as squealers by their coworkers and because there seems to be little reason to assume the responsiblilities reserved for supervisors who are paid accordingly. It is interesting that those cultural values that emphasize group loyalty, antagonism to authority, security, minimum work output, and the avoidance of responsibility are not too dissimilar to those described for the code of chronicity in hospitalized schizophrenics.

These, then, are only some of the problems a team leader must face in devising a treatment program and attempting to create a ward situation conducive to high staff morale and enthusiasm. However, other more serious problems further compound these difficulties. These problems pertain to the reactions evoked in staff while working for any length of time with chronic schizophrenics.

The Counterconditioning of Staff

We already have commented on a number of subcultural values and behaviors of chronic schizophrenics that tend to perpetuate the process of chronicity. In addition to these, the chronic schizophrenic also has at his disposal a variety of techniques exquisitely designed to dampen or quash the therapeutic enthusiasm of almost any staff within a short period of time. By employing these techniques, which we have labeled the weapons of insanity (Ludwig and Farrelly, 1967), the patient can preserve his prerogatives, continue to go his own way, and avoid being pestered about getting well and preparing for discharge. It makes little practical difference whether we regard the patients' use of these techniques as volitional or not, organically or psychologically determined. What does matter is that they exist and that their very existence tends to produce an invariable staff response.

It is very difficult to maintain or sustain any therapeutic zeal for these patients when almost every helpful or kind gesture is either repulsed, ignored, or unappreciated. Patients seem masters of counterconditioning and extinction techniques. When the staff try to rouse them from their apathy, correct their deviant behavior, or interest them in some constructive task, patients often respond by stubbornly ignoring, cursing, spitting, hitting, threatening, or assaulting them. Not only do patients seem ungrateful or even resentful of staff efforts, but some may even attempt to drive the staff further away with Mafia-like threats of maiming or destroying their families.

In a situation where the staff receive little feedback or gratitude from patients, the usual response is for therapeutic interest to wane or become extinguished. When patients drop all the social amenities, courtesies, and decencies, the predicted staff response is to gradually move from a position of helpfulness and concern to one of frustration and apathy.

When a patient does lose control of his behavior and strikes other patients or staff members, he knows that the staff cannot retaliate in like manner. Even when the staff feel that a good kick in the pants or a slap may be infinitely more therapeutic than a tranquilizer pill in controlling patient behavior, they are bound by the humane principles of kindness, understanding, or restraint. Physical punishment is taboo and has no place in modern therapeutic institutions. In the ongoing struggle for control between patients and staff, the staff must engage in battle with one hand tied behind. The patient can fight as dirty as he likes using alley rules (thumb in eyeball, knee in groin). The staff, so to speak, are conscientiously bound by the Marquis of Queensbury rules of having to fight back fair and square.

In addition to the limitations (well known by patients) imposed on the staff, patients may also utilize the weapon of "If you upset me, I'll make you wish you hadn't." Confronted by the staff, patients may implement this unspoken threat by losing hard-won therapeutic gains, staying up all night, and displaying bizarre behavior. When patients respond in such a way following staff confrontation, the staff inevitably assume that they have pushed the patient too fast and too far. The possibility of a patient getting upset is, in effect, a club held over the staff's collective head.

Other difficulties exist as well. For patients who by current clinical mythology are supposed to show poor reality testing, chronic schizophrenics reveal a remarkable degree of cunning and ingenuity in attacking the treatment programs at their most vulnerable points. They possess the ability to ferret out the staff's emotional sensitivities, but also are quite adept at pushing them to the point of loss of control and helplessness. It is humanly impossible to work with these patients over a long period of time without experiencing the whole gamut of primitive emotions related to instincts for self-survival. If the staff were to respond to these emotions in terms of the classical fight or flight reaction, the former type response would result in their dismissal from the hospital and the latter type response would result in decreased therapeutic intervention with patients.

We have found it a general rule with few exceptions that those more paranoid patients who become potentially violent or assaultive are uncanny in their ability to pick on people, either staff members or helpful patients, who are weaker than they or who present no serious threat of physical retaliation. The authority hierarchy on the ward also plays a great influence on this behavior—at least in circumstances in which patients are not absolutely panicked or completely out of control. In general, ward aides receive the most abuse, nurses less so, the head nurse or social worker even less, and the ward physician or psychiatrist hardly at all. There is some rationale for patients' actions because they are often aware that the higher the authority figure they attack, the greater the potential for massive retaliation in the form of frequent intramuscular injections of medication, electroconvulsive treatments, loss of privileges, seclusion, and restraints. Needless to say, the very fact that aides are exposed to the most hazards while receiving the least remuneration cannot serve as an incentive for them to confront and interact with these patients on their own initiative, regardless of program demands. It is more likely that they will choose to treat these patients gingerly and to keep a safe distance. Minimal involvement means minimal risk.

The Adaptive Staff Response

Part of the real difficulty in establishing an effective treatment and rehabilitation program for chronic schizophrenics resides in the very reaction of hospital staff toward working with these patients. Caught between what they have been taught represents good professional treatment and their own personal intuitive (often equated with bad) reactions provoked by the tactics and behaviors of patients, the staff eventually become incapacitated in their treatment efforts. The conflict is between how the staff are taught they should treat patients and how they spontaneously want to respond.

It is easy to understand the genesis of this bind. If the staff accept the view that the mentally ill patient is not responsible for his actions, it follows that the essentials of any humanitarian treatment approach must always be comprised of love, kindness, acceptance, and understanding; above all, it is professionally inappropriate to criticize strongly, react angrily, or punish patients for their behavior in as much as such behavior has been caused by factors beyond their control. On the other hand, day-to-day experience with these patients invariably arouses staff reactions that are diametrically opposed to those that they are expected to feel. Unfortunately (or fortunately, depending on one's bias), most staff members are neither saints nor stoics—they tend to react to provocation in a perfectly human way.

The basic interpersonal contradictions in the traditional treatment approach to chronic schizophrenics can be summarized in the following way: The staff is asked:

1. To be loving and kind toward patients who react to these gestures with rejection, rebuke, hatred, or physical assaults.

2. To be respectful and considerate of patients who show little or no personal human dignity, as defined by the qualities of conscious awareness, free will, and a sense of self-responsibility and social responsibility.

3. To feel compassion for people who do not seem to evince any emotional hurt and who, on the contrary, appear to be enjoying all kinds of special prerogatives in their status as mental patients.

4. To be therapeutic toward patients who do not want help and who continually work at extinguishing the flame of staff's therapeutic enthusiasm.

5. To be understanding toward those deviant patient behaviors that are more a reflection of the patients attempt to manipulate the environment than a search for succor.

6. To be helpful to patients who work at making them feel impotent.

7. To treat patients as human adults when these same patients often behave like infants or worse.

8. To regard patients as weak and fragile when it is obvious to them that patients are strong-willed, stubborn, and determined to get their way.

9. To provide empathy for patients who do not accept the blame or responsibility for their actions.

10. To invest trust in patients who may lash out at any moment and strike them.

11. To do nice things or personal favors for patients who give no thanks and who regard these favors as their due.

12. To respect the value system of patients which is antithetical to sane, responsible living.

13. To forgive deviant acts they cannot understand and to understand acts they cannot forgive.

14. To be "giving" to patients while they themselves are forced to live on marginal emotional subsistence from patients in appreciation for their efforts.

If staff attitudes must under all circumstances be those of patience, helpfulness, love, and acceptance, what options do staff members have when they frequently find themselves impatient, helpless, angry, and revolted by patients' behaviors? Not only is it difficult for the staff to act persistently one way when they feel another, but this same hypocritical facade weakens the therapeutic effectiveness of their efforts. Despite the loud and clear messages from their adrenals and viscera, the staff are permitted only a very limited response repertoire to the behavioral weapons employed by patients.

When working under these conditions for any length of time, the staff develop a kind of battle fatigue or shell shock and tend to resolve such conflicts by assuming an observable set of attitudes and behaviors that oftentimes complement those of patients. We have labled this characteristic staff reaction the syndrome of *chronic staffrenia.* The components of this syndrome include apathy, weariness, minimal personal involvement, decreased enthusiasm, lack of emotional investment, and markedly decreased expectations for patient rehabilitation. Also, because they are abused or attacked so often by patients, staff members come to develop a type of compensatory or adaptive paranoia (i.e., fear of walking down halls alone, not turning back on patients, not being in room alone with patients, fear of confronting obstreperous patient, etc.). Because of these continual stresses, it is not surprising to find that many staff members also come to feel depressed and anxious in their job situation. Staff attitudes soon become depicted by such statements as "Let well enough alone" or "To hell with it—it just isn't worth it." The staff increasingly tend to withdraw and engage in perfunctory therapeutic activities, which, regardless of their name, at best resemble good custodial care, and they become all too happy to settle for patient cooperation in lieu of patient rehabilitation.

The validity of our observations on this syndrome receives partial confirmation by Woodbury (1964) who dealt with similar phenomena under the heading of the *sucked dry syndrome.* Briefly commenting on his experiences at Chestnut Lodge during a replacement therapy era (i.e., love cures all philosophy), he noted that the "feeling of exhaustion, emptiness, despair, guilt, and underlying anger which personnel often felt at the end of a day's work on the unit" reached an epidemic level at times. The more the patients got from the staff, the more they demanded. In such a setting, staff crises were abundant and turnover of key personnel was high."

It is obvious that the successful conduct of any clinical treatment research program is ultimately dependent on the enthusiasm, cooperation, and dedication of those staff members directly involved in the day-to-day struggles with these patients. Unless staff morale is high and their therapeutic goals ambitious, it is unlikely that patients will receive full benefit from any treatment program. Therefore, it becomes incumbent on any person formulating a clinical treatment and rehabilitation program for chronic schizophrenics not only to concern himself with the efficacy of the techniques but also to create a working situation where the staff administering them can do so willingly and effectively.

The Liberation of the Staff

If the ward environment is to be optimally conducive to high staff morale, then certain general interpersonal principles must be adopted. Because we may regard the relationship between higher and lower echelon staff as the necessary condition and the relationship between ward staff and chronic schizophrenic patients as the sufficient condition for development of the syndrome of chronic staffrenia, these interpersonal principles must be capable of resolving the conflicts encountered with both types of relationships. Let us deal with the former type of relationship first.

One of the initial requirements in dealing with institutional aides is to recognize the realities of their job situation. This means that the ward leader need not play games of pseudodemocracy and professional equality when the facts dictate otherwise. Mental health professionals (doctors, nurses, social workers) make more money, have higher status, and possess more prerogatives because they are more highly trained, proficient in their specialties, and have greater experience in decision-making and the assumption of clinical responsibilities. This does not imply that they are better people than aides. Nor does it mean that their clinical contribution will be greater. It only means that they have chosen to work in an area in which demand exceeds supply and, therefore, one in which salary and status are relatively high. To pretend that this is not so is to do a disservice to the intelligence of all ward personnel, who, I believe, prefer honesty to mythology.

Despite the existence of this professional hierarchy, no matter how inequitable it may seem to many, certain practices can be instituted to lessen the resentment and increase the respect of the "have-nots" for the "haves," thereby providing a closer and more harmonious work situation for all ward personnel. One of the most important of these practices involves respecting people for their abilities and placing them in clinical situations in which they have the opportunity to exercise these abilities to the fullest. Although the team leader may not be in a position to reward meritorious work with money, he has by his very authority a very potent reinforcer at his command, namely, praise. It is my contention that lower level staff receive all too little of this cheap but precious commodity and that if it were dispensed more liberally and appropriately it would provide a powerful motivating effect. Almost everyone has a need to be appreciated and respected but in a credible way. It is simply not sufficient to play democratic games with lower echelon staff. What they lack in actual salary and status must be made up, to some extent, in appreciation for their clinical contributions and accomplishments.

Although high level staff are largely responsible for formulating the nature of the treatment program, handling administrative matters, and providing supervision, it is difficult to create a situation of high staff morale if the ward leaders do not occasionally pitch in and work side by side with aides in their various clinical duties. Generally, ward leaders tend to keep their hands clean by maintaining a safe administrative distance from the patients placed in their care. They may occasionally chat with patients during ward rounds or conduct general ward meetings, but they avoid such nitty-gritty activities as getting patients out of bed, encouraging personal hygiene and appropriate appearance, interacting with patients in the dayroom and hallways on an informal basis, feeding them, stimulating participation in recreational activities, and a host of other menial activities for which aides are largely responsible. However, the performance of patients in these very activities tends to be the best indicator of their current clinical status and their potential for discharge. If aides are to become convinced that their efforts expended in these various activities are clinically meaningful and important, ward professionals can only demonstrate their beliefs that this is so by periodically rolling up their sleeves and pitching in.

What must also be remembered in running a hospital ward is that daily routines are apt to get monotonous and boring. When the staff no longer get "kicks" from their jobs, they are apt to become either apathetic, querulous, or divert their interest to personal concerns. Therefore, in any treatment program it is not only essential that some provision be made for the staff to have fun occasionally but also that a sense of excitement and novelty be programmed into their daily activities. This often can be accomplished through creating a ward atmosphere in which learning and constant evaluation of therapeutic procedures are held at a premium and in which all staff members have the opportunity of participating in these processes. In other words, an active therapy program alone is insufficient for the stimulation of high staff morale; there must also be a commitment toward the honest assessment of this program and a willingness to try out new procedures and techniques.

These are only some of the necessary prerequisites for dealing with the problems of staff inertia and low motivation, and they apply to any type of treatment program for any type of patient. As indicated previously, work with the chronic schizophrenic is especially demanding and frustrating and creates a special set of problems—chronic staffrenia—above and beyond the general ones already mentioned. To resolve these problems, a particular kind of therapeutic philosophy is necessary.

Rights of Staff

Inasmuch as the staff have been commissioned to intervene therapeutically with these patients, it seems necessary to assume that they have certain rights consonant with their obligations. In our current and legitimate concern for the rights of patients, we often have overlooked or ignored the rights of those working with them. What currently obtains in most treatment programs is that the staff have the right to being cursed, threatened, mauled, ignored, or repulsed by ungrateful patients without being able to punish them for their actions or to vent openly their genuine feelings. However, it must be insisted on that the staff should and do have certain rights: the right to expect gratitude from patients and safety from physical harm, to interact honestly with patients, to be creative in and to derive a sense of accomplishment from their work. In other words, if patients are to be treated with respect and dignity, the lower echelon staff should be able to demand similar responses from patients (as well as from their supervisors). These are not idealized luxuries but absolute necessities for the treatment staff. Unless these necessary rights are encouraged, implemented, and ensured, no intensive, persistent, and concerted staff treatment effort can occur.

Another aspect of this problem pertains to staff interrelations. Because of the constant feelings of frustration, anger, and discouragement that arise in working with these patients, it is essential to provide opportunities for the staff to ventilate and share these feelings with one another. Because the staff live on a marginal emotional subsistence from patients, they must receive emotional sustenance elsewhere. When their therapeutic batteries are run down, encouragement, support, and suggestions from other staff members are often sufficient to recharge their enthusiasm for further encounters with these patients. Because the patients themselves do not express appreciation for the therapeutic efforts expended in their behalf, the staff must develop an esprit de corps of their own from which they can gather the necessary emotional strength to sustain a therapeutic rather than custodial orientation with these patients.

Pollyanna plus Scrooge

The staff should be encouraged to be genuine with patients. They need not be pressured to hide behind pseudohumanitarian treatment slogans that decree that love and understanding are the only appropriate responses to all patient behaviors and that anger and even occasional hatred are antitherapeutic. There is nothing inherently wrong in admiring and liking the good qualities of patients while, at the same time, disliking and rejecting their undesirable qualities. It is also possible to hate the crazy behavior of patients while liking them for what they have been or potentially could be in the future. If the staff are forced to conform to hackneyed therapeutic platitudes, their responses, at best, will consist of perfunctory love, phony acceptance, misguided kindness, or biased understanding. It seems most appropriate that the staff be allowed to give patients accurate and honest human feedback concerning the impact and social consequences of their behaviors. It is unreasonable to insist that the staff adopt inappropriate smiles or act kindly toward patients while brimming with anger. Love and understanding are not simply insufficient but, at times, actually incongruous and damaging in response to certain patient behaviors. For example, if the staff feel compelled to disguise their therapeutically taboo feelings of anger, disgust, or even hatred for certain repugnant patient actions with inappropriate, syrupy affect, they may make patients more confused and distrustful by re-creating the double-binding communicational interactions in the early life experiences of many patients. On the other hand, if these taboo but exceedingly human feelings (assuming they are not neurotically determined) can be expressed, the staff will also feel free to show genuine warmth and affection when the occasion demands. To be inhibited in the expression of anger is likewise to be inhibited in the expression of love. The freedom to express both positive and negative feelings toward patients will enable the staff to transmit much clearer and more believable cognitive and emotional messages to patients.

In short, then, the staff should be allowed and encouraged to use a whole relationship: to be positive, warm, and loving when patients behave sanely and well and to be angry, rebuking, rejecting, and punishing when patients are obnoxious or bad. The combination of Pollyanna plus Scrooge represents a more whole, integrated, human response; alone either response is a travesty.

Naturally, this does not mean that the staff be granted the complete license to behave in any way they choose and whenever they choose to do so. Granting the staff the freedom to interact honestly with patients saddles them with the additional obligation and responsibility of behaving humanely, impartially, and selflessly toward patients. Moreover, there is the further consideration that the staff gather from one another some consensual validation for their feelings toward a particular patient and that the emotional or verbal feedback given this patient be consistent for most staff members. The matter of group validation for reactions to specific patient behaviors is especially important in that it helps guard against idiosyncratic, impulsive, or counter-transference feelings peculiar to the particular staff member rather than objectively induced by the behavior of the patient. Only when trained staff members are united in their reactions and their responses systematic toward patient behaviors can patients experience the full impact of the staff's feelings. Consistent staff reactions, however, are not sufficent. They must be goal-oriented, always having as their primary purpose the constructive modification of patient behavior.

The Trap of Understanding

There is the general assumption among insight-oriented psychotherapists that if a patient can understand fully the psychological determinants of his behavior, he will then desire or be compelled to adopt more constructive ways of acting. There may be some validity to this assumption when applied to relatively well, highly motivated, neurotic, psychiatric outpatients, but it has little clinical pertinency when applied to hospitalized chronic schizophrenics. From our clinical experience, these patients receive little benefit in gaining insight or understanding about behaviors that they are unmotivated to change and that often pay off for them.

In their article, Talbot, Miller, and White (1964), refer to this overemphasis on insight as the *cult of psyche.* Instead of stimulating patients to maintain interest in newspapers and current events, keeping contacts with family and friends, and developing practical work skills, hospital staff, who give allegiance to the cult of psyche, tend to focus on dreams, fantasies, insights, and interpretations of the underlying causes of behavior. This concentration on intrapsychic processes tends to substitute for productive activities and interests. As a result, the insight-oriented therapy sessions come to assume such tremendous significance as the thrice daily temperature readings of the tubercular patients in Mann's *The Magic Mountain.*

There are two sides to the problem of psychological understanding—the patients' and the staff's. From the patients' perspective, knowledge of the psychological roots of their problems seems to bear little relationship to their willingness to alter behavior. We have encountered numerous patients who wallow in insights profound and dramatic enough to cause any psychoanalyst joy but that do not influence their behavior an iota. For many other patients, substantial behavioral change may occur without prior insight. In a more general sense, we feel on safe clinical grounds in claiming that for the majority of patients, the middle-class virtues of introspection and self-understanding are meaningless if not irrelevant concerns.

In many ways it seems obviously inappropriate for the staff to focus primarily on the hidden determinants of psychopathology with patients who are in a catatonic stupor, negligent in their personal hygiene or appearance, posturing bizarrely, grossly delusional, or stubbornly uncooperative. To give an extreme example, it seems ludicrous to even contemplate the notion of a therapist interpreting the meaning of a patient's assaultiveness while the patient is beating him up. For all these patients, we maintain that the major therapeutic problem is not one of having them understand why they are engaging in these undesirable behaviors but rather how to get them to stop doing so. From our clinical experience, the therapeutic paradox is that chronic schizophrenics have to be almost well before they derive any benefits from indulging in the luxury of wondering why they behaved as they did.

From the staff viewpoint, currently traditional approaches place great pressures on them to intervene with patients in a dynamic, interpretive way. If the patient openly defecates, masturbates, exhibits himself, or strikes out, the staff's customary role is to determine the underlying reasons for this behavior and then to impart this understanding to the patient in the hope that this will automatically correct the behavior. I do not argue against the notion that a dynamic understanding of the reasons for deviant behavior is essential in dealing with patients. On the contrary, it is difficult to conceive of an effective therapeutic program that makes no attempt to understand the genesis, precipitating causes or intent of patient behavior. The therapeutic danger, however, arises when nothing other than understanding is offered to patients— when understanding serves as an end in itself rather than a basis for developing potent techniques for modifying the deviant behavior. Moreover, through some false notion that understanding is synonymous with the Rogerian "uncondi tional positive regard" and a benign tolerance of crazy behavior, the staff may deprive patients of honest human feedback concerning the social and interpersonal repercussions of their acts. The therapeutic problem is that when the staff give perfunctory understanding rather than the appropriate human responses of anger, repugnance, or disgust, they reinforce the notion that patients are not responsible for their actions. If patients can be assured, as in fact they often are, that they will receive solace, benevolent understanding, and, therefore, instant forgiveness for their deviant behaviors, they are absolved of any guilt or shame (both potent motivators for change) they might feel or be made to feel for their actions. Therefore, automatic understanding, with its implication of instant forgiveness, unwittingly may contribute to the perpetuation of recalcitrant patient behavior.

Another more subtle but equally important aspect to this problem is that the strict use of a dynamic insight-oriented approach to deviant chronic schizophrenic behavior, aside from its general therapeutic impotency, can represent a way of avoiding or hiding from a meaningful encounter with these patients. By relating to patients largely through the impersonal, formal medium of some psychoanalytic or existential ideology, the therapist can avoid the more stressful, emotionally laden, and scary feelings associated with a direct, personal, involved, human confrontation, or reality-oriented interaction. From our clinical experience, it is the latter type of approach that seems to have the greater therapeutic impact.

The Popularity Question

The staff must resolve many other problems before any effective treatment program can be launched. One of these problems pertains to the ability and power of some patients to control and manipulate certain staff behaviors to a far greater extent than the staff can manipulate patient behaviors. If patients can emotionally upset the staff, command their attention, mobilize them into action, and demand some type of intervention by simply striking out or defecating, masturbating, or exposing themselves in the dayroom, it is largely the patients who are pulling the strings. As long as patients have more levers for provoking the staff than the latter have levers for evoking sane behavior from patients, the balance of power lies with the patients. Such a situation demands that the staff become aware of their own sensitivities to the tactics of patients and avoid falling into the trap of automatically responding in the predictable way to the variety of social push buttons employed by patients. This does not mean that the staff should not respond in a manner consonant with their true feelings; but that the staff should not lose control of their feelings and, thereby, behave in an irrational manner. In other words, the feelings evoked in the staff by patient behavior should be used consciously by them as an instrument of therapy (i.e., goal-directed and consistent) rather than as a whimsical response to the situation. Once this can be accomplished, the staff will be in a far better position to establish some type of regimen to reduce the effectiveness of the patients' maneuvers, as well as to offset their own sense of therapeutic impotency.

Furthermore, if the patient code of chronicity is to be broken, then so, too, the pseudotherapeutic code which dominates the current clinical scene. In essence, this latter code permits the awarding of rewards or goodies in the absence of good deeds and emphasizes the necessity of a continuing positive, empathic, accepting relationship with all patients, including chronic schizophrenics. It presumes that a mutually harmonious, warm relationship between patients and staff is much more conducive to patient rehabilitation than a relationship marked by friction and occasional ill will.

It would be nice if this presumption were so. Unfortunately, clinical reality conflicts with armchair idealism. All too often, a relatively conflict-free relationship with chronic patients can only be purchased at the cost of keeping them hospitalized. In fact, it is more the rule than the exception that staff popularity with patients is synonymous with poor therapy. To win such a popularity contest with patients, and thereby get in their good graces, all a staff member need do is to avoid confronting them and to cater to their whims or needs. To do otherwise is to incur their wrath or displeasure.

If the staff are dedicated to rehabilitating patients, they must anticipate and accept not only the likelihood of being unpopular but also of being hated. It is not unusual or even unreasonable for patients to resent staff members who strip them of their hard-won prerogatives, who force them virtually against their wills to begin making plans for leaving their comfortable hospital homes and facing the anxieties and fears associated with responsible living outside the hospital. Why should patients feel warmly toward staff members who attempt to induce them to relinquish everything they have come to covet, to change a way of life that has offered them comfort and security? Yet this is exactly what therapy with these patients is all about. And to accomplish this goal, the treatment staff must be willing to swallow the bitter pill of ingratitude and even deep resentment for all their treatment efforts.

It is my contention, based on our experiences with these patients and the staff charged with their care, that the principles and philosophies already outlined in this chapter are not only essential for providing maximal, healthy interaction with patients but also crucial in combatting the insidious development of the syndrome of chronic staffrenia. This in no way implies that the application of these principles will resolve all the problems involved in working with hospital staff or that staff relationships will always prove harmonious. Even under the most ideal conditions, it is difficult to imagine a situation in which there will not be periodic lulls in morale or frictions among the staff. However, if one is alert to staff needs and provides an environment in which these needs can at least be partially met and openly discussed, these lulls will end and conflict can be resolved. When chronic staffrenia is transformed into acute therapeutic enthusiasm, a treatment program has its optimal opportunity for success.

chapter 5

The Disruption of Chronicity

When a hospital ward milieu discourages responsible, socially adaptive behavior and fosters psychopathology and deviancy, it is anticipated that Le Châtelier's principle, pertaining to living systems, will be operative. This principle holds that a system in a steady state or equilibrium responds to the introduction of an external stimulus in such a manner as to counteract its effect. For example, a noxious stimulus presented to an amoeba will produce a contraction of the protoplasmic wall and some visible changes in the protoplasmic structure, but, after the stimulus is withdrawn, the organism will return to its original state. Only when the noxious stimulus is very powerful or applied for a lengthy period of time will permanent alterations occur. Translated into clinical terms, this implies that the introduction of even the most promising treatment approach for individual or groups of chronic schizophrenics has no more than a temporary beneficial effect when it is administered within the context of a chronic ward culture that acts to preserve the status quo. There may be some transient and sporadic signs of improvement in patients but, "after the dust settles," this improvement is likely to dissipate and all will be as before. If, in fact, this improvement is to be more permanent, drastic measures will have to be taken and applied over a sufficient length of time to disrupt the existing equilibrium of the chronic ward.

Tranquilization or Activation

When one attempts to construct a more healthy ward environment, one of the first matters to be resolved concerns the role of tranquilizer medication (mostly phenothiazines) in the treatment of chronic schizophrenics. It is unnecessary to cite the enormous amount of evidence attesting to the value of these drugs in the general treatment of schizophrenics. By now there have been sufficient studies to demonstrate the superiority of phenothiazine drugs compared to traditional forms of psychotherapy for acute and chronic schizophrenics (May, 1968; Pasamanick, et al., 1967). What must be commented on, however, are certain of the seldom-considered limitations of these drugs.

1. The demonstration of superior, statistically significant results of tranquilizer drugs compared to a placebo or traditional types of psychotherapy does not imply that all patients receiving these drugs respond well or even optimally to them. The significant results merely attest to the finding that these patients, as a group, do better than a comparable group receiving some other type of therapy or placebo. Thus, it is likely that some patients may be adversely affected by these drugs, while others respond minimally to them. Conversely, it is common to find that many patients given some type of control therapy will demonstrate considerable improvement, although not the same degree or extent as they would with drugs.

2. The finding that patients improve on these drugs does not mean that this improvement is sufficient in all cases to ensure their discharge from the hospital or their continued functioning in the community. Although the drugs may produce some lessening in psychopathology, many patients start at such a low level of socially adaptive behavior that the subsequent improvement only represents an iota of the amount necessary to alter their prognosis. In other words, statistical improvement in a large group of patients cannot be viewed as synonymous with practical clinical improvement.

3. Improvement related to the administration of tranquilizer medication may simply reflect the fact that patients are merely more manageable and tractable within the hospital than previously but may not be indicative that they have become more responsible and self-sufficient human beings. In essence, then, despite the contributions of these drugs, they cannot be viewed as panaceas for the treatment of chronic schizophrenics.

The patients who present the major treatment problem and who represent the bulk of hospitalized patients are largely those who may be regarded as pharmacological residues, in the sense that they have received almost every variety of phenothiazine tranquilization in varying dosages, often for many years, without any substantial change in their clinical status or in their ability to function in the community. For most of these patients, drugs continue to be administered mainly for management purposes or even out of force of habit rather than for active therapeutic purposes. In fact, it is my distinct impression that whatever benefits these drugs originally held for these patients have long since passed and that the continued administration of these drugs inadvertently produces adverse therapeutic effects. For many patients, pill-taking two, three, or four times daily begins to become a way of life and tends to foster an increased dependency on the hospital. The queueing up of patients at nursing stations to receive their daily pill assumes many features of a social event. As part of this medicated way of life, patients come to rely on drugs as a means for quelling all their feelings and to produce a state of emotional numbness. As a result, they never have the opportunity to resolve the anxieties and fears that originally brought them to the hospital and that continue to play an important role in their desire to remain hospitalized.

From the vantage point of the professional staff, the excessive reliance on these drugs absolves them of the obligation of becoming more intimately involved with these patients and actively searching for new and more effective treatment modalities. As long as staff prescribe drugs for these patients, it is assumed by administrators, family, and community that patients are receiving adequate therapy. The convenient dispensing of these drugs, then, tends to produce a therapeutic indolence and sense of complacency among the hospital staff, for they assume that they are doing all that can be expected of them, especially when they also expose these patients to some sort of nebulous, ill-defined milieu treatment program. Moreover, as part of this overreliance on drugs, professional staff are all too prone to resort to these drugs on a p.r.n. (give as needed) basis whenever patients appear upset or unmanageable rather than risk the emotional stresses associated with intense, interpersonal confrontations.

In our own work with chronic schizophrenics, we have decided to explore the possibility of abandoning all forms of tranquilizing and sedative medication in our various treatment programs for all the reasons listed above and to work with these patients primarily within a psychosocial framework. The general treatment conceptualization employed tends to run counter to traditional ones for it emphasizes the activation of dormant healthy behaviors, as well as suppressed psychological conflicts, as one of the first and more important steps in the overall treatment process. We have postulated that such an activation will likely occur through a combination of lifting the pharmacological lid and exposing patients to situations of increased interpersonal involvement and responsibility. Either approach alone may prove relatively ineffective. For example, it has been our experience that almost all our referred patients who have been on high maintenance doses of phenothiazine drugs over the years do not undergo a substantial change in clinical status when withdrawn from these drugs. Likewise, heavily tranquilized patients respond perfunctorily at best to situations demanding responsible, interpersonal activities. It is only when the drugs are withdrawn and patients are placed within a certain kind of ward milieu that interesting things begin to happen.

In brief, then, the basic treatment conceptualization advocated can be represented in an oversimplified manner (see Figure 5-1). Part A of Figure 5-1 depicts the notion that a given social stimulus of strong intensity (e.g., interpersonal communication, demand for responsible behavior, etc.) will elicit relatively ordered, predictable, and goal-directed responses in normal as well as neurotic persons. This same stimulus, applied to a heavily tranquilized, withdrawn, chronic schizophrenic, in the context of a traditional ward milieu, will produce either an attentuated response or a completely unpredictable one (see Figure 5-1, part B). It is difficult to take therapeutic advantage of these responses because they are so negligible, hard to observe, or unexpected. In behavior therapy circles, there is a principle known as dead man's law, which indicates the problems of modifying null behavior. For behavior to be altered, a sufficient amount must be present so that its frequency of appearance can be

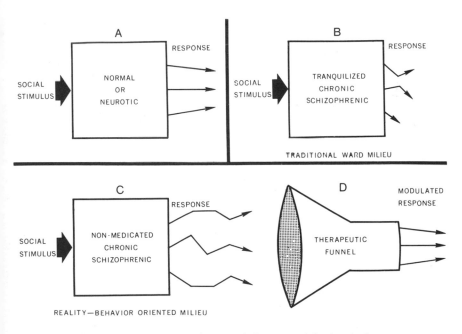

Figure 5-1: Response characteristics to social stimulation.

either increased or decreased through the application of appropriate positive or negative reinforcements. Therefore, it seems proper to employ procedures that will elicit the appearance of more behaviors, both in quantity and diversity.

In this regard, Figure 5-1 indicates that if the same chronic schizophrenic is withdrawn from psychotropic medication and placed in a ward setting where he cannot escape the implications of his actions or lack of actions, the given social stimulus will more likely evoke more exaggerated and varied responses (part C). Some of these responses will be appropriate whereas others will seem haphazard, meaningless, or bizarre. This phase of treatment represents the activation of chronicity and is the specific focus of this chapter.

The elicitation of these responses, however, must be regarded as an initial but essential step in the treatment process. There can be little definitive therapeutic value in producing a response for the sake of a response. If optimal results are to be obtained, a type of therapeutic funnel capable of shaping and channeling these responses in a more modulated, socially adaptive and constructive direction must also be constructed (see Figure 5-1, part D). The term therapeutic funnel refers to the specific treatment procedures designed to mold the evoked responses. A variety of these procedures may be employed; these will be described at length in subsequent chapters.

It must be emphasized that the primary rationale for this model pertains to the necessity for disrupting the therapeutically destructive equilibrium existing within a chronic ward culture. When the convenience of tranquilization is not readily available to patients and staff alike, when the dormant conflicts of patients are permitted to emerge, when the traditional quiet ward is no longer esteemed, a considerable burden is placed on the patients to find new ways of adaptation and on the staff to explore new therapeutic modalities and ways of relating to the patients. If the staff are forced to cope with the previously submerged iceberg of patient psychopathology, it is likely that they too will awaken from their institutional slumbers.

In employing this model, which not only eliminates or reduces the therapeutic role of tranquilizing medication but also stresses the simultaneous importance of increased interpersonal involvement and responsibility, clinicians must be aware of the likelihood of opening a Pandora's box. By lifting the pharmacological lid and introducing the notion of responsibility they can anticipate the reactivation of previously suppressed psychotic symptomatology as well as the reexperiencing of old fears and anxieties in patients. Undoubtedly, some clinicians will interpret the reemergence and resurgence of psychopathology to mean that patients become sicker under the stress and duress of these procedures. Although this is a legitimate possibility for symptomatic neurotic or agitated patients, such an interpretation does not seem appropriate when applied to most chronic schizophrenics. It must be remembered that the patients under discussion represent the hard core of chronic schizophrenics who have already been exposed to every variety of psychiatric therapy, with unsuccessful or negligible results obtained at best. From a clinical standpoint, the primary task is to get through to these patients, shake them from their complacency and chronic equilibrium, get them socially involved and more responsible, and challenge or disrupt the stability of their socially maladaptive habits and outlook—even at the cost of activating their psychoses.

There is some clinical support for this view in the literature. From their experience with chronic patients, Stone and Eldred (1959, p. 179) concluded as follows:

> Thus, it seems likely that in these chronic patients an imposed increase in frequency and duration of contacts with personnel was accompanied by the development of manifest delusions. This adds weight to the hypothesis that delusions represent restitutive symptoms, as psychotic attempts to deal with the interplay of internal forces and external reality. Unfortunately, this is often interpreted by nurse and doctor alike as a poor result. The patient becomes more agitated. His orderly routines break down. He is more demanding of staff time and attention. There may even be an increase in suicidal risk. . . . It should not surprise us that a patient whose wall of apathy has been breeched would revert to his old screen of projections and delusions, in order to cope with the stress of new relationships. We do not consider the increase of delusions to be necessarily a good or bad turn. We do think that it may be an inevitable occurrence in the rehabilitation of certain chronic schizophrenics.

Now that we have considered some of the arguments for the activation of chronicity, several qualifications must be made. Most of the above comments about tranquilizers pertain primarily to socially withdrawn, minimally communicative, or passive chronic schizophrenics. However, there are other types of chronics who are actively delusional, grossly bizarre, overly responsive to social stimuli, or who constantly seek out interpersonal interaction, albeit inappropriate, throughout most of their prolonged hospitalization—despite their being on high maintenance doses of tranquilizer medication. Obviously, the immediate therapeutic problem with these patients is not one of provoking responsivity but rather of dampening or shaping it. The appearance of too much psychopathology may present as many difficulties in treatment as the presence of null behavior; with both types of situations patients may prove equally unreachable. Therefore, for overly responsive patients, the removal of medication is not so essential as placing them in a ward environment that can channel and modify their behavior in a socially appropriate manner.

I do not mean to imply that medication has no role in the inpatient treatment of hard-core, chronic schizophrenics. In our own inpatient treatment programs, we have found the use of phenothiazine tranquilizers or sedatives extremely helpful in certain specific situations. These situations pertain primarily to dealing with instances of aggressive and assaultive behavior that endanger either the patient himself or others, especially when this behavior is not immediately amenable to other forms of therapeutic intervention. In such instances, we have chosen to employ medication only to reduce the immediate risk and, after this is accomplished, to resort to other nonsomatic procedures to prevent future occurrences. When medication is employed, it is administered vigorously and in sufficiently high doses. However, rather than keeping patients on pharmacological ice interminably for fear of a recurrence of the dangerous behavior, medication is only given for several days, after which time it is withdrawn. Aside from these specific situations, it has been our impression that the whole gamut of schizophrenic behavior can be handled quite effectively solely through the use of various psychosocial strategems.

Cultural Confrontation

Aside from a deemphasis on medication, clinicians who aspire to disrupt the therapeutically destructive influences of a chronic ward culture and arouse patients from their institutional stupors must adopt and then implement certain clinical tenets. These tenets must serve as the theoretical foundation for almost any psychosocial approach to treatment.

1. As stated previously, all patients are regarded as responsible and hence accountable for their behavior even though they may be considered insane by psychiatric and social standards. If pressed to do so, they can exercise the choice of getting well. This assumption may not conform to many notions regarding the biochemical etiology of schizophrenia, but inasmuch as no pharmacologic cure is readily available, the question of such an etiology is purely academic for the purposes of treatment. If clinicians are to act, they have little choice other than to adopt a psychosocial basis for patients' behaviors and psychosocial techniques to modify them.

2. Because all patients live together on one ward, the behavior of any one member, good or bad, reflects on and influences the whole group. Just as the deviant behavior of a family member can affect the welfare of the whole family, a similar phenomenon can operate within a hospital ward enviornment. Patients, in fact, must be regarded as their brothers' keepers, whether they like it or not, and they are obliged to intervene to prevent the deviant behavior of their fellow patients from affecting the welfare of all patients on the ward. Instead of the ward staff having the major burden for modifying patient deviant behavior, the patients themselves should be expected to assume much of this task. Moreover, it is presumed that in helping others they will be helping themselves.

3. There is no need to deluge someone with medication simply because he happens to be experiencing intolerable feelings of anxiety, fear, depression, or

insomnia. Patients must learn to live with and through these feelings without ready access to agents that tend to produce mental oblivion. They will have to find other constructive ways of coping with these feelings or just learn to bear some suffering if they are ever going to learn to live humanly and productively in the outside world. Naturally, there will be many exceptions to this view, but whenever possible, patients should be provided the opportunity of resolving their discomfort by means other than instant tranquilization.

4. Staff must provide as little reinforcement as possible for pathological or deviant forms of behavior. Patients should have their craziness pointed out consistently and insistently. Furthermore, the privileges patients receive are not automatically due them but contingent on the performance of desired behaviors.

5. Patients' present behaviors are judged all important. Although past experiences may have shaped much of their present conflicts and behaviors, such psychological genesis is deemed irrelevant for two reasons: (a) A variety of etiologically oriented treatment approaches have been tried with these patients and failed. (b) Present behaviors are the only ones the staff can see, measure, and attempt to eliminate or encourage.

6. To become well, patients will first have to think, feel, and behave in ways defined as healthy by staff. The concepts of normality and sanity as therapeutic goals are too intangible and vague; a deliberate attempt must be made to concretize these concepts by insisting that patients adopt the standards of appropriate behavior as specified by therapeutic staff. These standards may seem arbitrary and artificial, but they at least indicate a starting point for personal growth. The luxuries of self-actualization and individuality can come later, after patients demonstrate some semblance of human, socially adaptive behavior.

7. There is no need to play at democracy in therapeutic community meetings or at other decision-making functions; not the majority, but health and sanity, as defined by the staff, should rule. Citizens of the schizophrenic community have no voting privileges on the ward; to be granted a voice in ward affairs, they first have to go through the naturalization process of sustained, responsible behavior.

Undoubtedly, the enforcement and implementation of these assumptions will create an artificial ward society that, in many ways, does not conform to the expectations of society at large. In fact, it could be argued that the expectation that patients, for example, not engage in sexual activity with one another on the ward or that they show concern for the rights of others and assume responsibility for the behavior of fellow patients represents an unduly idealistic, moralistic position concerning appropriate human behavior. In our own experiences, several patients themselves objected that it was unreasonable for the staff to expect them to act in such an unnatural manner—in society, the normal thing for them to do would be to mind their own business. Although there is a certain validity in this objection, the critical problem for most of these patients is not related to the specific standards set for their behavior but rather their unwillingness to conform to any standards that demand of them some modicum of responsible, sane behavior. As long as staff members are in a position to establish appropriate standards for behavior, they may as well choose those they can admire not only in patients but in themselves as well. Moreover, it is assumed that if patients can learn to conform to the expectations of their small ward society, they will be in a much better position to cope with the expectations of society at large.

These assumptions, then, demand a radical revision in the customary conception of the psychiatric treatment of chronic schizophrenic patients. Because medications are not given except for uncontrollable, aggressive, or overly agitated behavior, when patients complain of insomnia they simply do not sleep. If they complain of anxiety, tension, or headaches, they will have to find ways to deal with these feelings without drowning them with drugs. If patients get upset when confronted by the staff with their deviant behavior, the staff can feel free to push them further, even at the risk of setting the patients back. If patients show no courtesy in their requests and assume a demanding attitude, the staff need not honor them. There is no reason to presume that chronic schizophrenics, by virtue of their illness, are incapable of preceding their requests with a "please" and following them with a "thank you." Mental illness and manners need not be antithetical.

Breaking the Code

At this point, I should like to change the focus of the discussion from the general to the specific and recount some of our own experiences in grappling with the code of chronicity. When I first began working with chronic schizophrenics, I was very much imbued with the virtues of insight and the necessity of providing understanding and acceptance to these "unfortunate," "deprived," and "socially-rejected" patients. However, it did not take long to realize that such an approach was both inappropriate and totally ineffective for such patients. In fact, such a therapeutic orientation held even less relevance to the problems of coping with the countertherapeutic forces operative in the chronic culture. If meaningful interaction with these patients was to occur, then a new orientation to therapy would have to be adopted.

At first, when patient problems arose on the ward, such as aggressive acts, destruction of property, or even failure to respond responsibly when necessary, we held numerous group meetings with all thirty patients present and talked at considerable length about these problems. These discussions and homilies had little if any impact. Appeals to reason failed, and attempts at compromise were either ignored or viewed as weakness by these patients. Obviously, if patients were to benefit from treatment, the cold war stalemate between patients and staff could not continue.

After a point in time, the treatment staff came to adopt the assumptions outlined above as an operational basis for relating to patients both individually and as a group. Not only were we interested in raising the price of chronicity by making it a luxury patients could not afford but also in creating a ward environment where chronic, socially maladaptive behaviors no longer paid off. Patients would be expected to behave responsibly in regard to their own welfare and that of fellow patients whether they wanted to or not.

Once we became firmly committed to these treatment goals we were left with the task of translating them into tactics and procedures aimed at undermining the unhealthy aspects of patient group solidarity and the group reinforcement of deviant behavior. One of the first strategies adopted, to put it bluntly, was that of divide and conquer. Inasmuch as it was virtually impossible to enlist the support and cooperation of patients as a group for our treatment goals, it seemed reasonable to try to fragment the group by deliberately playing patients off against one another. It simply would not be sufficient for staff to communicate verbally to patients how they were screwing one another up by their lack of concern for one another's welfare or by their irresponsible behavior; if the message was to prove meaningless and effective, it would have to hit home emotionally. From our vantage point, this could only be done by using the patients' God-given and taken-for-granted hospital privileges as treatment levers. Thus, if any given patient engaged in serious deviant behavior, he as well as the entire group of thirty patients would have to experience the consequences of this behavior. Patients as a group could no longer afford to encourage acting-out or to undermine the therapeutic ministrations of staff if they hoped to retain their usual prerogatives and privileges. In fact, if they showed foresight, they should be motivated to prevent certain therapeutically taboo actions that might jeopardize their privileges. In this manner, the ward culture was redefined so that any patient who behaved irresponsibly would be viewed as a betrayer rather than an esteemed member of the patient group.

Also, a basic issue to be settled with patients centered on the matter of control, namely, who was in charge. This issue was humorously and succinctly described in a "Miss Peach" cartoon:

> CAMP LEADER: "Look, children, if you prefer a camp wherein everyone runs amok and eats themselves sick on candy and stays up all night and gets boggy-eyed, well it's up to you!"
> CHILDREN (Holding protest sign, they shout in unison): "We do!"
> CAMP LEADER: "OH, REALLY? WELL, I'M RUNNING THIS CAMP, NOT YOU!"

Although the patients on numerous occasions requested the staff to let them run the ward, we had little doubt that any such undertaking would lead to chaos. One of the better integrated patients, in fact, predicted that if we were to comply with this request the ward would become another *Lord of the Flies.* Such an outcome almost did occur in a study discussed later. Therefore, to preserve some semblance of a therapeutic milieu, we persistently conveyed to patients that ward rules, as established by the staff, were the only appropriate standards for patient behavior during their residence on the unit. If, as happened on several occasions, patients protested certain policies and called for a vote, even when all thirty patients voted "yes" and three staff members voted "no," the "noes" would win. When patients protested that the staff were unfair in not obeying the majority decision, the common staff response was that fairness or democracy were not their concern—only sanity, responsibility, and decent behavior from patients. The staff were not interested in engaging in pseudo-democratic procedures of group rule but preferred rather to establish a system most conducive to getting patients well. Patient requests and decisions would be listened to, encouraged, and honored only when they were reasonable and consistent with ward policies. If patients did not like the way the staff ran the program, they were offered the option of getting better so that they might be discharged from the hospital. The staff were not running the ward for the patients' comfort and convenience but rather to help them get well.

In order to further undermine the chronic patients' value system, we decided to utilize many of the same concrete, meaningful, and immediate rewards and punishments that patients themselves employed to perpetuate it. Minor infractions of ward rules were met by the usual loss of certain privileges. However, if any member or members of the patient group went AWOL from the hospital or engaged in forbidden aggressive or sexual activities and no one attempted to intervene or inform the staff, the entire population would be restricted to the ward and lose all privileges for three days. For each additional infraction of these taboo behaviors occurring during their confinement, the patients would receive additional days of restrictions. In this manner, we attempted to make the total group of patients directly responsible for the behavior of each of its members.

Although we sanctioned and encouraged patients to vent their anger and to defend themselves appropriately against attack, to intervene and restrain other patients engaging in fights, and to prevent fellow patients from running away from the hospital, we never failed to insist that these behaviors be employed within the boundaries of moderation and discretion. The staff were always present on these occasions to guarantee that the boundaries would be observed. There was no clinically valid reason why the staff should always be expected to intervene in physical scrapes or conflicts between patients. In fact, we viewed the practice of having the staff automatically intervene in these incidents as having an adverse therapeutic effect for two reasons: (1) It conveyed the message to the patients that they were not competent or capable of coping with difficult situations. (2) It relieved patients of the obligation and responsibility for the welfare of their fellow patients.

In addition, we clearly communicated the value that squealing on or actively controlling other group members' unacceptable behaviors was good when it was against a bad code. Contrary to the generally ambivalent reactions of persons in authority toward informants, we offered sanctuary, concrete rewards, and staff approval for those patients who thwarted their own group's destructive values and behaviors. In short, our aim was to mobilize the potent but latent constructive forces of the patient peer group to modify inappropriate reactions, to encourage the assumption of responsibility, and to increase coping behaviors. Previously, these forces had manifested themselves only in an antitherapeutic manner.

In order to convey some flavor of the impact of these procedures on patients, selected excerpts of patient-staff interaction during general ward meetings are given below. The following interchange occurred shortly after we attempted to implement our policy concerning total group responsibility. As will be noted from the content of this interaction, patients were not only reluctant to accept the justice or fairness of ward restrictions for the sexual transgression of two patients, but also displayed many of the attitudes characteristic of chronic patients. However, even in this early meeting patients began breaking out of the code as they commented on the behavior of their fellow patients. This trend was to continue and become more pronounced during the ensuing weeks of this particular program.

> T-SW[1] [*addressing patient group*] : "What's everybody restricted for?"
> WM: "I don't want to be put on the defensive right off the bat. See, I was caught in bed with AF and the whole ward was restricted."
> KF: "I don't see why everybody in this building should sit in all day."
> BM: "We're supposed to do something [*referring to sexual transgression*] , but what the hell are you supposed to do?"
> T-P: "Are you saying this is upsetting?"
> BM: "Yes. I'm in the room with 'em. Who the hell wants to sit here on a nice day? Bad enough the first time they did it."
> AF: [*laughs*]
> T-P: "Does this make sense that everybody is responsible for what a few patients do?"
> EM: "We can't do anything about it."
> WM [*excusing his behavior*] : "I have trouble sleeping nights."
> T-P: "No wonder! Why does this bother you?"
> WM: "New environment. Living with women."
> MM: "AF isn't responsible."

[1] *"M" after patient's initial indicates male and "F" indicates female. "T" stands for therapist, with the following qualifications: "SW"=Social Worker, "N"=Nurse, "P"=Psychiatrist, "A"=Aide.*

MF: "If she's so sick, then WM should throw her out of his bed at night!"
WM: "I've got just so much will power."
MM [*angrily*]: "Then this is going to happen again?"
WM: "No, it's not going to happen again."
AM: "I don't think AF knows how to act. She's just so agitated she's looking for someone to depend on."
WM: "I suppose if I weren't so sick myself, maybe she could depend on me."
AF: "I'm so goddam tired. That's why we have these meetings—to get everybody up and out of bed."
DM: "How long were you restricted?"
WM: "Why restrict everybody?"
BM: "I suppose group pressure."
LF: "Why not take the guilty ones and lock them up?"
AF [*shouts*]: "Get off my hands!"
T-P [*interpreting*]: "Do you say your hands are being slapped?"
AF: "I wish somebody would wake me up!"
T-SW: "If AF is too crazy to stay out of somebody else's bed, it's up to everybody else to watch her."
JF: "I don't see what we can do."
MF: "It isn't that it is going on just now, but it will keep going on."
CM: "On other wards they never restricted the whole ward."
AF: "What are you going to do—bury us alive?"
MM: "You're not making sense!"
T-SW [*to AF*]: "Are you saying we can't stop you?"
AF: "Oh hell, I don't know."
MM: "I don't think AF is responsible. She's going through an act."
AF: "Act! It's no act!"
RM: "I don't think she knows what she's doing."
CF: "She knows damn well what she's doing."
AF [*to CF*]: "Get lost!"
CF [*to group*]: "What are we supposed to do—feel sorry for her?"
MF: "I was on the grounds and people thought I was AF. How do you think I felt?!"
MM: "I was in the VA hospital and there were boys and girls and there was no hanky-panky."
SF: "Maybe sex is like a new toy for AF."
MM: "I think there are guys on this ward that are in the same boat as WM. AF is the only girl who's lost her self-respect."
T-P [*to group*]: "It's a pretty scary thing to have responsibility for others!"
CM: "Yes, if you don't know what to do about it."
BM: "If you don't know how to help yourself, how can you help others?"
T-P: "Sometimes it's good to get involved in someone else's problems."
EM: "You tell them, but they don't pay any attention."
CM: "You want to help them, and they don't use the help."
KM [*annoyed at constructive talk and excusing WM's behavior*]: "Some people just have to have sex."
BF: "I haven't had relations for five years. I think you just have to think about something else."

After the first several times that the ward was placed on restriction, many patients began breaking out of their shell and directing their anger (at first expressed toward staff) at the offending persons. Interaction at ward meetings became heightened, and patients who previously had only the staff to reckon with, now had to take on their fellow patients as well. They soon came to see, in a very concrete way, that the behavior of other patients did truly affect them and that they had to cope with other patients to preserve their own rights and privileges.

Although patients still resented staff for this unfair infringement on their rights and privileges, at the same time they seemed to become more sensitized and aware of the behavior of their fellow patients, especially when this behavior portended a possible threat to their own privileges. Through this forced patient involvement and interaction, we were able to produce a situation wherein the partial power of the patient peer group could be unleashed and, hopefully, channeled in an appropriate and constructive direction to control and modify the irresponsible actions of other group members.

The following excerpt of patient interaction captures the reaction of the patient group to a female patient who had eloped temporarily from the ward, thereby putting the whole ward on restrictions. Even though the offending patient was known to be vicious and assaultive—terrorizing staff and patients on previous wards into not crossing her—her fellow patients now were able to throw caution to the wind and exert pressure on her to shape up. As a result of the therapist-nurse telling the group that they are all on three days restriction because of LF's behavior, several patients in the group acted disgruntled and angry.

> T-P: "Nobody has told LF about their feelings yet."
> CF: "She knows we all hate her!"
> LF: "I didn't know the whole ward would be restricted."
> T-N: "You knew it. You're not that crazy!"
> LF: "Yes I am!"
> CF: "She needs a good kick in the ass!"
> BM: "Now we can't go to the zoo."
> DM: "Take her down and sit on her and give her a hard time!"
> BM: "What are we supposed to do?"
> MM: "God damn it to hell, son of a beehive, Jesus Christ!"
> T-SW: "LF, are you crying?"
> LF [crying]: "I want to go to hell where I belong."
> MM: "LF, you ain't that important to take three days out of my life. Jesus Christ! . . . This is worse than an admission ward."
> LF [now threatening]: "I don't have to take this shit!"
> T-SW: "Oh yes you do!"
> MM: "Are you going to run away again?"
> LF: "I might."
> MM: "You'll get a kick in the ass!"

LF: "I'll kick you right back."
DM: "All this because of one dame. I don't like it a damn bit. Let's change the ward rules."
T-SW: "Let's change LF."
KM: "She doesn't want help."
T-SW: "She doesn't give a damn about any of you."
LF: "That's not true!"
MM [*referring to LF*]: "She's a bitch!"
LF [*shouting*]: "What did you call me?"

LF and MM got up from chairs and began fist fighting with each other. Several patients intervened and pulled them apart. LF got the worst of the fight. No one was seriously hurt. LF seemed considerably more subdued and less hostile. A heated discussion continued about LF's behavior with serveral patients agreeing they wished she had killed herself when she eloped. At end of meeting, one patient suggested that MM and LF shake hands and make up. MM's answer: "I wouldn't shake hands with that bitch!" In subsequent meetings, patients again confronted her vigorously, both forcing her to come to group meetings and keeping her from abruptly leaving them when she did not like what was being discussed.

Soon, patients began preventing others from eloping, either talking them out of it or informing staff of the proposed escape. At the encouragement of staff or on their own initiative, they intervened in fights, restraining the offending parties. They became offended at aberrant sexual behavior and reported instances of this to the staff.

At the same time, these instances were discussed openly at general ward meetings. The discussions seemed to become more meaningful, and the topic of responsibility, which at previous meetings seemed mainly of theoretical interest, now began to become a reality.

At one point patients had gotten little sleep for several nights because they were trying to control and calm patient DM who had been noisy and destructive on the ward. The focus of the following discussion is on responsibility and the relationship of the parents to the patients' illness.

CM: "I'd like to say something, Dr. L. I think last night was the first time in a long while we all got some sleep."
T-SW: "Many feelings were stirred up due to DM's behavior, but you all lived through it."
T-P: "Through this experience each and every one of you could put yourselves in your parents' and society's shoes and appreciate how frustrated they must feel with you."
RM: "I know they are disappointed in us."
CM: "My father expresses feelings of disgust with me. Calls me goofy in the head."
T-N: "People can't help being discouraged when you keep doing the same things over and over—flubbing up chances."

GM: "The rest of my family aren't like my father."

T-SW: "I think the rest of your family might be afraid of you and just go along with you."

BF: "I think families understand more today than they used to. They have better insight into mental illness."

KM: "I don't think families care. It's their fault. If we were raised right, we wouldn't be here."

GM: "I think you are just passing the buck!"

BF: "Many people come from poor environments and turn out O.K."

KM: "They're exceptions. There are exceptions to all rules."

T-P: "But you can change your present behavior."

CM: "You can't change the past. I didn't have a decent childhood."

T-SW: "Whose fault was that?"

AF: "Yea, whose?"

T-SW: "What counts is *now*. What you do, it's up to you."

KM: "Bullshit . . . I was afraid of a lot of people's parents until I grew up. I'm only afraid of psychiatrists now."

T-SW: "That's the first time I've ever heard you say you were afraid."

KM: "You should know the answers."

RM [*to KM*]: "It's partly your fault."

KM [*angrily*]: "It's not my fault!"

T-P: "It's your responsibility to get out of here. We can't come up with the answers for each one of you to get out."

KM: "There are certain key factors involved in my getting out . . . One is getting a job and holding it."

T-SW: "Every day, by the kinds of decisions you make, is the deciding factor in your getting out."

T-N: "It's up to you!"

CM: "The final decision is up to the staff. They have to release you."

T-N: "What do you think, LF?"

LF: "I don't agree with KM. You can't blame your parents. Our choice is our own." . . .

T-SW: "Each and every one of us has had experiences that were unfair and cruel. But what you do about them is what counts."

KM: "What do we get out of it? What does the state do for us? Treatment, bah!"

T-P: "What is your obligation? How can you help the staff or meet them halfway in order to get out?"

RM: "We've got to do our part and help all we can."

KM: "I don't go along with the state, the rules, etc. I'm not going to be broken."

T-SW: "That's what I get from what you say: 'They aren't going to break me.' If you haven't gained a thing, then the question is 'What can you do about changing?' "

MM: "You can compare us to Vietcong guerillas. I don't know how to play the game anymore. Some of us are trying to muscle our way through. Others are passive."

T-P: "We want to break you of craziness. We believe we can break this chronicity. Supposing you all win out with your iron will and break us. You can have hospitalization forever."

T-SW: "Most of you want freedom on your own terms."

KM: "You mean your terms!"

T-SW: "Society has terms."

PM: "It's obvious we are defeated. We've lost a lot [*referring to privileges*]."

KM: "I'm not defeated. Just slowed down."

T-SW: "I agree with you. You've won out from your family, staff on other wards, etc."

CM [*boasting*]: "We're too much of a challenge!"

RM: "We got to get this idea out of our head. We've got to work with the staff and change our ideas and get out." . . .

As the program progressed and as patient responsibility and involvement with others increased, several patients voiced the dilemma they were in by "squealing" on their fellow patients or acting toward them as staff would. They felt caught in a "no-man's land"—citizens without a country. They felt that if they betrayed their code, they would not know either who they were nor to whom they belonged. At least, by retaining the chronic patient's value system, they would have a ready-made identity.

We recognized their dilemma as painfully real; nonetheless, we actively manipulated ward situations and meetings in order to force them to stop procrastinating or straddling the fence between sanity and insanity or between responsibility and irresponsibility and to make the agonizing choice of whose values they would adopt—patients' or staff's. To help them make up their minds and to reduce the number of options available to them, we constantly rewarded their efforts to identify with the staff and removed privileges when they behaved too deviantly.

From our clinical impressions, it seemed that the psychosocial techniques employed were capable of stirring up a beehive of both socially appropriate and inappropriate behavior. Not only did many patients who were previously uninvolved and socially withdrawn show varying degrees of responsibility for others but they as well as others also demonstrated an activation of their underlying psychopathology. In these latter instances, much of the evoked behavior might have seemed random, haphazard, and purposeless, but it told us that these patients were not burned out, that they could still be reached through psychosocial intervention, and that their basic psychological conflicts could be activated and symbolically brought to the surface.

It would be false to give the impression that all patients were responsive to these techniques. Some, in fact, seemed too disorganized or uninvolved to respond to these techniques or even to attend seriously to what was transpiring; others responded beautifully and seemed much better integrated psychologically at the end of this particular treatment program. Overall, however, the majority of patients who began to break out of their shell of chronicity displayed much more emotion and activity, which, at least, could serve as a substrate or basis for further therapeutic intervention.

Undoubtedly, many other psychosocial procedures could have been employed to achieve the same results. I do not regard these particular techniques as inviolate, perfect, or even most efficient; at best they represent beginning attempts at breaking down the conditions and barriers that help confer therapeutic immunity on these patients. However, what must be regarded as inviolate is the assumption that unless the procedures, whatever their particular nature, are designed to cope with and resolve the socially maladaptive and destructive influences inherent in the chronic patient culture, most therapeutic efforts will prove futile.

The above discussion, then, as well as the specific clinical examples employed, pertain primarily to a theoretical and procedural basis for breaking through the barrier of chronicity and shaking up the system which perpetuates it. We have yet to deal with some other ways in which this may be accomplished and which may prove even more effective and efficient. Most important, we have still to consider the issue of the therapeutic funnel, namely, the specific techniques to be used in molding, channeling, and shaping the evoked behavior. As indicated in Chapter 1, the major therapeutic problems with chronic schizophrenics not only pertain to getting their attention but also in knowing what to do with it once it is attained.

part three

Modifying the Behavior of Inpatients

chapter 6

The Intricacies of Interaction

In current psychotherapy literature, there is the implicit assumption, especially within a group or ward setting, that interaction among patients or between patients and staff is, by virtue of definition, therapeutic. Interaction tends to be revered for the sake of interaction, and all meetings with patients are regarded as therapeutic to various degrees, depending on the extent of the interaction. The more patients talk and emote, the more they become involved with one another, the more they participate in scheduled activities, the more they supposedly will be helped. It is as though the concept of interaction has become imbued with a sacrosanct and inviolate quality. Seldom is the possibility entertained that the resultant interaction may prove destructive, meaningless, or even superfluous. Even when the interaction proves appropriate and constructive, it likewise may have little bearing on subsequent behavior.

To some extent, this emphasis on interaction as a direct indicator of therapeutic benefit has some justification in the case of chronic schizophrenics. Anyone having worked with these patients for any length of time cannot help be impressed by the paucity of interpersonal interaction, lack of social involvement, social isolation, and lack of concern for others, including fellow patients. As a result, it is presumed that almost any procedures that heighten interaction among patients must also prove therapeutic.

It seems essential to provide a fuller description of the social lives of chronic schizophrenics within a hospital ward setting in order to understand why the goal of interaction is emphasized in most treatment programs. In our own studies, we have had the opportunity to evaluate the activities of patients in some detail. Employing a modification of the Location Activity Inventory (LAI), a rating instrument developed by Hunter, Schooler, and Spohn (1962), we obtained daily observations on thirty patients for a four-month period. These spot observations pertained to the behavior of patients on the ward during unscheduled activities. The number of observations totaled 3,136. The results of our observations showed remarkable agreement with those obtained by the authors of the LAI who made observations on 100 deteriorated chronic schizophrenics over a period of six months.

Table 6-1. LAI PERCENTAGES

Location	%	Posture	%
Bathroom	9.14	On floor	1.08
Own room	47.22	Lying on bed, etc.	36.73
Other patient's room	0.72	Sitting	32.61
Hallway	15.01	Standing	19.07
Dayroom	27.91	Walking	10.50
Position	%	*Activity*	%
Facing wall	5.93	Pathological behavior	32.16
Back against wall	59.20	Sleep	20.11
Facing window	2.21	Null behavior	22.87
Facing mirror	2.00	Functional, nonsocial	8.50
Away from wall	30.65	Parasocial	10.63
		Social game	1.59
		With one or more persons	4.13

The selected results of our observations are given in Table 6-1. The four general categories of patient behavior include location, position, posture, and activity. For present purposes, it is only necessary to comment on this last category. As we can see, patients spend the largest percentage of time (32.16 percent) engaged in pathological behavior (e.g., self-manipulation, nongoal-directed activity, nonfunctional object manipulation, and nonsocial verbal, gestural, and laughing behaviors). They also spend a considerable amount of time sleeping (20.11 percent) and engaging in null behavior (22.87 percent) (e.g., sitting, staring, etc.). About 8.5 percent of their time is spent in such functional, nonsocial activities as personal care, excretory functions, and functional object manipulations, whereas parasocial activities, such as reading, writing, television viewing, nonsocial games, etc. occupy 10.63 percent of their time. It is dramatic to find that social interactions, consisting either of games or discussions with other patients, represent by far the smallest portion of the time (5.72 percent) spent by chronic schizophrenics. Although we have no data on a control group of patients of other diagnostic categories, this cannot alter the fact that chronic schizophrenics demonstrate virtually no appropriate social interaction or any inclination to engage in this behavior when left to their own devices.

In attempting to account for this severe paucity of social involvement, some authors have postulated that withdrawal from fellow patients may have a realistic basis, as in situations where better integrated patients seek to avoid their more regressed and occasionally assaultive fellows (Rowland, 1938). However, this hypothesis cannot account for the equal lack of relatedness among nontroublesome patients. It is also unlikely that one can level blame for this withdrawal solely on the effects of institutionalization; this behavior seems characteristic of many of these patients even prior to the onset of acute symptomatology or shortly after hospitilization.

Schooler and Lang (1963) advanced five hypotheses to explain the negative reaction of these patients to social contact, as well as their avoidance of responsibility-bearing, decision-making roles. These hypotheses focused on (1) the fear of showing positive feelings toward others, (2) the fear of receiving positive feelings from others, (3) the fear of showing negative feelings toward others, (4) the fear of receiving negative feelings from others, and (5) disturbance by the mere presence of others. It is difficult to find fault with hypotheses as comprehensive as these; it is even more difficult to validate them. In any event, these etiologic possibilities help little in the practical treatment of these patients. Regardless of how, why, or when this social isolation begins, the immediate therapeutic task is to remedy it.

Interestingly enough, there have been several controlled studies with chronic schizophrenics in which the effects of high and low social interaction situations were compared. The results of these studies raised considerable doubt or qualifications about the overall therapeutic value of interaction. Pace (1957), for example, found that the exposure of patients to increased interactions produced an increase in unrealistic interactions. Assuming that increased interactions were, by definition, desirable, regardless of their unrealistic nature, he concluded that the greatest advantage of the treatment program appeared "to be in resocialization, and not the correction of psychopathology per se."

Sanders, and co-workers (1962) obtained rather similar results. The design of this study compared the therapeutic impact of four different treatment conditions. Condition 1 pertained to an intensified, social interaction program emphasizing small-group therapy and patient government. In addition, patients received certain core activities, such as a social skills course, and participated in therapeutic community meetings. Condition 2 pertained to a program consisting of core activities and therapeutic community meetings. Condition 3 included therapeutic community meetings only. Condition 4, the main control, represented the program on an ordinary hospital ward.

The results indicated that the three experimental groups showed a graded increase in social interaction in the predicted direction. In other words, the greater the opportunities and expectations for social interaction, the more the interaction. However, regardless of this differential response, there were no differences among the groups in terms of motivation for treatment or psychiatric status. These authors concluded that "there is no simple relationship between intensity of interaction and remission of psychotic symptoms."

In order to emphasize the consistency of these results, I should also like to summarize the results of a study by Fairweather and co-workers (1964). These investigators compared the effects of small, task-oriented groups of about fifteen members. The group composition was heterogeneous in that a substantial number of nonpsychotic and short-term psychotic patients were included with the chronic schizophrenics. Because of this heterogeneity, and the fact that the authors did not attempt to distinguish the effects of their experimental program on different diagnostic types of patients, generalizations to chronic schizophrenics could not be made. Nevertheless, although the results indicated an increase in the intensity and amount of verbal interactions in the small-group program, the changes in psychopathology between experimental and control groups proved relatively unimpressive.

The results of these studies have several important implications concerning the treatment of chronic schizophrenics. Although it is apparent that these authors are biased concerning the value of increased interaction and have interpreted their respective programs as successful because such interaction can be demonstrated, the results of these programs do not seem particularly impressive. Essentially, all that these studies demonstrate is that if chronic schizophrenics are exposed to situations fostering social interaction, an increase in social interaction can be found. These authors tend to gloss over their own data, indicating that the resulting increased interaction does not produce a corresponding decrease in psychopathology. This would indicate that the value of interaction, as defined in these studies, is limited and that perhaps other procedures are necessary.

In our own behavior modification studies with chronic schizophrenics, we have had the opportunity to assess the value of interaction in several contexts. As a result of our findings, we have gained a far better appreciation of the potential role of interaction in the total treatment process, as well as the conditions under which its impact is optimal or minimal. As we shall see, the term interaction is far too broad and superficial to be of any clinical or scientific value. If interaction is to be appraised, then operational descriptions of the kind, amount, duration, and context in which it occurs must be made in order to interpret the results. It is not only possible but also likely that different types of interaction will produce different types of results.

What we shall do now is to consider the results of two different interactional treatment programs, one unsuccessful and the other successful, and then attempt to account for these discrepancies. By contrasting these programs, we should be able to arrive at certain general treatment principles regarding the efficacy of interaction.

Small-Group Responsibility

The first experimental treatment program may be designated as the *small-group responsibility* model (Ludwig, Marx, Hill, and Hermsmeier, 1967). In a sense, the inspiration for this program derived from our experiences with the already described *total-group responsibility* program devised to combat the code of chronicity. As mentioned previously, we discovered a marked but latent potential in chronic schizophrenics to overcome their self-imposed isolation regarding their cohorts when forced to take responsibility for others through the withholding of privileges. This artificial imposition of group responsibility produced striking and almost immediate results, especially in the prevention and curtailing of some of the more drastic behaviors, such as aggression, destruction of property, sexual acting-out, and elopement from the ward. The resultant patient response clearly seemed to be a matter of "whose ox was being gored." When patient acting-out only provided discomfort or annoyance for the staff, it was ignored or openly encouraged by fellow patients; when patients themselves experienced discomfort or inconvenience because of the actions of their fellows, many of the patients were transformed suddenly into mental health activists. Because this particular program was geared more toward dealing with the most blatant and serious forms of deviant behavior and did not focus on more specific forms of psychopathology or deviancy, such as bizarre mannerisms, social withdrawal, unwillingness to participate in ward activities, self-care, and personal hygiene, it was felt that a more comprehensive treatment program was called for. Moreover, whereas the total-group responsibility program represented an exploratory, informal clinical study, we attempted to streamline our procedures and evaluate certain aspects of interaction within the context of a formal experimental treatment program.

Because previous clinical experience dictated that these patients could not be expected to interact with one another in a meaningful, constructive way simply by telling them to do so, some motivational levers seemed necessary to ensure that patients would follow through on these therapeutic expectations. We therefore constructed a treatment program of forced small-group responsibility in which all patients not only would be obligated to cope with and take responsibility for fellow patients within their assigned groups but actually would be rewarded or penalized according to the extent that they successfully met this obligation.

The Study Proper

Thirty chronic schizophrenics—sixteen males and fourteen females—were used in the study. The experimental treatment population consisted of five groups of four patients each, with two males and two females in each group. Within each group, one member of each sex represented a high scorer on one of the behavior rating instruments while the other member of each sex represented a low scorer. The magnitude of these scores corresponded directly with the level of general behavior or psychological integration of patients. The remaining ten patients, who individually were regarded as responsible only for themselves, constituted the control group. The program lasted fifteen weeks. Suitable rating scales were employed to measure both the process of treatment as well as its outcome.

For each group of four a number of steps were taken to enhance group cohesiveness and interaction. All patients within a particular group received a ward work assignment that they were required to carry out as a unit. They also sat together at meals, received recreational therapy together, and met with staff as an intact group. Each of these groups was assigned a staff consultant who would meet with it on both scheduled and unscheduled occasions. The basic rule set forth to govern the consultants' relationships with group members was essentially a deemphasis on one-to-one staff-patient involvement. Consultants were asked, whenever possible, to meet with the entire group rather than with the individual member, even in situations where the individual had requested a meeting to talk over something personal or where an individual's rather than the group's drastic behavior required staff intervention. The essential message we desired to impart to the group patients was "you no longer have any problems as an individual—only group problems."

Another principle governing staff-patient relationships was that the staff remain relatively passive with their assigned groups in order to provide them the opportunity to solve either their ongoing problems or special incidents that might arise. In other words, comparable to task-oriented or problem-solving groups, these groups would be regarded as self-sufficient and capable of coping with any of their internal difficulties.

The basic motivational lever to foster group involvement and interaction pertained to the privilege system. Once a week, each group would meet with the entire ward staff to receive feedback about its overall performance and to receive privileges based on an assessment of that performance. This rating procedure was fairly unique in that each member in the group was evaluated separately on a special rating form, the STU Behavior Report (see Chart 6-1), and the scores of all four members were summed and averaged. This average score determined which of the seven privilege levels the group would be assigned for the entire following week. There was also a special punishment category pertaining to more drastic behaviors, such as aggression, to which the entire group would be assigned for a day at a time if any of its members transgressed in this manner. By establishing a privilege system such as this, we hope to impress on patients that their destinies were, in fact, intertwined and that the behavior of any member in the group affected the welfare and prerogatives of the entire group. Moreover, if

Chart 6-1. STU BEHAVIOR REPORT

NAME _____ FOR WEEK ENDING _____

0 POINTS	*2 POINTS*	*4 POINTS*
Personal Appearance		
1. Dirty	So-so	Clean
2. Sloppy	So-so	Neat
3. Bad taste (clothes)	So-so	Good taste
4. Lousy posture	So-so	Good posture
5. Piggy	So-so	Civilized
Personal Housekeeping		
6. Dirty	So-so	Clean
7. Sloppy	So-so	Neat
Work		
8. Goof-off	So-so	Dependable
9. Snotty	So-so	Respectful
10. Inefficient	So-so	Efficient
General Behavior		
11. Crazy	So-so	Sane
12. Sourpuss	So-so	Friendly
13. Big mouth	So so	Tactful
14. Hating	So-so	Considerate
15. Belligerent	So-so	Peacemaker
16. Greedy	So-so	Generous
17. Irresponsible	So-so	Responsible
18. Stubborn	So-so	Cooperative
19. Close-mouthed	So-so	Open
20. Glob	So-so	Alive
21. Passive	So-so	Initiative
22. Blah	So-so	Creative
23. Vulgar	So-so	Polite
24. Tramp	So-so	Modest
25. A. Queer	So-so	Masculine
B. Lesbian	So-so	Feminine

Total behavior points _____
Less 3 points for each venial sin _____
Total score _____

the two better functioning patients within any group desired to obtain higher privileges, they would have to work more intensively with their poorer functioning brethren and improve their performance so that the group's average weekly score would be higher.

Results

The above, then, constituted the rationale and procedure for the study. Unfortunately, despite our high therapeutic expectations, the overall results turned out to be a dismal failure. Not only did the small-group patients fail to show any greater improvement than the controls or an enhancement in performance at the end compared to the beginning of the program, but a number of the experimental patients actually got worse. Inasmuch as we obtained weekly behavior ratings on all patients, we were in a position to evaluate (through regression equations) the direction and rate of change in behavior for each patient. Statistical analyses demonstrated that for the small-group patients, seven showed a significant deterioration in behavior whereas two showed a significant improvement; for the control patients, one showed a significant deterioration whereas four showed significant improvement.

Aside from these general findings, a number of more intriguing ones were to emerge. The first of these pertained to the differential responses of the high or better integrated and the low or lesser integrated patients within these groups. Originally, we had wondered whether the better members in each group would help to bring the poorer members to a higher level of functioning or whether the poorer members would tend to drag down the better members. The results indicated, as a generalization, that the better members tended to get worse while the poorer members tended to improve. In other words, within each group there was a tendency for the behavior of members to approach the average level of functioning for the total group, a behavioral regression toward the mean. The behavior of patients within each group changed, but the group itself, viewed as a unit, tended to remain stable. We might portray these results as shown in Figure 6-1.

Such a treatment response was intriguing because it corroborated related findings of Sanders and associates (1962), whose general treatment study was described above. Similar to our own results, the better patients in their two most intensive, interactional programs did worse whereas their poorer patients did better.

In retrospect, these findings appeared to make good clinical sense. The deterioration in functioning of the originally better patients attested to the fragility of their behavioral equilibrium or adjustment within the hospital. Once placed in a stressful situation in which they would experience the frustration, anger, discouragement, or failure associated with interpersonal involvement, psychological and behavioral decompensation could be expected to follow. This was especially so when these patients were obligated to assume the initiative in

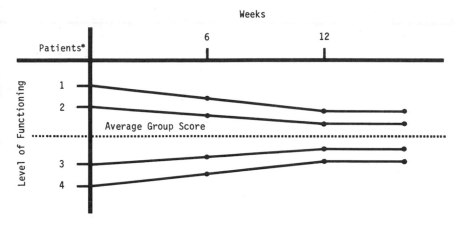

Figure 6-1: Group treatment response. (The numerals* stand for patients and their relative standing in the group in terms of behavioral functioning.)

coping with difficult situations with only minimal guidance and structure provided by staff. On the other hand, for the originally sicker patients (who could not sink much lower), the intense, interactional group situation could not help but rouse them from their profound psychotic withdrawal and cause them to show more vitality and response. With this display of increased responsivity to external stimulation, these patients were apt to receive higher behavioral ratings.

In an attempt to gain some objective information on the tendency of this particular treatment model to foster group closeness, we measured the physical distance that group patients chose to maintain among one another during the thrice weekly general ward meetings. The chairs in this meeting were arranged in a large circle within the ward dayroom and patients were free to choose any seat they wished. The number of seats interposed between group members constituted the scores used. Surprisingly, rather than finding group members congregating together over the course of the program, the tendency was for them to sit farther apart from one another over time.

Of further interest to the analysis of group dynamics were our findings that the behavior rating scores of all individuals within any group tended to be significantly related on a week-to-week basis over the course of the program. This correspondence in scores was especially marked in the case of the two leaders within each group. Although these results indicated that patients, in fact, were highly involved with one another and that the behavior of any given group member tended to affect all members of that group, this did not mean that this involvement was necessarily beneficial. It merely indicated that group members tended to influence one another for better or for worse, but, as the general results revealed, mostly for worse.

In interpreting the results of this program, I must first stress that there can be no question that the treatment model employed fostered heightened interaction. In fact, the interaction among group members was at times so intense as to make us quite apprehensive about its outcome. I shall say more about the quality of this interaction (see p. 121). For the present, suffice it to say that social interaction per se, as employed in this program, could not be regarded as therapeutically beneficial. In fact, there was some indication that it could produce adverse therapeutic effects in our population of patients.

As we pondered over the reasons this program failed, several possibilities suggested themselves: (1) An apparent shortcoming related to the staff's inability to capitalize on all possible opportunities for therapeutic action because they were instructed to play more of a passive role in their relationships with patient groups. The staff's behavior was structured in this way to grant the group patients maximum possibilities for autonomous action and also to permit the opportunity for a process study of patient coping maneuvers. Because of this relative nondirective approach on the part of the staff, it appeared likely that the experimental treatment model was not given a completely fair test in terms of its potential effectiveness. With more structured, goal-directed, and persistent intervention from the staff, it was possible that better therapeutic results might have been obtained. (2) Despite the relatively small size of these groups, it seemed that the interaction among patients was extremely confusing and undecipherable for the patients and staff alike. Group dynamics often became so complex that it would have been difficult even for a skilled therapist to channel the group forces in a constructive direction. Therefore, it was possible that the patients and staff would have found groups of even smaller size easier to deal with. (3) We also entertained the hypothesis that patients were delegated too much responsibility for their peers. Whereas the total-group responsibility program only obliged patients to cope with the more drastic behaviors of their fellows, the small-group responsibility program held them accountable for all of each other's behaviors. It was difficult enough for staff to shape the behavior of chronic schizophrenics; retrospectively, we came to realize that it might prove far more stressful for patients assigned a comparable duty for three other patients. As a result, this treatment model was apt to foster frustration, discouragement, and withdrawal on the part of patients because their prospects of success were, in reality, limited. We attempted to test all these hypotheses by conducting, at some later time, another experimental treatment program which represented a refinement and modification of the small-group responsibility model.

The Buddy Program

The new interactional treatment model we chose to employ had a natural, social basis and was less artificial than the small-group model. This new program was designated the buddy system (Ludwig and Marx, 1969). It was interesting that such a naturally occurring and socially widespread relationship between peers had neither been formally tapped nor systematically studied in the treatment of mental patients, especially chronic schizophrenics. Aside from the spontaneous, natural formation of buddy friendships, especially among teen-agers, there were countless other instances where the buddy system has been used to a practical advantage both for each member of the buddy pair as well as for the organization sponsoring them. In many of these instances, the pairing of buddies proved arbitrary or involuntary, but this had little effect on what could be accomplished by this relationship. For example, in the armed services, scouting patrols, scuba or deep-sea diving, YMCA camps, school outings, etc. the formation or assignment of buddy pairs safeguarded the mission or task as well as minimized the risk to the participants. In these situations, each buddy assumed responsibility for the welfare of the other, making certain that no harm befell his partner or, if it did, offering immediate succor and seeking help. Not only were buddies safer with each other, but they had the advantage of their combined strength and foresight as well.

These practical features represented only part of a cooperative, dyadic relationship. Less obvious were the commonly developed by-products of buddyship, such as companionship, the caring attitude, friendship, mutual trust, cooperative teamwork, and awareness of another person's worth and contribu-tions—all qualities seldom encountered in the chronic schizophrenic. In order to exploit the potential advantages of this relationship, as well as to remedy the lacks of the small-group program, we decided to investigate the effectiveness of a buddy system for mental patients.

As with the forced small-group responsibility program, our clinical experience dictated that buddy relationships and the mutual assumption of responsibility would not automatically take place among patients simply by instructing or encouraging patients to move in this direction. Left to their own initiative, patients would prefer to remain alone, isolated, and unbothered by the problems of others. Therefore, if buddy relationships were to develop, the staff would have to intervene in some manner by creating a situation, albeit contrived, conducive for this to take place. In our view, one of the first steps would be to ensure a high degree of exposure and joint activity of each selected buddy with another. This we attempted to do by insisting that the designated buddies share the same room, perform the same work detail, eat next to each other at the same table, receive recreational therapy and psychotherapy together, and be regarded in all staff-patient interactions as a unit rather than as two separate individuals.

This high degree of forced exposure would be relatively impotent to provoke mutual interaction between patients were it not for the imposition of an additional feature, namely, forced shared responsibility. From our previous observations of these patients, we have been impressed by the paucity of social involvement existing between long-time roommates, tablemates, or workmates. Chronic schizophrenics could live closely with one another for years without developing even a semblance of a socially appropriate or rewarding relationship or without even knowing one another's names. It was for this reason that we instituted the practice of paired responsibility whereby each buddy would share or experience the privileges or restrictions earned by the combined efforts of the two. As in the small-group program, these privileges or restrictions were determined on the basis of weekly behavioral ratings. For certain taboo behaviors, the restrictions would be imposed immediately on the buddies.

Another modification in the program design pertained to the staff relationships with patients. In the small-group responsibility program, the staff would only be available as a last resort in offering advice or help to group leaders in coping with a troublesome cohort. As we came to learn, patients seldom solicited assistance from their staff consultants even though the patient leaders' influencing techniques with difficult cohorts proved relatively inept. Rather, if their methods for the control of fellow patients were not immediately effective, patients would tend to become easily discouraged and withdraw from further interaction. In order to counter this defeatist behavior, as well as to supplement the limited repertoire of influencing techniques available to patients, we modified the staff functions. Instead of waiting to see how patients would handle difficult situations, the staff assigned to each buddy pair would actively intervene when indicated and provide structure, guidance, and encouragement for faltering patients.

To implement this more active staff role, two types of meetings were established: (1) An assigned staff member would meet with each buddy pair after its weekly rating and discuss specific ways by which the pair could improve its overall performance so that it might attain more privileges the following week. (2) The staff member met daily with each buddyship for half hour paired-therapy sessions. The buddies had the opportunity to bring up any meaningful material during these sessions; if no meaningful material was forthcoming, the staff member would attempt to provoke meaningful inter-action and constructive discourse.

The predominant themes emphasized in the paired-therapy sessions were that patients could no longer be regarded as isolated individuals, that their destinies were intertwined no matter how much they preferred to deny this, that their buddies could either turn out to be helpmates or hindrances depending on how they dealt with them, and that they were stuck with this relationship until "discharge do them part." As a result, patients could not longer blame the staff for their privilege status and predicaments—only their own behavior and that of their buddies determined their ward welfare and status.

Fourteen pairs—seven male-male and seven female-female—were selected for study. Similar to the small-group program, each pair was composed of one better and one poorer functioning patient. The rationale for this type of pairing pertained not only to our desire to balance and equalize the therapeutic difficulties among all buddy pairs but also to provide some nucleus, in the form of the better integrated patient, for constructive activity within each pair. Because we had eliminated much of the interactional complexity and reduced the responsibility of each patient to one other patient rather than three as was found in the small-group responsibility program, we were not certain whether the better patient would pull the worse patient up or the worse patient would drag the better patient down. Naturally, it was our hope that both patients would benefit considerably from this new treatment model.

One other factor concerning the formation of the buddy pairs pertains to our rationale for limiting the pairs to members of the same sex. Our reasons for this choice were based more on practical than theoretical considerations: (1) The generally accepted notion of buddies related more to members of the same sex. A relationship with members of the opposite sex would be often complicated (or enriched as the case may be) with the sexual urge, expressed either openly or covertly. Moreover, we presumed that a closer relationship would be more apt to develop in same sex pairs because their socially or biologically determined interests were more similar. (2) Social and moral taboos prevented us from obtaining the degree of exposure between males and females we felt necessary for the development of buddy relationships. For instance, males and females could not share the same bedroom, handle a similar bathroom detail, groom or shower together. (3) There was some evidence in the experimental literature that male and female chronic schizophrenics performed differently in different task situations. In a study assessing affiliation among schizophrenics, Carmi Schooler (1963, p. 445) concluded that "theories based on experimental findings with one sex cannot be generalized to explain the behavior of chronic schizophrenics of the other sex." Partly for this reason, we were interested in learning what differences there would be between the two types of buddy pairs.

The actual experimental treatment program lasted for sixteen weeks. For an analysis of results, patients served as their own controls in that their performance during the experimental program was compared to their performance during a prior baseline period consisting of exposure to a traditional hospital therapy program.

Results

In contrast to the small-group program, the therapeutic effects of the buddy system proved dramatic. Not only did the total group of patients comprising the buddy pairs show steady, significant improvement in their level of functioning over time but, when the behavior of individual patients was assessed, regression equations revealed significant improvement in twelve patients over time. Only two patients became significantly worse. Of the remaining fourteen patients, ten showed an improvement and four showed a deterioration in behavior; the regression values, however, were not sufficiently high to reach statistical significance. There was no appreciable difference in the response of males or females to this program, both sexes as separate groups showing a significant increment in performance over the course of the program. A graphic portrayal of the results of this program, compared to the baseline period, may be seen in Figure 6-2.

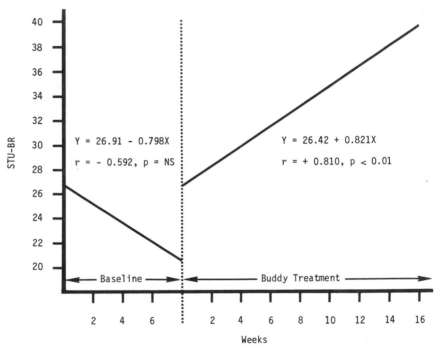

$Y = 26.91 - 0.798X$

$r = - 0.592, p = NS$

$Y = 26.42 + 0.821X$

$r = + 0.810, p < 0.01$

Figure 6-2: Total group regression lines for baseline treatment periods (n=22).

Unlike the small-group responsibility program, we were to find no significant differences in the amount of improvement shown between the originally better and worse patients. The regression to the mean phenomenon observed previously was not at all characteristic of this program. Instead, the gradual progression of the behavior rating scores of buddies upward indicated a distinct departure from the response to the small-group model. It was difficult to determine whether the better or worse members of the buddyship were primarily responsible for the improved scores of their partners. Rather, it seemed that both responded favorably to the constant companionship and mutual responsibility fostered under the buddy system.

That the buddies tended to be influenced strongly by the presence and behavior of one another was demonstrated by the weekly intercorrelations of their rating scores. With six of fourteen pairs showing significant positive intercorrelations and six others showing weak positive intercorrelations, it seemed reasonable to conclude that the constructive behavior of one member either produced or was accompanied by constructive behavior on the part of his buddy, and the converse. Therefore, despite the arbitrary assignment of buddies and the artificiality of their forced relationship, it indeed appeared that this treatment structure was able to produce some sort of mutual relationship. These findings further attested to the ability of chronic schizophrenics to form powerful relationships with one another provided that the setting is conducive.

Given this situation, we decided to evaluate whether liking the assigned buddy made any real difference in terms of treatment outcome. From our initial hypotheses, it seems natural that patients who were relatively happy with their assigned buddies would work better with them and therefore improve more than patients who were discontented with their partners.

In order to investigate this assumption, one member of our staff met individually with each patient at one, eight, and sixteen weeks after the start of the program and made the following statement: "We are considering the possibility of changing buddies. If we could arrange it, would you like a different buddy? If 'yes,' whom would you like?" A "yes" response was scored "+" and a "no" response "0".

After quantifying this data, we proceeded to perform a correlation analysis between the combined behavior rating scores of each buddy pair and its combined buddy preference score. Contrary to our original expectation, results of this analysis indicated that the greater the dissension within buddy pairs (in terms of their desire to change partners), the higher their combined behavioral functioning at the termination of the treatment program. This was a clear indication that patients need not like each other to function well together. In fact, the best functioning buddy pairs seemed to be those characterized by having at least one activist buddy who would prod, pester, and keep after his cohort to perform constructively. Therefore, if given the chance to change partners, the prodded patients seemed to welcome the opportunity of surcease from annoyance while the prodder patients seemd happy to be relieved of their involuntary burden. On the other hand, the buddies who performed poorly were those who were most content with each other because they were more apt to leave each other alone.

Another specific aspect of buddy behavior pertained to the voluntary association of pairs in situations where they were not compelled to be together. This we attempted to evaluate by recording every week at the general ward meeting the number of pairs whose members voluntarily chose to sit next to each other. Inasmuch as there were approximately forty seats available and patients were free to select where they would sit (the number of choices diminishing as the seats were gradually taken), we would expect pair members to distribute themselves randomly throughout the meeting room perhaps with only one or two buddies seated together by chance. Anticipating this to be the case, we predicted that the structure and expectations of the therapeutic program would induce more and more buddy pairs to show physical proximity in their seating patterns over the course of time.

Neither our anticipation of initial distance among buddies nor our prediction of greater closeness over time were confirmed by the data; in fact, just the reverse was to occur. The first finding to impress us was the large number of buddy pairs who chose to sit together periodically during the sixteen-week program. This number of pairs ranged from three to eleven in any given week (mean = 7.9), far above the number expected to pair together by chance. The total number of weeks any given pair sat together ranged from one to thirteen with a mean of 8.1.

These findings were interesting because they attested to the strong expectational set of togetherness imposed on patients by the buddy treatment model. Even though staff were specifically instructed not to tell patients where to sit, we had to assume that patients either felt that they were expected to remain together for this large ward meeting or they desired to remain together or they simply stayed together out of habit.

This, however, was not the total picture of their behavior. Another intriguing finding was the significant tendency for the number of buddies seated adjacent to each other to diminish gradually over time. This was especially so for buddy pairs who demonstrated high interaction. In other words, the more interaction patients had with their partners, the less their tendency to sit with them as the program progressed or, to put it differently, the more they chose to distance themselves from each other when they had the chance.

As far as an overall appraisal of the buddy treatment model, the program could be regarded as a qualified success. The complex and confusing interaction among patients noted during the small-group program became much simpler and comprehendible with the paired relationship. Moreover, the possibility that the burden of responsibility for other patients was too great in the previous small-group and total-group responsibility phases was eliminated in the present program in which patients had only one other person to be accountable for—a fair and reasonable load of responsibility. In fact, it was our impression that patients were much better able to cope with their partners when they desired to or were made to than previously. Involvement in the affairs of others, meaningful interaction, the promotion of a helping and caring attitude, and even companionship became present to varying degrees and at various times.

The Many Faces of Interaction

By now it should be apparent that the concept of interaction cannot be automatically imbued with therapeutic sanctity and regarded as immune from critical examination. Inasmuch as both the above-described treatment programs fostered increased interaction and led to almost diametrically opposite results, it seems reasonable to suppose that different kinds of interaction were operative. By contrasting and comparing the conditions under which these divergent results can be obtained, it may be possible to sharpen the concept of interaction and to define the situations under which it will be associated with optimal improvement in patients.

1. The value of interaction must be qualified by the kinds of patients for whom it is intended. Whereas an increased involvement, both verbally and nonverbally, with one another may automatically prove beneficial for neurotic or character disorder patients (although this remains to be demonstrated), this can not be regarded as inevitable with chronic schizophrenics, patients who seem unduly threatened by encounters with others. Therefore, the matter of group composition will undoubtedly play a role in determining the effects of interaction. This factor is noted by Sanders and his colleagues (*in* Fairweather, 1964, p. 209) in their study of the influence of group compositions on treatment outcome. These authors conclude that "groups of mental patients have many of the characteristics of a servomechanism . . . Once the composition of a group is optimum, leaders emerge, problems are solved, participation of all members occurs, and the level of social activity of all members within the group increases." It should be pointed out that these authors are referring to the addition of nonpsychotic and acutely psychotic patients to groups of chronic schizophrenics.

2. The extent to which interaction is artificially forced or imposed on patients will be related to the rapidity and degree of mutual involvement among patients. With chronic schizophrenics, it is much more likely that interaction will occur under conditions of high exposure to one another and joint activities rather than under conditions where patients are permitted to "do their own thing."

3. The quality of the interaction will be determined by the degree of interpersonal responsibility associated with it. We already have demonstrated that increased interpersonal involvement will occur in chronic schizophrenics whenever their privileges and prerogatives are made contingent on the behavior of fellow patients; the nature of this involvement, however, will be dependent on the number of patients encompassed within the sphere of responsibility and the kind and frequency of patient behaviors for which others will be held accountable. For example, in the total-group responsibility program, designed to

undermine the code of chronicity, patients were regarded as accountable for the behavior of fellow patients only in respect to more blatant, potentially destructive behaviors (e.g., aggression, sexual acting-out) which did not have a high frequency of occurrence. Our impressions indicated that they were able to cope with this responsibility quite adequately. However, in the small-group program, this accountability extended to the whole gamut of pathological or socially maladaptive behaviors for both themselves and three other patients as well. This may have been far too great a burden of responsibility to place on their shoulders and, undoubtedly, contributed to their buckling under the pressure. When this type of responsibility was reduced to only one other patient, as in the buddy system, patients had a far easier time in accepting and managing it. In other words, it appeared that the more blatant and the less frequent the behaviors for which patients were held accountable, the greater the ability of the group to deal with these behaviors and the more group members who could be regarded as mutually responsible. Conversely, it was also apparent that the more subtle and the greater the frequency of the behavior to be controlled and modified, the greater the need to narrow the extent of mutual responsibility if constructive interaction was to occur.

4. Group size must be taken into account in assessing the influence of interaction. From our observations, it appears that the larger the group of chronic schizophrenic patients, the greater the forces working toward group homeostasis or resistance to change. We already have described such forces at work in the patient culture at large. In the small-group program, we observed these homeostatic forces in operation within each group in the regression to the mean phenomenon, whereby the two better members showed a deterioration and the two poorer members showed an improvement in performance during the course of the program. This phenomenon tended to ensure group stability and the status quo. By breaking up the patient population into subunits of two, as in the buddy system, we were able to weaken as well as overcome many of these destructive, homeostatic forces.

5. The quality of interaction also plays an important role in the effectiveness of behavior modification procedures. Our clinical observations and experimental data strongly indicate that affection, warmth, and kindliness are not only unrealistic emotions to expect from chronic schizophrenics but also may not prove to be most therapeutic. In fact, anger or annoyance with one's fellow group member or partner tends to serve as a better basis for mutual involvement and responsibility than a caring attitude. Given the clinical fact that chronic schizophrenics resent any invasion of their privacy and especially resist the development of meaningful interpersonal relationships, we should have anticipated the very thing we found. If the behavior of a patient is to improve, this simply cannot take palce without considerable prodding, supervision,

confrontation, cajoling, badgering, and persistent intervention on the part of a fellow patient. Such behavior cannot help but irritate both the initiator and recipient; it threatens the very thing each wants most—namely, peace and quiet, security, and isolation. A frictionless, harmonious relationship between buddies tends to be one in which neither member cares enough to do anything about changing the behavior of the other.

6. The influence of the quantity dimension was very apparent in the buddy system program. From our daily work with patients, the two most disturbing problems encountered in fostering a working relationship between buddies concerned the matter of too little or too much interaction. In the former instance, it was difficult to elicit even minimal cooperative endeavors or teamwork. In the latter instance, teamwork could be accomplished for brief periods of time but would soon break down owing to squabbling, arguing, and fighting between buddies. In these high interaction situations, patients had difficulty in controlling the rising tide of their emotions and would tend to explode or withdraw from the ecounter. To some extent, it was interesting that patients tended to attenuate the prospects for high interaction in a natural way. This was reflected in the significant trend for small-group and buddy patients to avoid one another over time at the general ward meetings. It appeared, therefore, that there existed an optimal range for involvement and interaction, whether ambivalent, hostile or affectionate, and interaction above or below this range did not seem to promote a constructive working relationship.

From this discussion, it should be apparent that the phenomenon of interaction is both complex and multifaceted. Just as it is possible to produce interaction that will be purposeless, senseless, and even destructive, it is possible to produce interaction that will be meaningful, relevant, and beneficial. To ensure that the latter will occur, it is first necessary to provide an operational definition of the specific kind of interaction desired and then to devise techniques for eliciting it. The production of interaction for the sake of interaction makes little conceptual sense and has even less practical therapeutic justification.

Although the production of therapeutic interaction should represent an essential feature of any therapeutic program for chronic schizophrenics, it cannot be regarded as the sole goal of therapy. An adequate therapy program for these patients must also include many other elements. These will be dealt with in the following chapters.

chapter 7

Interpersonal Influencing Techniques of Patients

There is a good deal written in the psychiatric literature about the individual psychopathology of schizophrenics but hardly anything about their interpersonal behavior. Questions pertaining to how patients relate to one another in different contexts, how they get other patients to carry out their bidding, how they work toward a given goal, how they react when thwarted, how they exert leadership, etc. require answers if a fuller understanding of patient behavior is to be obtained. It is unlikely that any treatment approach can prove maximally effective if it is not steeped in clinical reality. As we shall see, clinical reality dictates that chronic schizophrenics demonstrate severe deficits in the interpersonal sphere; a major therapeutic problem pertains to finding specific solutions to remedy them.

In the previously described small-group responsibility program, we have had the opportunity to study firsthand this relatively untapped and neglected

Adapted from A. M. Ludwig and A. J. Marx, Influencing techniques of chronic schizophrenics. Arch. Gen. Psych., 18:681-688, 1968, with permission.

dimension of chronic schizophrenic behavior—namely, the techniques and strategies patients themselves employ to influence, control, and manipulate one another. In a sense, the structural aspects of this particular treatment model were ideal for studying the interpersonal behavior of patients because it forced interaction, provided small-group units in which this interaction could be highlighted, defined a common goal toward which groups were to work, and, most important, permitted only a minimum of staff interference and intervention in the group process. As a result, this treatment model brought into sharp focus many unsuspected obstacles preventing effective teamwork and cooperative endeavors among patients. It also served to portray in bold relief the numerous inadequacies and deficiencies in the coping mechanisms and interpersonal influencing techniques of patients.

Because it would prove both cumbersome and confusing to describe all the influences at work among members of each group and between groups, it seemed more valuable to adopt an arbitrary framework within which these influences could be categorized and described. This framework essentially pertained to the relationships between the group leader(s) and their fellow patients.

It soon became apparent that those patients who assumed group leadership bore little resemblance to a Spartacus, Joan of Arc, or other charismatic prototypes. It seemed more appropriate to use the word "leader" in a very special and relative sense; within these small groups of chronic schizophrenics leadership was determined by the relative psychological intactness or verbal skills of each member ("In the land of the blind, the one-eyed man is king") or relegated by staff to the patient or patients who seemed most receptive and cooperative to the demands of the program. In some cases, patients assumed this role by default when no other group member showed any initiative. In other instances, leadership was shared simultaneously or alternated from week to week among different patients within each group.

Throughout the program, it was difficult to tell at times whether the real leader or leaders of the group were those who worked for the group's betterment or the apparently more disorganized patients who seemed bent on actions inimical to the group's welfare. Although I shall devote some discussion to the negative group influences observed, the bulk of the following remarks will pertain to the struggles of the group leaders to gain greater group privileges, curb the incidence of privilege transgressions, and prevent members of their groups from committing aggressive, destructive, or sexual offenses.

Techniques for Interpersonal Control

Verbal Manifestoes

It should not be surprising that even chronic patients employ language as the primary means for controlling one another. What is of clinical interest, however, is the particular nature of this verbal behavior. Among our group of chronic schizophrenics, it was rare to hear one patient make a polite, courteous request of another. It was much more common for the group leader to employ simple commands, direct orders, declarative statements, or unqualified requests, much in the manner of papal edicts or royal manifestoes, in order to produce constructive behavior in his fellow patients. Such statements as "Do this," "Stop it," "Stay here," "Stand in line," and "Clean your room" were issued without explanation or rationale, much as a commanding officer might do with a subordinate. Not all orders or commands were specific and relevant; many tended to be limp, euphemistic, and global in character. For example, in his attempts to influence the behavior of a troublesome patient, the leader, either on his own initiative or at the behest of staff, would direct his charge to "Shape up," "Act sane," or "Be good."

Although we assumed that there were a multitude of verbal influencing techniques potentially available to patients, we were impressed by the paucity and primitiveness of those actually employed. Almost completely missing from their repertoire of verbal influences were such techniques as persuasion, coaxing, and appeals to reason. On infrequent occasions, when explanations were offered for constructive behavior change, they always pertained to the acquisition of greater privileges (e.g., "If you behave, we'll get dessert tonight"). Never did any patient attempt to influence his cohort by referring to the presumed rewards of mental health or the prospects of hospital discharge for sane, responsible behavior.

The Snowball Effect

When the direct verbal statement or order proved ineffective, there was a rather predictable sequence of procedures leaders employed to deal with the recalcitrant patient.

With the failure of simple verbal language, the leader would often try to modify, control, and direct the behavior of another patient through simple language. At first, these physical influences included gentle but firm physical restraint, pulling, tugging, or pushing the patient to prevent him from striking out, to get him to his work detail, meetings, and meals, to make him shower or clean his room. However, if these procedures failed, the leader characteristically would choose one of two alternatives: He would either withdraw completely from the frustrating situation and adopt a "to-hell-with-it" attitude or else would continue his influencing efforts but with an increasing loss of self-control.

At this critical point, if the latter course was taken, the *snowball effect* seemed to take over. The leader might first resort to threats (e.g., "Do this, or else . . . ") or he might begin to curse, shout, roughly handle, or vigorously restrain the offensive patient. If these methods also failed and if staff could not intervene in time, the leader was apt to get carried away and begin to hit, slap, punch, or kick the obstreperous patient. Apparently, this snowball phenomenon was not solely a function of protracted frustration; examples of it were noted almost immediately after the program began.

Schizophrenogenic Leadership

We presumed that one of the functions of an effective leader was to serve as an idealized model with whom his followers could identify. Although several group leaders on occasions fulfilled this function admirably, they tended to destroy the potential effectiveness of their leadership by inconsistent, confusing, and seemingly contradictory behavior. Even though their fellow patients showed a willingness to respond constructively, certain tactics of the leader often kept them in a state of confused uncertainty, made it difficult for them to know just how to respond, and weakened the possibility of a constructive identification.

A number of behavioral patterns seemed typical of all group leaders:

1. They were apt to show the common hypocritical "Do as I say, but don't do as I do" attitude. They seemed to be very perceptive and critical about the maladaptive behavior of others but were defensive and blind to their own faults. They would see the necessity of punishing others for "bad acts" but regarded themselves as blameless for their own misbehavior.

2. They characteristically had low frustration tolerance. When everything was going well with the group, they would function admirably. However, once they encountered some frustrating situation with which they felt unable to cope, they were apt to withdraw from the therapeutic arena and leave their fellow patients stranded and without leadership. Rather than take advantage of the opportunity for staff consultation and guidance, the leaders frequently chose to drop group problems in the staff's lap, making such comments as "It's your job . . . , " "You're getting paid for it . . . . "

3. It was often difficult for patients to know with certainty where the loyalty of their leaders lay or under which flags they served. In many respects, the leader seemed to function in the role of a double agent or fickle turncoat. When the leader was coping well with his group, he appeared to identify with the therapeutic program and was offended by crazy or deviant behavior in his peers. At these times, he seemed a firm, reliable ally of the treatment staff. However, under the pressures of temporary, unresolved group conflict, he peremptorily might break this therapeutic alliance and regard his former staff allies as his new enemies, expressing such irrational recriminations as "It's your [the staff's] fault that we have these problems."

4. Group leaders characteristically imparted to their group a confusing, contradictory philosophy concerning the nature of their illness and the underlying reasons for their behavior. On some occasions, when a fellow patient acted out directly against the leader or threatened to jeopardize the group's privileges, the leader would regard this behavior as conscious, volitional, and purposive and respond accordingly. On other occasions, in apparently similar

situations, he might plead their case to the staff, exonerating their behavior by insisting that they were crazy, that they could not help what they did, and that they were not responsible for their actions.

With all these inconsistencies in leadership, it was not surprising to find that the more regressed patients failed to make a sustained identification with the positive attributes of their leaders.

The Group Scapegoat

Within each group, there seemed to be a very special relationship between the best and worst functioning members. Some part of this relationship undoubtedly was determined by the realistic demands of the program which held the better group members responsible for the behavior of all group members. This would necessitate that the group leader would be forced into great interaction with the most difficult patients in the group because they represented the most serious threat to the whole group's privileges. Aside from this consideration, there seemed to be other, more subtle aspects to this interaction.

From our vantage point, it appeared that all groups needed to maintain at least one patient in the role of scapegoat who would serve as an outlet for their pent-up frustrations and anger and as a convenient focus of blame for their predicaments. Often, there was a realistic basis for the leaders' antagonism toward these patients, but their reactions appeared overdetermined and far out of proportion to the specific provocation. Clinically, the resultant appeared as a sado-masochistic interaction in which the leader took every opportunity to berate or physically punish the troublesome patient and the troublesome patient took great pleasure in provoking the leader to the point of loss of control. This behavior would persist even after numerous staff attempts to point out the self- and group-defeating results of this interaction.

Whether leaders did so wittingly or unwittingly, the result of their interaction with the group scapegoat was to keep him or her in a "one-down" role. The leader showed no inclination or desire to work with him constructively when he was not creating trouble. At work or at room-cleaning details, occasions in which the leader tended to play a supervisory role, he not only failed to compliment these patients for their small gains but frequently showed impatience with their efforts, derogated their accomplishments, of did their work for them, thereby reinforcing their feelings of ineptness and inadequacy.

Another supporting observation for the scapegoat concept pertained to numerous instances when the staff, temporarily disgusted with the attitudes and behaviors of the group leader, might (as a therapeutic tactic) begin to regard the sickest member of the group as the potential leader. This often became an intolerable situation for the former leader who frequently responded with renewed initiative, constructive motivation, and increased group involvement.

Whimsical Reinforcement

Regardless of the efficacy of the patients' influencing techniques or the intuitive rationale underlying them, one observation was crystal clear—these patients were strict, card-carrying behaviorists in their interactions. They showed little or no interest and concern in what their fellow patients thought or felt; their only concern was in what others did. However, it was obvious that none of these patients ever read psychology texts on learning theory and reinforcement procedures; they tended to violate most of the basic principles for conditioning behavior.

In general, we might characterize the reinforcement practices of patients as follows:

1. Patients were much more likely to resort to such negative reinforcements as scolding, shouting, or physical punishment for bad behavior than they were to offer warmth, praise, or concrete rewards for good behavior. The result of this practice was to give other patients much more attention when they were behaving badly than when they were behaving appropriately (as well as fitting into the apparent need of these patients for castigation), thereby reinforcing some aspects of this crazy behavior.

2. Even when negative reinforcements were administered, they were seldom contingent on specific behavior or moderated in intensity. There tended to be an all-or-nothing response to the many gradations of behavior stimuli. Sometimes minimal provocation would evoke an exaggerated response; at other times blatant, reprehensible behavior would produce no response. In other words, either little happened at all or else all hell would break loose. In a situation where the punishment might far outweigh the crime and where the criteria for a crime continually changed, it was difficult for the offender to be certain just why he was being punished.

3. Aside from problems in quantity of response, there were also problems related to its inappropriate quality. The leaders, as well as the led, demonstrated a type of chaotic emotionality, transforming one kind of emotion into another. For example, as soon as patients began to experience warmth or affection toward one another, these emotions abruptly would give way to seemingly unwarranted and inappropriate ones. It was our impression that patients were severely deficient in their ability to distinguish among the spectrum of their own emotions and those of others toward them and, as a result, could not use or sustain an appropriate emotion for any length of time. Affection became confused with love, love with sex, sex with fear, fear with anger, and anger with persecution. Because of these rapid emotional metamorphoses, patients never knew where they stood with one another and never could establish a well-defined or stable relationship—a prerequisite for exerting effective interpersonal influence.

4. The application of the reinforcement was seldom systematic, consist-

ent, and persistent. Over a period of time leaders would have many sporadic spurts of enlightened, constructive activity which would peter out long before they had tested the mettle of their techniques. They seemed to lack the staying power for the long haul of producing behavioral modification in another patient.

5. There was the tendency to respond in a global rather than specific manner to particular behaviors. For example, in order to guard against a patient striking out, the group might confine the patient to a small physical area where he or she could be continually watched and walled off from any interpersonal contacts. In other words, the group might impose the punishment of total interpersonal isolation for a variable period of time to prevent the recurrence of a specific form of taboo behavior. Unfortunately, the offending patient might interpret this restriction as a punishment for the inoffensive or good behavior he displayed during this time as well, thereby weakening the immediacy and specificity of the negative response to the undesirable behavior.

6. Patients showed little perceptiveness or interest in responding to the danger signs of impending trouble. As long as there was no actual difficulty, they were content to let well enough alone. They seldom took prophylactic action and were much more prone to act after than before the fact. Because of such a practice, the milder influencing techniques, which might have proved effective in preventing a blow up, became relatively impotent once this had happened.

The Breakdown of Behavioral Controls

Placed in a stressful situation of forced group interaction and responsibility, chronic schizophrenic patients were more disposed to act out in ways detrimental to themselves and fellow patients than when they were held accountable for only their own behavior. This could be documented in the significantly greater incidence of serious offenses committed by the group responsibility in comparison to the individual responsibility patients (see Table 7-1). This greater incidence was accounted for almost entirely by aggressive attacks on fellow patients and staff members.

Table 7-1. INCIDENCE OF SERIOUS OFFENSES (15 WEEKS)

	Strike Staff	Aggression	Total
Group ($n=20$)	91	123	214
Individuals ($n=10$)	22	14	36
$p <$	n.s.	.01	.01

Although the treatment model appeared to promote greater social interaction among patients, it became obvious that this interaction could not always be regarded as desirable or appropriate. To some extent, we must share the blame for these results. What we had not realized in the formulation of this treatment program was that the potential for destructive interaction would be as great if not greater than that for constructive, social interaction.

From these observations, we became convinced that without strict limits and the restraining and supervisory presence of staff, the harsh, Draconian code of patients, which often alternated with a completely laissez faire one, might have led to an anarchistic, totalitarian social system. Even though staff were not expected to intervene in the affairs of patients, there were numerous occasions where intervention became absolutely necessary in order to prevent patients from seriously harming one another.

Unfortunately, not until the closing weeks of the program did we fully recognize that the treatment model invested far greater power and authority in the more recalcitrant, uncooperative members of each group than in its leaders. Because these group saboteurs could bring their entire group crashing down into privilege restrictions with a single slap, they were in excellent position to emotionally blackmail the group leaders into leaving them alone. Should the group leader press them too much in their work details or other ward chores, they could easily get him to give up or become wary of upsetting them by striking a staff member or another patient, thereby expunging all prior group gains. This acting-out against the group was not only a function of avoiding stress; there were numerous instances when these recalcitrant patients seemed to derive a perverse pleasure at frustrating and discouraging the more cooperative patients from achieving greater privileges.

The group leaders could not be completely exonerated from the plight of their groups. In many instances it was clinically apparent that these uncooperative patients would have responded to kind, patient, and persistent leadership, but this was seldom forthcoming in their encounters with group leaders. Not only were group leaders generally inept in handling these patients, but they seemed to contribute both indirectly and directly to the aggressive acting-out within their group. This was also compounded by their general lack of affection or concern for the welfare of other group members and their impatience and hostility toward these difficult patients, even when they were attempting to behave well. Directly, the leaders themselves also were responsible for instances of aggression either by exceeding the bounds of discretion in dealing with other patients or by striking out whenever they became discouraged.

Therapeutic Implications

As we assess the impact of this experimental treatment model on patient behavior, several generalizations seemed warranted. These patients can and do exert powerful influences over one another, especially in a situation where they are forced to interact and their destinies are intertwined. Many of these influences may prove beneficial, others may start out with positive intent and fizzle out, others are completely ineffectual, and still others may be solely destructive and motivated by malevolence. Comparing these antagonistic influences to lines of force, we suspect that the ultimate impact on any individual patient is determined by the resultant of these varied interactions operating simultaneously and over time. Unfortunately, in the long run, the contradictory, confusing, and double-binding nature of these influences tends to inhibit any major gains.

In our observations of patient relationships within their respective groups, it is also apparent that patients have only a limited repertoire of influencing techniques at their disposal. Confronted with diversified situations, they tend to handle them with stereotyped, relatively inflexible patterns of responses instead of systematically exploring other alternatives. When these responses fail to show any immediate results, patients either withdraw from the stressful situation or begin to lose self-control. When patients resort to either of these alternatives, the potential effectiveness of any of their procedures is bound to become seriously undermined.

On the assumption that the behaviors noted within the context of this model are caricatures if not characteristics of the same difficulties patients show in coping with any stressful interpersonal situation, we may metaphorically regard chronic schizophrenics as interpersonal cripples who are seriously handicapped in the style and diversity of their influencing techniques and social skills. This conceptualization presents an alternative way of understanding the long-noted avoidance of interpersonal contacts by the chronic schizophrenic. Traditionally, this avoidance of interpersonal relationships has been considered a function of underlying fears and anxieties ("smothering, double-binding mother," "latent homosexual conflict," etc.) of close relationships. Our interpretation implies that this avoidance, to some extent, is based on the lack of appropriate skills to handle these interpersonal situations. Whether this lack is based on a primary deficit (either environmentally or genetically induced), is secondary to the withering effects of chronic hospitalization, or is in response to willful patient behavior may be almost beside the point in terms of treatment and rehabilitation. Should this conclusion prove correct, it would argue for the introduction of a new, relatively ignored dimension in the treatment of these patients, namely, the intensive training in basic interpersonal influencing techniques and skills. Such training would have to go far beyond the usual practices, even in active treatment situations, of relating to these patients with the hope that they will acquire these interpersonal skills by example or osmosis.

In the buddy system program, we made some initial advances in overcoming these difficulties. In the daily paired-therapy sessions, as indicated in

Chapter 6, staff actively employed role-modeling, had patients rehearse behaviors, continually pointed out inappropriate interactions, and demonstrated effective interpersonal influencing techniques in an effort to remedy the patients' lacks in this area. Despite the exploratory, informal, and unsystematic nature of these techniques, it was our impression that they proved invaluable and contributed to the general success of the buddy treatment program. However, these techniques are not the only ones for teaching patients how to exert effective interpersonal control. In Chapter 8 we shall consider other more formal, systematic, and specific techniques for accomplishing this goal.

chapter 8

Chronic Schizophrenics as Behavioral Engineers

There is by now a considerable body of research attesting to the efficacy of techniques based on learning theory as a means of shaping, influencing, or changing behavior, both animal and human. In fact, for many theoreticians, learning theory provides a parsimonious explanation for almost all behavior modification practices, from child-rearing and teaching to psychotherapy. Presumably, the extent to which these practices explicitly or implicitly capitalize on learning theory principles will determine the degree to which they will prove effective and efficient.

If we can accept this presumption, it seems reasonable to make the further assumption that training people to become proficient in the application of certain behavior modification practices based on learning theory will likewise help them become adept at influencing others. Therefore, if therapists desire to

Revised and adapted from A. M. Ludwig, A. J. Marx, and P. A. Hill. Chronic schizophrenics as behavioral engineers. J. Nerv. Ment. Dis., 152:31-44, 1971, with permission.

remedy some of the interpersonal deficits of chronic schizophrenics, a reasonable starting point would be to teach patients to understand and apply certain simple, basic principles of behavioral engineering. Moreover, if patients can master this, it would raise the practical possibility of using them as an ancillary source of help in the treatment of other hospitalized patients.

The Two Types of Learning

Although there are several different schools of behavior therapy based on learning principles, the essential therapeutic goals of all schools may be regarded as similar. In terms of behavior modification, most behavior therapists tend to pose three questions (Ullman and Krasner, 1965): (1) What specific patient behaviors are maladaptive and what behaviors need to be increased or decreased in frequency? (2) What environmental contingencies currently support the patient's behavior in the sense of maintaining the undesirable behavior and decreasing the likelihood of performing adaptive behavior? (3) What environmental changes, usually in terms of reinforcing stimuli, can be manipulated to change the patient's behavior?

Most forms of behavior therapy derive from two basic concepts of learning—classical and operant. Central to both concepts is the assumption of a functional connection between an environmental stimulus and some response by the subject. In classical or Pavlovian conditioning, a stimulus evokes a response; in operant or Skinnerian conditioning, the subject must emit a response to a situation prior to an environmental event (i.e., reinforcement) that becomes associated with it and changes its frequency of occurrence. In order to clarify this distinction, especially for the purpose of later discussion, a very brief review of these concepts seems necessary.

In classical conditioning, a stimulus—the *conditioned stimulus*—that initally has no power to elicit a given response—the *unconditioned response*—may acquire such power if it is repeatedly associated with the presentation of a stimulus—the *unconditioned stimulus*—that has the power to produce the given response. This repeated association of the unconditioned stimulus with the conditioned stimulus may be regarded as *reinforcement* of the conditioned stimulus. The conditioned response, once formed, may be expected to undergo changes in strength depending on certain environmental events. For example, if the unconditioned stimulus is repeatedly withheld, the conditioned response gradually diminishes until *extinction* occurs. Once a conditioned response has developed, the phenomenon of generalization, whereby similar stimuli evoke the same response, may occur. The less similar the second, third, etc. stimulus to the original one, the less the generalization. A complementary process to generalization is *discrimination*. When two stimuli are similar, conditioned discrimination may be obtained by the selective reinforcement of the one stimulus and extinction of the other. In this way, the one reinforced will elicit the given response whereas the one extinguished will not.

In general, the responses evoked in classical conditioning studies concern the involuntary musculature; in contrast, operant behavior is associated with the voluntary musculature. In operant conditioning theory it is held that individuals make many random responses or operate from birth on their environment. An operant behavior closely followed by a pleasant stimulus (positive reinforcement) tends to increase in frequency whereas one followed by an unpleasant or noxious stimulus tends to decrease in frequency. Withdrawal of an aversive stimulus may be regarded as a positive reinforcing event. The repeated absence of reinforcement tends to lead to *extinction* of the learned behavior whereby its frequency of occurrence returns to a rate similar to that observed prior to reinforcement.

In operant theory, the concept of *discriminative* stimuli is also essential. These are stimuli that mark the time or place an operant behavior will have reinforcing consequences. Whenever a particular stimulus is repeatedly associated with or is similar to the reinforcement, it tends to assume many of the reinforcement stimulus qualities, a phenomenon known as *operant stimulus generalization.* Money represents a good example of a discriminative stimulus systematically associated with a primary positive reinforcer (e.g., any stimulus, such as food, that relieves a basic drive). Stimuli that have acquired their reinforcing powers through their prior function as discriminative stimuli are called *secondary,* or *acquired, reinforcers.*

This limited discussion cannot do justice to the complexities of either classical or operant conditioning theory. Its only purpose has been to serve as an entré to our work in this area. The study to be presented will highlight another important dimension in the treatment of chronic schizophrenics. Initially, though, let us acknowledge other relevant work in this area.

Although operant conditioning procedures have been employed extensively in the treatment of the mentally ill, most work has been done on a single case rather than group program basis (see Ullman and Krasner, 1965). The *token economy,* developed by Ayllon and Azrin (1965), represents one of the first total ward programs designed to reinforce appropriate social behaviors of chronic schizophrenic patients in a systematic manner. Variations of this program have been carried out by others (Atthowe and Drasner, 1968; Gericke, 1965).

In the token economy, the staff provide secondary reinforcers (i.e., tokens) contingent on patient performance of designated activities. For example, in the Ayllon and Azrin study, tokens were awarded for self-care activities, such as grooming, bathing, tooth-brushing, exercises, and bed-making, as well as for on-ward and off-ward jobs. With the tokens earned, patients could purchase a variety of reinforcers. These included the following categories: (1) privacy—e.g., selection of rooms, personal chairs, cabinets, choice of eating group, etc.; (2) off-ward privileges; (3) social interaction with the staff—e.g., private audience with chaplain, nurse, physician, psychologist; (4) attendance at religious services; (5) recreational opportunities; and (6) commissary items. Although these authors seem to regard their program as an unqualified success, careful scrutiny of their results can lead to other interpretations. (1) Approximately 39 percent of their forty-four patients were on phenothiazine medication. It is quite possible that such medication may have profoundly affected the responsivity of patients. (2) Only a relatively small proportion of their patients accounted for most of the tokens or secondary reinforcers earned whereas the majority proved relatively unresponsive to token reinforcers designed to motivate self-care activities or participation in off-ward jobs. This would point up the necessity of designing a program for reaching patients unaffected by secondary reinforcers. Perhaps, for this subgroup, primary reinforcers may have proven more effective. All told, their results argue more for the limited rather than unlimited efficacy of their procedures for the total range of hospitalized, chronic schizophrenics.

The Double-Conditioning Model

The study we conducted pertained to a double-conditioning therapy program designed to operantly condition chronic schizophrenics to become behavioral therapists or operant conditioners of other chronic schizophrenics. It was hypothesized that such a program might prove helpful both to those patients doing the conditioning, in terms of teaching them interpersonal influencing techniques, as well as to those being conditioned.

In contrast to previous operant conditioning programs, such as the token economy, the double-conditioning treatment model was unique in the following ways: (1) separation of chronic schizophrenics into two subsamples (i.e., more and less socially responsive patients) with application of different kinds of reinforcement procedures for each, (2) the simultaneous modification of behaviors of completely different levels of complexity for these two subsamples, and (3) the systematic utilization of patients themselves as behavioral therapists for other patients.

On the basis of global behavior ratings of fifteen male and twelve female patients, we selected the top two-thirds (representing the more socially responsive patients) to serve as behavioral therapists for the remaining third (representing the less socially responsive patients). We then paired up two members from this pool of more responsive patients (hereafter called "guardians") and assigned them one patient from the pool of less responive patients (hereafter called "charge" patients), thereby forming nine triads. Each triad was required to work together as an intact unit for twenty weeks, the predetermined length of the experimental program.

At this point, some explanation must be offered for the division of patients into these two subgroups. The rationale for this was twofold: (1) The results of the token economy program (Ayllon and Azrin, 1965) indicated that the majority of patients were relatively unaffected by the use of secondary reinforcers as motivators for constructive behavior. (2) Our own prior clinical experience indicated a basic distinction among patients regarding responsivity to social cues. The charge patients for the most part tended to be more regressed, withdrawn, and refractory to ordinary verbal communications. In most ways, they behaved in a socially and psychologically primitive manner. Although they would act purposefully to relieve basic drives, such as hunger, excretory functions, and the need for sleep, their behavioral repertoire was deficient in some of the most simple, elementary social behaviors, such as attending and responding to simple verbal requests. Because of the concrete or nonsymbolic way in which they related to the world, it seemed that more immediate and tangible reinforcers would be necessary to shape their behavior. In contrast, the guardian patients for the most part represented the more socially active, psychologically intact, and responsive subsample. They could attend and respond to most verbal communications and possessed an adequate repertoire of behaviors for engaging in limited work and social activities within a hospital setting. Their primary social handicaps lay in their difficulties in initiating or sustaining appropriate conversations and their lack of proficiency in constructively influencing others in an effective and efficient manner. Because they seemed capable of some degree of abstraction, as well as the postponement of gratification, less immediate and tangible reinforcers seemed suitable. Hence, the establishment of two different treatment goals and the use of different kinds of reinforcers for these two general types of patients seemed appropriate.

Prior to the initiation of the program, movies, videotape demonstrations, reading material, seminars, and practice sessions were employed to train the nursing and aide staff in the basic principles of learning theory and operant conditioning as they applied to our particular program. Also, during this preparatory phase, an intensive effort was made to determine the individual likes and dislikes of all patients in terms of food and goodies (e.g., ice cream, candy, fruit, cigarettes) in order to find the most powerful primary reinforcers. In some cases, relatives were contacted to determine what foods or treats patients liked best. Where a patient's food or goodie preferences were not obvious, we employed Premack's (1959) principle of recording high-rate behaviors which, in turn, might later be used as reinforcers for other desired behaviors.

Conditioning of Guardian Patients

At the start of the experimental program, assigned staff met with each pair of guardian patients, explained the purpose of the program, gave them instructions and demonstrations on the operant conditioning principles and procedures to be used, and informed them that they could earn coupons on the basis of both performance and effort in conditioning their charge patient. These coupons would be redeemable for treats, thereby serving as secondary reinforcers. In order to avoid the sense of frustration and failure that might be encountered when working with a recalcitrant, unresponsive charge patient, the guardians were informed that the amount of coupons earned would not be related to obtaining positive results with their charge, but would be dependent entirely on their own efforts and performance.

Behavior therapy sessions were scheduled once a day, six days per week. These sessions consisted of nine three-minute blocks during which time the operant conditioning procedures were employed. An assigned staff member conducted a scheduled conditioning program for the first three-minute block in order to model the appropriate procedures for the guardian patients as well as to reestablish the response level of the charge patient attained on the previous day. Each of the two guardian patients then alternated turns for the remaining eight three-minute blocks. During each of these time blocks, the assigned staff member provided positive social reinforcements (i.e., praise) to the guardian whenever appropriate and corrected procedural mistakes whenever they occurred. If the guardian refused to complete a given time block, the staff member intervened and worked with the charge until time was up and it was the turn of the other guardian to proceed. At the end of each three-minute time block, the staff member could award the guardian from zero to two coupons (i.e., one coupon awarded for effort and one for accurate performance). Because each guardian had four turns, he or she could earn daily up to eight coupons which could be cashed in each evening or saved for future use. The exchange value of these coupons is given in Chart 8-1.

Four specific operations were required of the guardian patient for each conditioning trial with his assigned charge: (1) He or she had to present the stimulus to which the charge patient could respond (e.g., the name of the patient, questions of varying complexity, objects for identification). (2) He was required to distinguish between appropriate and inappropriate response and then to provide immediate, brief social reinforcement (e.g., "Good, Peter") for appropriate response. (3) He had to remain aware of the primary reinforcement schedule being used at each stage of the charge's conditioning. (4) He had to administer the primary reinforcement as quickly after the social reinforcer as possible and according to the prescribed schedule. These operations carried out efficiently and in the proper sequence remained the basis for judging and rewarding the performance of the guardian.

In addition to the one staff member who was reinforcing and providing systematic feedback to the guardian about his or her performance, a second staff member was assigned the task of recording the number of presentations of the stimulus, the number of correct responses by the charge patient, keeping time, and recording the amount of coupons earned by guardians. As guardians became

Chart 8-1. COUPON EXCHANGE VALUE

Item	Coupons Required
3 pieces of small candy	1
2 cookies	1
1 stick of chewing gum	1
1 miniature candy bar	1
1 sucker	1
1 cigarette	2
1 doughnut	2
1 glass of pop, milk, juice, Kool-Aid	3
1 apple, orange, banana	3
1 bag of popcorn	3
1 regular candy bar	3
1 roll of life-savers	3
1 bag of M&M's	3
1 ice cream bar, Fudgsicle, Popsicle	4
1 box of Cracker Jack	4
1 bag of potato chips, corn chips	4
1 piece of pie	6
1 drumstick, frozen malt	6
1 package of cupcakes, Twinkies, cake rolls	6

more proficient in administering the conditioning procedures, we planned to have them assume more and more of the functions of the second staff member.

At the termination of each session, a fifteen-minute time period was set aside for the purpose of (1) providing feedback to guardian patients about their overall performance in the behavior therapy session, (2) informing them what they would have to do to earn more coupons, (3) reviewing the progress of their charge patient, and (4) attempting to elicit from them suggestions as to how to accelerate their charge's progress.

Conditioning of Charge Patients

Whereas guardians were rewarded with secondary reinforcers (i.e., coupons), the charge patients were offered primary reinforcers (e.g., various foods, sweets, soft drinks, drags of cigarettes) contingent on correct responses and in accordance with a predetermined fixed ratio reinforcement schedule. Because of the large number of conditioning trials carried out in each behavior therapy session, only very small portions of the reinforcer were to be given for correct responses in order to avoid satiation effects. As previously noted, the guardians were required to provide social reinforcement (i.e., praise) for all correct responses by their charge and immediately preceding the awarding of a primary reinforcer. Because most charge patients initially were unresponsive to ordinary social stimuli, the pairing of the social reinforcer with a primary reinforcer was for the purpose of eventually having the social reinforcer take on the positive valence associated with the primary reinforcer.

From extensive observations of patients prior to the program, we collected a list of behaviors we felt needed to be built in or shaped in these regressed charge patients. From this list, we constructed a hierarchy of response levels proceeding from the most elemental, simple behaviors (e.g., eye contact in response to calling the patient's name) to progressively more complex behaviors (e.g., structured social conversation). This hierarchy of behaviors was appropriate for all charge patients. There were five major levels to this hierarchy, each level having several sublevels (see Chart 8-2 for a description of levels). The use of this hierarchy for all charge patients rather than individual hierarchies for each of them simplified the mechanics of the program for staff and patient alike and permitted comparison of progress for the nine charge patients against a given standard.

Chart 8-2. RESPONSE LEVEL HIERARCHY

I. *Eye Contact*
   A.   Quick glance when name is said
   B.   Holds glance for one second in response to name
   C.   Holds glance for three seconds in response to name
II. *Appropriate Sitting Posture*
   A.   Head up
        1.   For three seconds in response to simple request
        2.   For ten seconds in response to simple request
   B.   Shoulders back
        1.   For three seconds in response to simple request
        2.   For ten seconds in response to simple request
III. *Simple Verbal Response*
   A.   Appropriate "yes-no" responses to simple verbal questions
   B.   Naming objects
   C.   Naming staff and patients from pictures
   D.   Specifying functions of simple objects
   E.   Simple memory tasks
IV. *Simple Social Response*
   A.   Greetings and salutations
   B.   Opinions and small talk
V. *Elimination of Individualized Peculiar Behaviors*
   A.   Removal of mannerisms, bizarre gestures, verbal productions, etc., depending on which are predominant in a given patient, primarily by rewarding only appropriate responses to requests

Other procedural details of the behavior therapy sessions were also established on a necessarily arbitrary basis. For each of the behavior sublevels, a response rate of 80 percent correct during an entire conditioning session or twenty correct consecutive responses represented the criteria for judging whether that response was satisfactorily established. For any given response sublevel, there were four consecutive fixed-ratio primary reinforcement schedules of correct responses as follows: 1:1, 1:2, 1:3, and 1:5. This provided for the gradual thinning out of primary reinforcers. Social reinforcement for correct responses was always provided on a 1:1 schedule. When the charge patient met the criterion of successful establishment of a given behavior on a 1:1 primary reinforcement schedule, the guardians, under the guidance of staff, proceeded to a 1:2 reinforcement schedule, etc. up to a 1:5 schedule for that behavioral level. Once the necessary performance was obtained at this most attenuated primary reinforcement schedule, the operant conditioning program would shift to the next higher level of the response hierarchy and begin over on a 1:1 reinforcement schedule. Once this level of behavior became established, attenuation of reinforcement would again take place, etc. It should be noted that a correct response at a higher level in the behavior response hierarchy incorporated all the lower level behaviors.

The reinforcement procedure was also standardized to deal with instances when the rate of correct responses remained consistently low over a period of time for any given response sublevel. When this happened, the conditioners would first switch to different primary reinforcers. If this had no noticeable effect, the conditioners were to move down to a more frequent or thicker reinforcement schedule (e.g., from 1:3 to 1:1). If there was still no significant progress by the charge patient, the guardians would then drop back one sublevel on the behavioral hierarchy, etc.

Response of Charge Patients

The individual response patterns of the nine charge patients are depicted in Figure 8-1.[1] The information contained in the figure represents an effort to reduce the enormous amount of data into some interpretable results. The ordinate indicates both the response level and differential reinforcement rates within that level, while the abcissa indicates the number of three-minute time blocks over the twenty-week program. A vertical line from one fixed-ratio reinforcement schedule to another or from one response level to another represents successful establishment of that behavior for a given reinforcement schedule. A horizontal line represents failure to establish the behavior for a particular level or reinforcement schedule over a certain number of three-minute blocks. A vertical drop from the horizontal line indicates that the patient slipped back to a lower level in the response hierarchy or to a thicker reinforcement schedule.

The study of these patient response patterns revealed varying rates of progress. With four patients—C, E, G, and H—there was slow but steady progress up the response hierarchy, with each patient showing different ceilings and

---

[1]*Because of serious clinical problems outside the behavior therapy sessions, such as not eating and aggressive behavior, we had to start patients D and I on Prolixin Enanthate during the program and have employed arrows to indicate the points of intervention.*

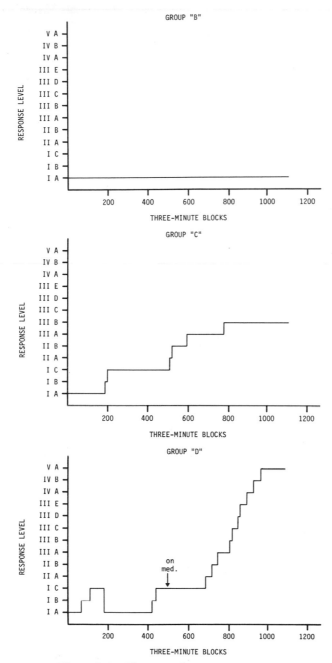

Figure 8-1: Charge patient response patterns.

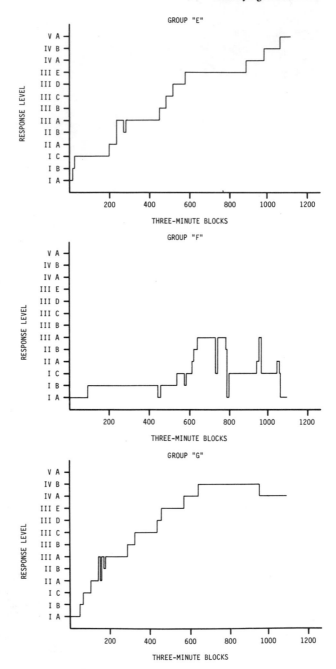

Figure 8-1 (cont.): Charge patient response patterns.

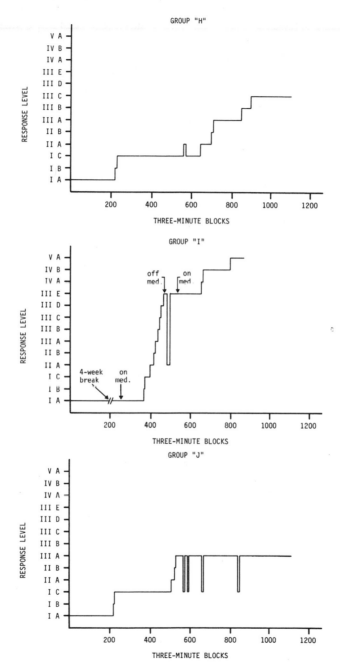

Figure 8-1 (cont.): Charge patient response patterns.

differential rates of response for different levels and reinforcement schedules. Another three patients—B, F, and J—showed virtually no response to the operant conditioning procedures. With patient B every possible primary reinforcement was used, attempts were made to increase drive level through withholding of meals, and the technique of reinforcing successive approximations to even the simplest behavior was used, all to no avail. Patients F and J, on the other hand, did at least respond to the point of reaching somewhat higher ceilings on the response hierarchy, but there were frequent and wide fluctuations in their responses. Patients D and I, who were treated with Prolixin Enanthate, manifested a very dramatic increment in their response rate and progress shortly after administration of the drug. This increment was even more pronounced in patient I, who had medication discontinued at one point with a marked drop in response level and then showed continued progress following its being restarted. Although we can make no definitive statement about the mechanics of the drug effect on these patients, the evidence is strongly suggestive that it played some role in facilitating correct responses to the conditioning procedures.

Some additional results bear mention. Figure 8-2 summarizes the highest levels in the response hierarchy achieved by the charge patients, the number of trials in each sublevel (contained within each block), and the total percent of correct responses regardless of level (in parentheses). For the nine patients over a twenty-week period, a total of 142,869 trials were recorded, the median being 15,625. There was no consistent pattern to the number of trials necessary to establish any given level of behavior regardless of its simplicity or complexity.

GROUP	(Per Cent) (Correct)	I A	I B	I C	II A	II B	III A	III B	III C	III D	III E	IV A	IV B	V A	TOTAL TRIALS
B	(22.1%)	20,246													20,246
C	(55.7%)	3,471	224	6,509	131	861	1,545	2,884							15,625
D	(65.0%)	6,366	1,081	4,808	364	231	500	90	291	78	236	261	264	680	15,250
E	(58.7%)	283	125	3,256	862	102	2,258	340	301	575	2,749	773	501	662	12,787
F	(41.0%)	3,037	8,660	4,642	407	254	1,373								18,373
G	(66.0%)	975	257	579	471	29	1,889	441	1,309	174	785	1,570	2,669		11,148
H	(59.5%)	4,307	325	6,960	615	63	1,497	526	1,678						15,971
I	(47.7%)	10,563	70	456	307	95	84	99	89	109	1,093	84	743	732	14,524
J	(41.9%)	4,750	34	6,592	221	113	7,235								18,945
GRAND TOTALS		53,998	10,776	33,802	3,378	1,748	16,381	4,380	3,668	936	4,863	2,688	4,177	2,074	142,869
MEDIANS		4,307	241	4,725	386	108	1,521	391	301	142	939	517	622	680	15,625

Figure 8-2: Number of conditioning trials at each response level.

Aside from these objective findings, there were a number of intriguing clinical observations. The behavior of the charge patients in behavior therapy sessions was usually anything but passive, mechanical, and perfunctory. Rather, charge patients often played an active role in shaping what went on with their guardians to the extent that there were many times when we could not be certain who was conditioning whom. This was perhaps best demonstrated by the charge patients who would remind their guardians in a chiding manner about the prompt and proper awarding of primary and social reinforcers. For example, one charge patient criticized her guardian for spilling some soda pop on the floor and said "Don't spill it on the floor, feed it to me!" Others would indicate when they were full or would urge the conditioner to slow down in the administration of reinforcers: "What do you want me to do? I am eating as fast as I can!" On certain occasions, they would indicate their preference for particular primary reinforcers to the conditioners and would refuse to respond unless they got their way: "If I can't have a cigarette for a reinforcer, I won't say a thing."

Charge patients also exerted control over the conditioners in other ways. For example, some patients demonstrated an apparent stubbornness by keeping their heads turned away or closing their eyes at times when eye contact was required, thereby showing a far lower rate of eye contact in response to the presented stimulus than might be expected to occur on the basis of random eye movements alone. Furthermore, many charge patients showed definite preferences among their conditioners, both staff and guardians, responding much better for one than the others, regardless of the efficiency and skill of the conditioner during the sessions.

Response of Guardian Patients

For the most part, the performance of guardians as behavioral therapists within the behavior therapy sessions far exceeded our initial expectations. During the twenty-week period, the seventeen guardians (one had eloped from the hospital and had to be supplanted by a reserve patient whose performance could not be subjected to a valid statistical analysis) had earned 12,960 coupons, representing 58 percent of the total number that could have been earned for perfect performance and persistence. The mean number of coupons earned by patients was 554.8 with a standard deviation of 208.6. Only one guardian, who earned a total of sixty-one coupons, could be regarded as extremely unresponsive. In this case, there was a total refusal to administer the conditioning trials after the third week of the program.

Although the guardians as a group, especially during the initial part of the program, committed many procedural errors and had to be corrected frequently by the staff, this relative ineptness did not necessarily hamper their ability to elicit correct responses from the charge patient to the presented stimulus. In fact, we were surprised to find that with five of the nine charge patients, one or both guardians obtained a higher percentage of correct responses over all conditioning trials than did the assigned, trained staff. With only four charge patients did the staff obtain a higher correct response rate.

From the many analyses performed, the best predictor of guardian performance as behavioral therapists appeared to be their level of functioning in a ward setting prior to the start of the experimental program. It was also interesting to note that for about one half of the guardians, their level of functioning within the behavior therapy sessions was significantly related to their general level of functioning on the ward on a week-to-week basis. This finding was suggestive of the existence of a generalization effect.

From a clinical standpoint, it appeared that most of the guardians were relatively cooperative in the behavior therapy sessions and even seemed to relish the roles they played. One patient remarked "It's fun; it's almost like a game."; several other patients voiced similar sentiments. However, cooperative participation was not constant for all guardians and for all times, and on a number of occasions the guardian patients would remind us of their schizophrenic illness by manifesting their customary symptoms. One patient, who refused to participate after the third week, claimed he needed help more than the charge patient; another patient would periodically moan about "the strange feeling in my head"; another would hallucinate at times; one patient occasionally claimed the procedures were too ridiculous to perform; two other patients, when angry at the staff for some reason, would go off on no-work sitdown strikes for several sessions. (Rather amusingly, one of the guardians consistently refused to use cigarettes as reinforcers for his charge because he felt it was medically unethical to use tobacco for a nonhabitual smoker.) Nevertheless, considering the severity of psychopathology of all these patients, their performance in these sessions during the course of twenty weeks could be regarded as relatively successful.

It was interesting that for the first several weeks of the program the guardians had considerable difficulty in comprehending the rationale for the conditioning procedures despite numerous staff explanations. Most commonly, the guardians seemed to regard the behavior therapy sessions as a time to feed their charges rather than as an opportunity to induce behavior change through the use of food as a reinforcement. For example, instead of simply presenting the stimulus (i.e., the patient's name), the guardian might say "Bernice, do you want some ice cream or candy?" or "Charlotte, it's important for you to eat, come on and eat now."

We found that the ongoing training of patients as behavioral therapists required an enormous amount of staff effort. Many of the guardians, whether because of preoccupation, confusion, anxiety, stubbornness, or inadequate pretraining, tended to commit a variety of procedural errors during administration of the operant conditioning procedures. The most common types of errors committed by guardians were as follows: (1) forgetting to present the stimulus (i.e., name of charge, question, object for identification); (2) either forgetting to supply the social reinforcer after the correct response or supplying it for the incorrect response; (3) forgetting to supply the primary reinforcer immediately after the social reinforcer for correct response or supplying it for an inappropriate response; (4) providing the primary reinforcer before the social reinforcer; (5) manifesting difficulty in keeping track of the differential primary reinforcement rates, especially when the reinforcement schedule became progressively thinned out, and (6) permitting too great a time lag between the eliciting of a correct response and the administration of the social and/or primary reinforcer. During the program, staff were relatively effective in reducing many of these procedural errors through negative reinforcement (not awarding coupons), direct corrective verbal feedback, and role-modeling, as well as through praise for appropriate, efficient behavior.

Other unanticipated and less straightforward staff problems arose in training the guardians as behavior therapists; more complex behaviors were expected of the guardians as their charges advanced on their behavior hierarchy. In many instances the guardian would appear confused or become inappropriate when expected to ask the charge patient a question that required a simple "yes" or "no" answer. For example, the guardians would formulate questions that could not be answered by "yes" or "no" (e.g., "Are my pants gray or black?"). To further confuse the issue, some of these guardians would then demand a "yes" or "no" response to this type of question. Silly or inappropriate questions were also noted: "If I'm wearing a watch, am I wearing a watch?" "Do you see my ass?" "What do you think of the King of Diamonds?" In order to resolve these problems, the staff had to extemporize training devices or learning aids for the guardians, such as formulating long lists of standard questions to be used by the guardians in working with their charges.

As the guardians became more proficient in all these techniques, we gradually expanded their duties to include timekeeping and recording responses. Twelve of the seventeen patients were eventually able to do a reliable job of timekeeping, whereas six became able to perform the even more complex task of recording responses. These accomplishments were particularly impressive in that only social reinforcers were used for rewarding guardians for these behaviors; there was no materialistic payoff, and they were rewarded solely by staff approval and praise.

A number of observations of the fate of the guardians' secondary reinforcers (coupons) were of interest. There was little question that most guardians coveted the coupons, because they eagerly awaited the scheduled evening time when they could cash them in for treats. However, there were some practical difficulties outside the behavior therapy sessions stemming from using a currency-like reinforcer. Some patients started stealing coupons from others or conning their fellows out of them; other patients gave their earned coupons away out of fear, to please other patients, or to demonstrate defiantly to the staff that these reinforcers held little value for them; still others hoarded and refused to part with their coupons.

General Remarks

The interpretation of these findings must be tempered somewhat by several methodological and practical deficiencies inherent in a relatively large operant conditioning program of this sort.

1. Although the general milieu outside the behavior therapy sessions reinforced appropriate behavior, no attempt was made to implement total control of the environmental contingencies of reinforcement for specific behaviors on a twenty-four-hour basis. Although ideal, this situation would have been exceedingly difficult to achieve because of the limitations of available staff, money, and time as well as the demands of the experimental program itself. As a result, it was possible and perhaps even likely that many of the gains made by patients within the time-limited behavior therapy sessions had dissipated outside these sessions owing to inadvertent negative reinforcement of the acquired behaviors or positive reinforcement of undesired behaviors.

2. Even within the behavior therapy sessions, it was not feasible to ensure precision control of the reinforcement procedures; as had been anticipated, guardian patients committed many procedural errors. Moreover, in shaping the performance of guardians as behavior therapists, the staff likely employed some subjective criteria in awarding the coupons. The very nature of this type of clinical program made it difficult to employ the degree of precision and objectivity commonly found in laboratory studies involving behavior modification techniques.

3. Several aspects of this program were designed more for the practical convenience of the patients and staff than for their strict scientific merit. The standard hierarchy of response levels, the different fixed-ratio reinforcement schedules, and the time-limited behavior therapy sessions were all constructed to facilitate administration of the program because it was felt that use of highly individualized response hierarchies, flexible and aperiodic reinforcement rates, and conditioning sessions of indeterminate length would tend to confuse both patients and staff alike.

4. In regard to the matter of primary reinforcers, we were bound by certain ethical and administrative considerations that, in turn, might limit the efficacy and potency of the reinforcers. Assuming that the strength of a reinforcer would be directly related to the underlying drive level of the organism, we were not in a position to enhance the attractiveness of food reinforcers by the prior exposure of patients to prolonged food deprivation

outside behavior therapy sessions. Patients still were entitled to three meals a day regardless of their performance within these sessions. Needless to say, we also were not able to evaluate the effectiveness of a wide range of potentially aversive stimuli for the modification of patient behavior.

Given these problems, all of which mitigate against the optimal modification of behavior, we are better equipped to comment on the various findings and to offer some speculations concerning their clinical implications. Initially, it must be acknowledged that a comprehensive appraisal of this program is difficult inasmuch as it succeeded in some respects and failed in others for both charges and guardians alike. For the charges, although all but one patient showed at least a minimal response to the conditioning procedures, no consistent pattern of response characteristics prevailed. The results indicated that all patients reacted in a somewhat different manner to the same conditioning procedures in terms of rate of learning, the stability or instability of the learned response, and the highest behavior ceiling reached.

For this subgroup of patients, it was apparent that a conditioning program of this sort seemed a highly relevant way of attempting to remedy their clinical deficits. As indicated in Chapter 1, the first clinical problem to be resolved in treatment pertains to getting the attention of patients. All else is superfluous if this cannot be accomplished. Therefore, in our response hierarchy, eye contact represented the first level of behavior we hoped to establish. If this foundation could be achieved, it seemed likely that more complex behaviors could be built in. In a sense, the conditioning program with charge patients represented a systematic attempt to lay the building blocks of appropriate socialized behavior—from the most elementary to the more complex.

From the results obtained, the outcome of these procedures seemed highly variable and unpredictable. For some patients, the laying of the behavioral building blocks proved to be an exceedingly slow, tedious, and laborious process. Thousands of clinical trials were necessary to elevate patient behavior several notches. For several patients, these building blocks would periodically fall down and construction would have to begin anew. For other patients, there appeared to be distinct limits on the number of building blocks that could be layed. Once an optimal response level was established, all efforts to evoke and build in higher levels of behavior proved futile. There were also a couple of other patients for whom pharmacological cement, in the form of phenothiazine medication, had to be added before it was possible to construct a behavioral edifice. If this cement were removed, the whole structure would crumble. And yet for others, the laying of these building blocks proceeded in a smooth, progressive manner. All this indicated that the best way of predicting the nature and extent of patient response to these procedures would be post hoc—after exposing patients to these procedures.

For the guardians, who represented a more socially intact subsample of chronic schizophrenics, the results proved far more impressive. For the most part, their behavior as operant conditioners could be substantially shaped through social and secondary reinforcers. Most of the guardians demonstrated a steady reduction in procedural errors during the course of the program, as well as an increase in competence to perform more complex procedures. In fact, some guardians not only were eventually able to perform the conditioning procedures as well as the staff, but also were successful in obtaining higher response rates from their charge. These results pointed to the feasibility of such patients serving as a source of ancillary personnel for conditioning programs conducted within a mental hospital. They also supported our hypothesis that these patients could be taught to relate to other patients and develop effective interpersonal influencing techniques under the appropriate conditions.

Despite the progress of most guardians within the behavior therapy sessions, there were a number of shortcomings in terms of their optimal functioning as behavior therapists. Although some guardians seemed to grasp the essential principles underlying the operant conditioning procedures and even displayed considerable improvisation and creativity, the majority of guardians became more proficient in a rather rote and mechanical fashion with little appreciation of the rationale for their activities. As a result, these latter guardians tended to perform in a rather fragile, inconsistent manner and would become easily confused and rattled at spontaneous or unanticipated responses on the part of their charges. Moreover, many guardians proved to be unreliable therapists in that they periodically would become uncooperative or uninvolved in their duties with a marked diminution in the motivating power of the previously potent secondary and social reinforcers.

The Dead Ends of Operant Conditioning

At this point, it seems essential to comment on some of the practical and theoretical limitations of operant conditioning as noted in our study despite its several methodological deficiencies. One of the most important developments of this study related to the clinical and statistical findings indicating that a strictly mechanistic learning theory explanation of patient behavior was either untenable or too limiting. The behavior of neither the guardians nor the charges could be accounted for solely on the basis of the classical black box model of stimulus input and response output without involving some explanations for what took place within the black box. The spontaneous, willful, and innovative responses to the conditioning procedures of both the charge and guardian patients often bore little resemblance to those usually recorded for laboratory subjects or animals exposed to classical or operant conditioning procedures. From our experience, there are several clinical pitfalls in relying solely on a strict operant conditioning paradigm.

1. One clinical pitfall relates to certain aspects of chronicity. For example, to understand the behavior of many chronic schizophrenics, it is important to appreciate that they simply may not wish to demonstrate improvement because of the frightening consequences associated with it. As these patients fully realize, marked improvement in behavior may lead to the loss of security and the increase in responsibility associated with hospital discharge. These aversive prospects may be continually at work in counteracting the potential potency of primary and secondary reinforcers employed in any conditioning programs. This would permit them to progress only so far and no further. It is as if these patients appear able to delay gratification in a perverse sense—that is, they seem willing to give up the immediate gratification of a spoonful of ice cream for the more long-range rewards associated with continued hospitalization.

2. For an operant conditioning program to be maximally effective, it is vital that the reinforcers offered be attractive or potent enough to induce patients to respond. During the course of our program, we became painfully aware of how relatively ignorant we were about the concept of reinforcement for chronic schizophrenic patients. For some patients there was no such thing as an absolute positive reinforcer for all times, for all situations, and for all behaviors. Not only would the positive valence of a reinforcer expectedly diminish as a function of satiation, but it might, from one day to the next, in a quite unpredictable manner appear to develop neutral or even negative qualities for the patient being conditioned. Moreover, the problem of reverse social polarity of reinforcers further compounded the difficulties—that is, in some patients the use of positive social reinforcers (e.g., praise) might result in a deterioration of performance, whereas negative social reinforcement or verbal censure might result in an increased efficiency of performance. Often this problem was further complicated by vacillations between reverse and appropriate social polarity of reinforcers within the same patient. I shall say more about these matters in the next chapter.

3. If cognizance is taken of a possible underlying neurophysiological deficit in at least a subpopulation of chronic schizophrenics, it may be appropriate to consider the existence of varying optimal behavior ceilings in these patients. Some patients may have relatively low ceilings whereas others may have relatively high ones. Moreover, because many mental hospitals provide an environment in which psychopathology is reinforced or appropriate behavior is not reinforced, the patient's actual level of performance may be well below his optimal potential level of performance. It can be presumed that operant conditioning procedures are likely to prove more effective in modifying behavior below the patient's optimal ceiling than at or above it. To change behavior further, it may be necessary to raise this ceiling through the use of psychotropic medication, electroconvulsive therapy, or other nonoperant procedures. Once this ceiling is raised, as in the case of our two patients given drugs, the introduction of operant procedures may facilitate further progress. It must be

emphasized, however, that the limitations of the structure and function of the organism determine the maximal ceilings for any behavioral repertoire. Perhaps certain chronic schizophrenics cannot be transformed into emotionally mature, creative, and socially adaptive individuals no matter what therapeutic measures are taken.

In summary, despite the inherent rigor of learning theory for delineating laws of behavior and prescribing methods for its modification, it seems that theory sometimes breaks down in practice with patient subjects such as chronic schizophrenics. In theory, if a person possesses the potential for manifesting certain behaviors, it would be possible to shape and establish these behaviors through operant conditioning procedures provided the subject's drive level is sufficient and the reinforcers are appropriate. In practice, this is exceedingly difficult to accomplish in many chronic schizophrenics (1) who manifest too scanty a behavioral repertoire to permit the use of operant procedures, (2) who are not responsive to available reinforcing stimuli, (3) whose current life situation would be adversely changed by successful response to treatment, (4) whose deviant and socially maladaptive behaviors are maintained by factors or reinforcers unknown (but apparently more potent than those that can be utilized to condition prosocial behaviors), or (5) whose underlying neuro-chemical dysfunction severely limits learning (see Kaufer and Phillips, 1966).

What, then, can be said about the operant conditioning techniques in the treatment of chronic schizophrenia? (1) It is apparent that the specificity and explicitness of these procedures, as well as the quantifiable nature of the data generated by them, offer a much more efficient way for administering and evaluating therapeutic procedures than can be accomplished by many traditional hospital practices. Also, the theory underlying these techniques provides a more parsimonious way of explaining the perpetuation of many of the pathological behaviors of patients. (2) There are many practical difficulties in the implementation of an ideal operant conditioning program within the context of a hospital ward setting. Because it is unlikely that total control of the environmental contingencies of reinforcement on a twenty-four-hour basis can be developed, powerful levers be employed, or strong drive states generated, a clinician employing these procedures for relatively large populations of these patients will have to settle for a good deal of "noise" or inefficiency in his work. (3) Although these procedures offer considerable promise for building in simple, fundamental behaviors in very deteriorated patients and as a means for training more socially intact patients certain interpersonal influencing skills, they do not seem capable of completely filling the therapeutic bill. As indicated previously, some patients seem to go only so far and no further in their improvement in response to these procedures.

As a final note, I feel obliged to point out that we have borrowed heavily from operant conditioning theory in terms of the general therapeutic philosophy espoused in previous chapters. Although I have employed a more colorful and less precise terminology in accounting for some of the deviant behavior of patients and procedures for correcting it, this cannot detract from the underlying similarity to learning theory. Phrases such as "patients behave in ways that pay off for them" or "not rewarding socially maladaptive behavior" could be translated easily in operant conditioning language. However, as illustrated in this chapter, operant theory cannot be invoked to account for all aspects of patient behavior or suggest ways for remedying them. From our clinical and research experiences with chronic schizophrenics, I do not see how it is validly possible to explain and cope with many aspects of deviant behavior without employing certain additional but yet necessary concepts as volition, responsibility, ward culture, or even the possibility of an underlying neurophysiological deficit, all of which are foreign or superfluous to learning theory. In other words, it is my contention that if learning theory is to prove more relevant to a true understanding of patient behavior and if the techniques based on it are to prove more efficacious, it is necessary that clinicians also consider and develop techniques to deal with interpersonal, intrapsychic, and neurophysiological factors.

chapter 9

Of Fulcra and Levers

Archimedes reputedly claimed that if he had a lever long enough and a fulcrum on which to rest it, he could move the earth. The optimistic clinician may make a similar claim concerning the treatment of chronic schizophrenia. The clinician's fulcrum is a situation whereby total control of all environmental responses to patient behavior can be planned, monitored, and enforced. His magical levers are rewards or reinforcers attractive or potent enough to induce patients to work for them and punishments or aversive stimuli unpleasant and noxious enough to induce patients to avoid them. Theoretically, the extent to which these ideal conditions can be achieved will prove directly proportional to the efficiency and successful outcome of any treatment program.

Just as Archimedes could not find his magical fulcrum and lever, the clinician must remain somewhat frustrated in his quest. Although it is possible to conceive of the clinician attaining this goal, a number of realistic and legitimate obstacles bar his way. These obstacles pertain to conflicts between the ideal and the practical, between what may be therapeutically effective and what is ethically feasible, and between the rights of the individual and the rights of society. Even more important, they pertain to certain major discrepancies between theory and clinical reality. Nevertheless, the clinician is charged with the care and treatment of these patients and he cannot relinquish his responsibility simply because he cannot achieve the ideal conditions under which behavior control and modification take place. If he cannot be completely successful in his quest, at least he can be partially successful.

The issue of fulcra and levers is especially relevant to the treatment of chronic schizophrenics. Unlike the cooperative, outpatient neurotic who seeks help for internal distress and who displays the ability to function autonomously outside the treatment sessions, most chronic schizophrenics actively avoid help, are uncooperative with the help offered, and do no act in a socially adaptive way. Moreover, unlike the neurotic who still shows striving or conative tendencies, the chronic schizophrenic acts in an anticonative manner, settling for behaviors far below those of which he is capable. In other words, the neurotic works at getting better whereas the chronic schizophrenic seems to work at remaining ill. Essentially, then, one of the major treatment problems with chronic schizophrenics is how to motivate them to improve. This problem may be stated in other terms, such as how to induce patients to pull themselves out of their altered state of consciousness, how to shed their socially maladaptive habits acquired during prolonged institutionalization, or how to abandon their tactics designed to ensure the continuation of hospital privileges and prerogatives; regardless of the conceptualization used, the issue basically boils down to how to get them to do something they do not want to do. For the clinician to accomplish this task, environmental control and behavior levers must enter the treatment picture.

Privilege Systems

One of the chief levers used for instituting or encouraging behavioral change in chronic schizophrenics is the privilege system. Almost all mental hospitals employ such a system, either formal or informal, explicit or implicit, consistent or inconsistent. Most often, the privileges employed refer to open or closed wards, the degree of supervision required for patients leaving the ward or walking about the hospital grounds, the availability of the canteen, recreational activities, etc. Though many clinicians claim that these or other privileges are prescribed or given not as rewards but according to the clinical status of patients and the degree of freedom they can tolerate, this does not alter the fact that patients tend to perceive these privileges as rewards for appropriate behavior, thereby serving as potential motivators for change.

Despite the extensive use of privilege systems, it is relatively rare to find them applied in any systematic manner and contingent on the performance of specific behaviors—essential criteria for optimizing their effectiveness. Moreover, it is even rarer that clinicians have a consistent, clinically relevant rationale for the privileges employed or have explicitly grappled with the many knotty conceptual problems inherent in the very nature of privileges, especially for chronic schizophrenics.

Privileges and Rights

In the development of a clinically meaningful privilege system, one of the first questions to be answered relates to what constitutes a patient's rights in contrast to his privileges. Many hospital administrators and clinicians insist that all mental patients are not merely entitled to but have the inalienable rights of food, clothing, shelter, and medical care, as well as of access to religious services, recreation, and occupational therapy. Undoubtedly, this is a very humanistic view and seems appropriate for the bulk of mental hospital patients. However, in the case of chronic schizophrenics the treatment paradox is that if patients are well fed, comfortable, and satisfied in all their needs, there is little inducement for them to change. By automatically regarding all these usual services as rights, the clinician is not left with much that can be used as motivating levers, and the residual tends to have weak, if any effects.

This conflict between rights and privileges is not one that can be resolved by reason or even research; the resolution will be dependent on the biases and treatment goals of the clinician. My own views on this matter are perhaps overly simplistic, but they have the advantage of avoiding endless philosophical debate. I am primarily interested in the one right of patients that supersedes all others: The patient is entitled to the most effective type of treatment available, the one that offers him the best possibility of some day functioning as a socially responsible citizen outside the hospital setting. The type of treatment administered, however, must be subject to two qualifications: (1) The health and welfare of the patient should remain a foremost concern. (2) Nothing must be done deliberately to cause him physical or psychological harm. Aside from these qualifications, all else should be regarded as potential treatment levers—provided that they are offered in some consistent, goal-directed manner in an effort to help the patient improve.

Although this viewpoint broadens the range of available levers, it does not permit complete therapeutic license; administrative or social sanctions may prohibit the use of certain procedures or require that certain privileges be regarded as rights. For example, patients cannot be starved in order to maximize the effectiveness of food as a reward for appropriate behavior nor can they be deliberately deprived of sleep in order to use rest as a positive reinforcer, even though these procedures may prove highly effective in modifying their behavior.

In other words, some social realities transcend therapeutic zeal, regardless of whether a clinician regards particular procedures as legitimate levers or certain services as privileges. A clinician must operate within the framework of these social realities, even if this requires that relatively inept procedures be used and less than optimal results obtained.

Privileges and Deprivation

Associated with privileges is the question of deprivation. Generally, it is assumed that privilege systems represent the graduated awarding of more rewards to patients as their behavior improves; punishments or deprivation are not considered integral parts of such systems. In actuality, this assumption is entirely false. Implicit in all privilege systems is the concept of deprivation, and this concept, in turn, is intimately related to the adopted definition of patient rights. In any instance where the privileges meted out to patients are less than those associated with their rights (as accepted by patients or others), deprivation can be said to exist. It is difficult to imagine an active treatment program for chronic schizophrenics in which their rights are not infringed on to some extent—at least according to somebody's definition of their rights.

It is also common to find that hospital administrators and clinicians differ considerably with patients in their views about patient rights and deprivations. For example, even if clinicians hold a fairly liberal view of patient rights and attempt to meet all patient needs, the patients themselves may feel abused and deprived of their freedom through involuntary incarceration. In other words, it is possible and even common for professionals to feel morally wholesome about honoring all the basic rights of patients but for the patients themselves to feel they are being deprived of even more basic human rights.

In any privilege system, therefore, we may assume that deprivation exists when the patients themselves believe they are not receiving certain services regarded as rights of patienthood, despite how hospital professionals choose to interpret the situation. In other words, if patients feel entitled to ground or town privileges and the staff deny them these privileges, patients in actuality are being deprived. This is an exceedingly important distinction in that it indicates that deprivation (often equated with punishment) represents an integral part of any privilege system, regardless of the euphemistic terminology used. The practical aspects of this matter pertain to the degree to which deprivations or punishments can be used in a privilege system to motivate patients to forego their deviant behavior and act in a socially appropriate manner. From a treatment viewpoint, the more privileges patients consider as rights, the more levers are available for modifying their behavior. Awarding or withdrawing these very privileges will have the greatest impact on patient behavior.

The Tendency to Staffomorphize

One inherent difficulty in the construction of many privilege systems is the tendency of clinicians to impute their own motives and desires to patients—in a sense, to *staffomorphize* patient needs. Because the staff would hate being hospitalized, it is assumed that patients would love to be discharged; because the staff enjoy socializing or listening to music, it is assumed that patients would enjoy this too; because the staff like recreational activities, it is assumed patients like to play games; because the staff enjoy occasional privacy or decorative garments or colorful rooms, it is assumed patients enjoy similar things; because the staff prefer insight into their problems and strive to achieve mental health, it is assumed that patients would prefer this; etc.

One unfortunate consequence of this tendency to staffomorphize is that the very privileges on which the staff place the highest premium and which are regarded as the penultimate of rewards may turn out to be relatively meaningless and poor motivators for chronic schizophrenic patients. These patients may care little whether they ever achieve the abstract and intangible goals of insight or whether they are permitted to socialize or engage in recreational activities. The essential clinical problem then pertains to what constitutes a reward or punishment and for whom.

In one of our early experimental treatment programs (Ludwig, 1968), we constructed a privilege hierarchy with seven different levels (see Chart 9-1, p. 164). At level 7, patients received a variety of privileges and opportunities unprecedented within the traditional hospital setting and these privileges reflected what staff themselves held in highest regard. Patients could stay up as late as they liked, watch television whenever they chose, secure passes for town at their bidding, and have first priority for all free tickets donated by various organizations to sporting events and shows within the nearby city. In addition, various staff members would invite them shopping, to their homes, or on special outings. On the ward, they would be regarded as special staff and be invited to participate in all coffee breaks and staff meetings. They also were encouraged to function as staff in making recommendations for solving various ward problems. Unfortunately, we made the mistake of conveying to patients that once they attained level 7 they would be eligible for the ultimate of all rewards—namely discharge. This created all sorts of unanticipated problems.

There was little question that the prerogatives, privileges, and status associated with level 7 served as a strong incentive for constructive performance on the part of many patients. However, as we were soon to learn, this level represented a very precarious, unstable, and emotionally uncomfortable perch for patients. The rewards of achievement were not without the punishments associated with increased responsibility and status. (1) The patients who attained this level were subjected to considerable amounts of ridicule, taunting, and teasing, as well as occasional physical abuse, from fellow patients at lower privilege levels. As a result, the level 7 patients often felt isolated and alienated from the remainder of their group and ill at ease with staff. (2) The greatest part of their dilemma had to do with the equation of level 7 with discharge, and the prospect of discharge hung like a sword of Damocles over their heads. One of our best female patients, a persistent self-mutilator, expressed her feelings as follows: "I can't wait until this program ends so that I can start beating myself again." Other patients found an equitable solution to their dilemma by slipping down to lower privilege levels where the pressures were not so great, where they could still maintain their identity with the patient group, where they still could command a sufficient number of privileges, and where, hopefully, the threat of discharge was minimized. A few other patients resolved this dilemma in more dramatic ways: They took a nose dive into more acute forms of psychosis to escape the implications of doing so well.

What holds for the highest privilege levels likewise holds for the lowest. For example, in one of our treatment programs a mush diet was used for all patients who committed a serious ward rule infraction, such as hitting others. The mush was a mixture of all the food of the regular meals, and its appearance could be regarded as highly unappetizing. Many of the ward staff were so repulsed by the appearance that they claimed that they would prefer not eating at all to having to eat the mush diet. Interestingly, we found that many patients, who originally regarded their mush diet with repugnance, began eating it wtih gusto, returning to the food cart for second and third helpings. Obviously, for these patients, the mush diet could not be regarded as aversive.

It therefore appears that the ordinary form of any privilege hierarchy may be upside down when applied to chronic schizophrenics. If the highest privilege level, equated with increased responsibility and the possibility of discharge, represents most severe punishment and if the lowest privilege level, such as mush diet, is a treat for some patients, clinicians must be willing to reappraise their preconceptions of effective motivators for chronic schizophrenics. Although it is often true that clinicians can legitimately employ the mechanism of empathy to decide what rewards and punishments will prove effective with patients, in many situations this does not work. The adage of "One man's meat is another man's poison" seems especially true for chronic schizophrenics. If a clinically relevant privilege system is to be devised, the therapist must sometimes be willing to travel "through the looking glass" and see the world through the eyes of his patients. Clinicians should base privilege systems on observations of the patients in their natural ward habitat rather than on their own staffomorphic outlook. Privilege systems should be tentative and subject to modification after empirical trials.

This whole problem is related to a more general one—the *reverse polarity of reinforcers*—mentioned briefly in Chapter 8. Essentially, this refers to the tendency of patients to attribute a valence to either social or primary reinforcers opposite to that of normal people. As a result, paradoxical effects may be encountered in patients when the usual rewards or punishments are administered. For example, most normal people respond well to affection and praise and continue to engage in behaviors that tend to elicit these reactions; they also are upset by hostility and criticism and try to avoid behaviors that elicit these reactions. By contrast, some chronic schizophrenics will behave in an entirely different manner. They will continue to engage in those behaviors that produce anger or sanctions and avoid those behaviors that elicit warmth and approbation from the staff. Unless the professional staff can diagnose situations such as these and respond accordingly, it is unlikely that their usual treatment programs for these patients will have much effect.

Let me illustrate how such knowledge can be used in devising a treatment program for a particular patient. The patient in question was a thirty-year-old, paranoid schizophrenic who was highly threatening and assaultive. It was noted that any time the staff showed affection toward her or approval for her appearance or behavior, the patient would shortly become belligerent, mess up her hair, or change into more dowdy clothing. On the other hand, when the staff reacted angrily toward her or chided her, she would seem almost relieved and function well for a period of time after which she would again display aggressive outbursts. In order to control her behavior, we instituted a hate therapy program in which several treatment staff members would meet with the patient twice a day and tell her how horrible she was and how much the staff disliked her. On no occasion during the six-week program was the staff permitted to express approval or affection for her. As predicted, in a short while the patient's agressive outbursts diminished and her appearance and general level of functioning became much improved. Although this clinical program demonstrated the types of reinforcers necessary to control and shape the patient's behavior, it still presented many conceptual dilemmas about where to go from that point.

The problem of reverse polarity of reinforcers is further complicated by the fact that for some patients the valence of a reinforcer, either social or primary, may change several times during the course of a single day or during a period of days. For example, a patient may be pleased by staff approval in the morning, angered by it in the afternoon, and unresponsive to it in the evening. There are a number of patients who for weeks on end center almost their entire existence on acquiring food, even raiding garbage pails or eating leftovers on other patient's plates, but then suddenly lose all interest in food, having to be coaxed to eat or even force fed. Naturally, when the effects of reinforcers prove paradoxical, quixotic, and unpredictable, the treatment problem becomes exceedingly complex.

The Three Dimensions

Generally, we may refer to three dimensions of any privilege system: kind, degree, and duration.

1. It is obvious that the rewards included within a privilege system should be both clinically appropriate and relevant to chronic schizophrenics in terms of providing incentives for appropriate, socialized behavior. From our many experiences with different privilege systems, it may be concluded that the most important and powerful motivators for patients are not the more esoteric, abstruse, futuristic, and intangible goals of self-knowledge, mental health, privacy, appreciation of the arts, religious values or socializing but rather the more specific, concrete, immediate, and tangible ones centering around food, desserts, cigarettes, visits to the canteen, and passive entertainment, such as watching television. For most of these patients, the former goals are luxuries not worth working for, whereas the latter goals are necessities. Only when patients begin to display an adequate repertoire of socialized behaviors and coherent thought processes do the more intangible, middle-class, professional aspirations assume import and, hence, motivating power.

2. Once the kind of privileges are decided on, the dimension of degree must be considered. To construct a privilege system, it is essential that each privilege level in the hierarchy be discrete and conform roughly to a meaningful set of desired behaviors or overall level of functioning in patients. The privilege levels should be graduated in regard to increased rewards and of sufficient number to provide patients with the possibility of success experiences for progressive increments in their overall functioning. If the gap between two privilege levels is too wide and there are only two or three levels possible, patients are apt to become discouraged over the expenditure of effort required for them to move to the next rung on the privilege ladder. A well-defined privilege system holds other practical advantages as well by ensuring that privileges are awarded objectively according to level of functioning. This tends to prevent staff from responding in a whimsical, inconsistent, or biased manner by alloting privileges on the basis of subjective criteria. The behavior displayed by a patient determines his collection of privileges whether the staff like him or not. (See Chart 9-1 a typical privilege system employed in several of our treatment studies.)

3. How soon after the display of appropriate behavior should privileges be awarded and for how long should these privileges last? In our own studies, we have had the opportunity to evaluate the use of weekly and daily privilege systems, as well as the use of immediate awarding of positive reinforcers. With the weekly privilege system, patients would be evaluated for their behaviors over the preceding week and be awarded privileges for the ensuing week. With the

Chart 9-1. PRIVILEGE SYSTEM

1. **0-24 Points**
   a. No privileges: restricted to ward
   b. No visitors
   c. No money
   d. Three meals per day; no desserts; one cup coffee or milk at each meal
   e. One pack state tobacco per week; no other tobacco
   f. No recreational therapy, unless prescribed; no television

2. **25-44 Points**
   a. Escorted groups
   b. Visitors on ward
   c. $1.00 per week for canteen (out of own funds)
   d. No desserts; one cup coffee or milk at each meal
   e. One pack cigarettes or state tobacco every three days (to be purchased by patient's canteen allowance)
   f. Movies with the group; no television

3. **45-59 Points**
   a. Escorted groups
   b. Visitors on ward
   c. $1.00 per week for canteen (out of own funds)
   d. No desserts; coffee and milk at meals only
   e. One pack cigarettes or state tobacco every three days (to be purchased by patient's canteen allowance)
   f. Television permitted

4. **60-74 Points**
   a. White card
   b. Visit on grounds
   c. $2.00 per week for canteen (out of own funds)
   d. Desserts permitted; coffee between meals okay
   e. Cigarettes and other tobacco products as finances permit
   f. May attend dances and athletic activities in the evening, with escort only

5. **75-84 Points**
   a. Blue card
   b. Rides off grounds
   c. $5.00 per week (out of own funds)
   d. Evening snacks
   e. Full cigarette privileges
   f. Recreational therapy trips and visits

6. **85-94 Points**
   a. Daytime pass for off-grounds trek to town
   b. Whole day off grounds with family
   c. $10.00 per week (out of own funds)
   d. Full privileges: snacks, cigarettes, etc.
   f. May attend football and basketball games, shows, concerts, etc., with escort

7. **95-100 Points**
   a. Evening pass to town for movie, etc. by self
   b. Overnight with family, only if suitable arrangements have been made
   c. Full privileges: money, snacks, cigarettes, etc.
   d. Free tickets to play, concert, game
   e. Sit with the staff in the behavior and privilege clinic, various other meetings, etc.

daily privilege system, the privilege status of patients on any particular day would be determined by ratings of their behavior on the preceding day. With the immediate reinforcement program (i.e., the conditioning sessions with the charge patients) patients would be offered positive reinforcers immediately after evocation of the desired response. As indicated in previous chapters, there are a variety of formal ways of employing a particular temporal privilege system for all patients or different temporal privilege systems for different kinds of patients. In the buddy and small-group treatment models, poorer functioning patients were assigned to better functioning ones and each buddy pair or group was rated and given privileges once weekly. With these models, it was assumed that the better functioning patients, who fully comprehended what the acquisition of greater privileges would entail, would be forced to work with their more regressed partners on a more constant daily basis to ensure higher rating scores and, hence, more privileges for all. With the double-conditioning model, charge patients received immediate rewards for desired behaviors whereas guardians could only capitalize on the fruits of their labors at the end of each day.

From these varied experiences, some generalizations seem warranted: (1) There are both practical advantages and disadvantages to any of these temporal systems. The weekly privilege system is much more expedient and economical in terms of staff time, especially in a general ward setting, because it frees the staff to engage in other therapeutic activities. Its major disadvantage lies in the relative lack of precision and the more global ratings of patient behavior, both of which may be partially remedied in the daily privilege system or the immediate application of positive reinforcers. However, with these latter practices, so much of staff time is taken up by providing supervision and feedback to patients that little time is left for other program activities. (2) It seems a truism that the more psychologically intact and socially appropriate the patients, the longer the time lag possible between the performance of certain behaviors and the assignment of privileges based on this performance; the more psychologically deteriorated and socially inappropriate the patients, the shorter the time lag possible. The weekly privilege system presupposes that patients possess some ability to abstract and make temporal connections between their behavior during one week and their privileges the next or can be taught the ability to postpone gratification; the use of daily or immediate rewards presupposes that patients are deficient in these areas.

Naturally, the use of any privilege system, regardless of kind, degree, and temporal duration, demands some mechanism for providing patients with specific feedback about their behavior and informing them which behaviors will have to be altered to reach the next level on the privilege hierarchy. It is not sufficient to simply assign patients to a particular privilege level without being certain that they explicitly know which constellation of their behaviors, both good and bad, warranted such privileges. In most of our treatment programs, a chief mechanism for providing this kind of feedback pertained to a behavior and privilege clinic in which patients would have the opportunity to meet with the ward staff at regularly scheduled intervals to learn the reasons for receiving their particular level of privileges. Other mechanisms involved direct supervisory critiques at work details and other ward functions for patients or countless informal comments about patient appearance and behavior throughout the day.

My impressions of the value of a graduated, well-constructed privilege system coincide with those of workers at Medfield State Hospital, who have pioneered in the use of a seventeen level step system for the rehabilitation of chronic schizophrenics (Isaac and LaFave, 1964, pp. 11-12). These workers describe their experience as follows:

> In additon to the concrete rewards (privileges, money) and symbolic rewards (higher step or status), the "Step System" has become the backbone of the rehabilitation research-service program by providing a systematic means of enhancing communications between the patients and the staff as well as by providing a program of incentives and rewards in ward and work areas. The rating schedules spell out, concretely, what the patients are expected to do, how they have done, where they need improvement and how others see them functioning. This replaces the more ambiguous, inconsistent, and often unspecified demands which patients traditionally must meet in order to be considered well enough to leave the hospital. The "Step System" ties its demands to the demands of the nonhospital world (that is, to appearance, behavior, conversation, quality of work and punctuality). In this manner, the patient relearns useful social and work skills and does not have to guess what is expected of him from one week to another.
>
> Not only does the "Step System" spell out a tangible, or concrete definition of "sick" behavior, but the social meaning and course of action to overcome the illness is also defined. The staff course of action to overcome the illness is also defined. The staff can devote its attention to definable and limited areas, and can note progress in these areas. The patient thinks in concrete terms, rather than abstract concepts, about his illness and his daily experience. He can handle the concrete demands and know if he is making progress, such as making his bed better or being able to work a longer day. The reward and punishment aspect of the system helps the patient to learn what he must do to get a reward and what he will lose if he fails to do these things. The staff renders decisions involving rewards and punishments on the basis of the program leading to consistency among the staff and reduces the likelihood of favoritism, manipulation or other highly subjective elements.

The Provision for Punishment

Chronic schizophrenics who are heavily tranquilized and left relatively alone are less apt to act out than those who are nonmedicated and exposed to an active treatment program that demands some modicum of responsible behavior from them. In the latter case, almost all such instances of acting-out can be attributed to two situations: (1) when patients are prevented from doing something they want to do and (2) when patients are pushed to do something they do not want to do.

For all practical purposes, we may assume that the degree of acting-out demonstrated by patients will be indicative of the slippage or ineffectiveness of the treatment program. The more patients can act out in socially deviant ways and thereby avoid dealing with their conflicts or feelings in socially adaptive ways, the less impact the treatment program will have on them. Acting-out and acting responsibly are incompatible.

In an elaboration of this point, mention should be made of the concept of *functional incompatibility*. According to Risley (1968) there is an inverse relationship between the presence of stereotyped deviant behaviors and the establishment of new, socially appropriate ones. Therefore, as long as these stereotyped behaviors remain present it is extremely difficult to positively reinforce the appearance of more adaptive ones. For these new behaviors to become established, the stereotyped behaviors must first be reduced or eliminated.

We have found this concept of functional incompatibility to be invariably true in most of our clinical work. As long as patients are permitted to vent or act out their feelings in some bizarre, aggressive, sexual, or harmful manner, it is unlikely that they will be able to deal with conflicts or frustrations in more socially adaptive ways. The law of psychic economy dictates that patients or people in general will always take the path of least resistance or one determined by habit if they have a choice in the matter. Therefore, if prosocial, constructive behaviors are to be built into patients or permitted to emerge, the more maladaptive outlets for discharging their feelings must be blocked. This is much easier to advocate than to accomplish because patients do not easily give up behavior patterns that have served them well in the past. If a privilege system is to be employed, it must provide for coping with this problem.

Needless to say, it is practically impossible to control all kinds and degrees of acting-out behaviors, especially with large groups of patients. If this could be done, the treatment problem would be easy. It is much more feasible to distinguish between the behavioral felonies, such as potentially dangerous or socially taboo acts, and the behavioral misdemeanors, such as bizarre mannerisms. For the former behaviors, because of their serious nature, a special punishment category (i.e., minimal privileges) may be suitable whereas for the latter behaviors the general privilege system should prove appropriate.

Those behaviors we have regarded as the equivalent of felonies can be grouped under the heading of the three F's—fighting, fornicating (heterosexual or homosexual), and fleeing (eloping from the hospital). Because these behaviors potentially endanger the welfare of the patients or the integrity of any treatment program, every effort must be made to curtail them or reduce their frequency.

In several of our treatment programs, we have adopted the practice of placing patients on *mortal sin restrictions* for the display of any of these behaviors. This colorful, emotionally charged term was deliberately employed to impress on patients just how seriously we viewed these acts. Essentially, these mortal sin restrictions were as follows: (1) confined to ward; (2) no visitors or presents; (3) no money; (4) no desserts, milk, or coffee; (5) no tobacco; (6) no recreational activities or television; and (7) none of the other usual hospital privileges.

We have experimented with imposing these restrictions on individuals, buddies, or small groups of patients up to three days, after which time they would automatically resume the general level of privileges earned. It has become our impression that the optimal time for mortal sin restrictions is one day at a time. If restrictions are imposed for longer than this, numerous difficulties seem to arise.

1. If these penalties are given for three-day periods and levied consecutively rather than concurrently for each offense, it is possible for patients to bury themselves in restrictions for a series of aggressive behaviors displayed during one day. For example, if a patient hits out ten times in one day, he may find himself placed on mortal sin for thirty days. Obviously, in such situations as this, the punishment far outweighs the crime. Because it becomes virtually impossible for patients to extricate themselves from this inordinate sentence except through sustained good behavior with no rewards, they display little incentive to mend their ways. In order to offer the possibility of therapeutic redemption, it makes much more sense to impose these penalties concurrently and for briefer periods of time, even though some patients may take advantage of this.

2. In an ideal sense, if punishment is to be used to discourage potentially dangerous or socially intolerable behavior, it should be administered immediately contingent on the occurrence of the offensive act and should be relatively brief. The longer punishments are, the more inefficient their results because patients are also inadvertently negatively reinforced for the good behaviors they may demonstrate during periods of restriction. It is for this very reason that I am opposed to the use of prolonged seclusion or physical restraints, as employed in many mental hospitals. During this period of confinement, patients receive no approval or rewards for the performance of appropriate behavior and, therefore, have little incentive for its continuation. These practices can be justified on the basis of patient management but not on the basis of patient therapy.

This presents somewhat of a dilemma in the administration of punishment. Obviously, it is not administratively or professionally feasible to employ brief, aversive stimuli, such as emetic agents (apomorphine, emetine), muscle paralytic agents (anectine), or faradic shock, as conditioned punishments for serious acting-out behavior, even though there may be an excellent scientific rationale for their use and they may produce some dramatic clinical results (Ludwig,

Marx, Hill, and Browning, 1969). In most mental hospitals, punishment can only be administered through the manipulation of privileges rather than through the application of aversive agents. Therefore, if the withdrawal of privileges or the imposition of restrictions is to have any impact on patients, these penalties must remain in effect for some suitable time period—long enough to get the message of punishment across to the offending patient but not long enough to discourage his behaving constructively. To illustrate, it does not make any sense to withdraw television privileges or desserts immediately after a patient strikes out if he is not watching television or eating at that time. If the punishment is to have any meaning, it must overlap the times when patients ordinarily receive certain privileges.

3. Another problem pertaining to the use of a special punishment category pertains to the matter of adaptation. In general, we have found that the effects of deprivation of desserts, cigarettes, television, etc. is maximal for the first day or so after this is instituted. However, the longer this deprivation is enforced or the longer the patient remains at these lower privilege levels, the weaker the motivation of patients to work for more privileges. Most chronic schizophrenics display an amazing ability to adjust to environmental deprivations and, after a period of time, begin to accept what they are getting as their due rather than work to change their status. When faced with the prospect of having to expend considerable energy to acquire greater privileges or continuing to engage in their same behaviors with minimal privileges, they are apt to choose the latter alternative. Naturally, with the advent of adaptation, the original power inherent in the lever of deprivation tends to vanish.

To counter this problem, we have employed a variety of maneuvers. Most simply, the key to preventing adaptation is to keep patients from remaining on lower privilege levels for any length of time. To accomplish this, the staff must work intensively with patients who have settled in a lower behavioral niche. These patients must be continuously prodded, encouraged, and even forced to engage in constructive, socially more adaptive behavior. Often, patients will begin demonstrating constructive behavior which can then be rewarded with the usual privileges, if for no other reason than to get the staff off their back. As indicated in earlier chapters, this responsibility need not fall entirely on the staff. The formal structure of the treatment program can be designed so that the major responsibility for dealing with recalcitrant patients falls on the shoulders of other patients or even the entire patient group.

The Implementation of Control

Intimately related to the use of privilege systems is the issue of control. If a privilege system is to work, some mechanism must ensure that patients obtain only those privileges that they have earned or that are assigned to them. If patients can obtain the gamut of privileges usually reserved for higher levels of functioning, there is little incentive to work harder. When rewards are forthcoming with minimal effort, it is unlikely that patients will strive to obtain the same rewards generally given for greater outputs of energy. Unfortunately, this very problem is involved in the implementation of most privilege systems.

In our various treatment programs, we have found it extremely common for patients to break their own privilege status or to help other patients break theirs. It has been my long-standing impression that, if patients devoted a small portion of the energy expended in getting their way toward getting well, the treatment program would be immeasurably simpler. I have already described some of these patient activities pertaining to the code of chronicity. Patients are anything but passive and docile when it comes to getting something they want. If their privilege status dictates that they are not entitled to cigarettes or dessert, patients will often steal these items or be given them by other patients. Obviously, as long as a privilege system is impossible to enforce, it has no motivating power and is therefore therapeutically impotent.

This is no easy problem to solve. The administration of a privilege system requires the constant correction of flaws, the elimination of loopholes, and the effective monitoring of patient activities in order to prevent patients from obtaining contraband articles for themselves or for others not entitled to them. It is essential that staff remain at least one step ahead of patients if a relatively fail-safe privilege system is the goal.

Although there are a number of alternative methods for discouraging the subversive tactics of patients, I should like to mention the one employed in much of our work. Essentially, this was to equate all such privilege infractions with *venial sins*. To impress on patients the notion that this type of behavior was bad, we penalized them by deducting a fixed number of points for each incident from their overall behavior rating scores. The final score received determined the level of privileges assigned. Therefore, it was possible that if patients accumulated enough venial sin offenses, they might receive privileges at one or two levels below those they ordinarily would be assigned. Although this practice could not be regarded as completely successful in curtailing these offenses, it did considerably curb their incidence.

Aside from a formal control procedure of this sort to aid in the implementation of a privilege system, there are many more informal ways control must be exerted. One of these pertains to the necessity for staff to present a united emotional front in all dealings with patients. The reactions of staff members can be employed as powerful levers for modifying, shaping, or changing patient behaviors provided that they are congruent, appropriate, and goal directed. Idiosyncratic emotional responses of staff members to particular patients undermine the relative strength of their potential influence. Chronic schizophrenics, like normals, prefer clearly defined messages; ambiguity and inconsistency provide sanctuaries for continued deviant behavior.

The use of tranquilizer and sedative medication may also play an important role in controlling patient behavior. Although we have deemphasized the use of psychiatric drugs in our various treatment studies, they still provide a type of therapeutic insurance when all else fails and, under special circumstances, represent the therapeutic procedure of choice. These special circumstances pertain mostly to severe aggresive or destructive behaviors that cannot be substantially deterred through the use of the regular privilege system, the ordinary forms of punishment, or the intervention of fellow patients. In these instances, drugs become indispensable not only in breaking the vicious circle of escalating aggressive behavior on the part of a patient but in preventing serious harm to others. Once the patient is brought under effective control, the drugs may be withdrawn and the usual therapy program reinstated.

What I have hoped to convey in this relatively brief discussion of treatment levers and environmental patient control is that most privilege systems can become much more clinically relevant and hopefully more effective in modifying patient behavior if they are employed in an explicit, specific, systematic, and goal-directed manner relevant to the desires of the patients rather than those of the staff. Privilege systems, whether openly acknowledged or not, exist in virtually all hospital treatment programs for these patients. The prime issue, however, pertains to whether they will be used in ways that can potentially benefit patients the most.

Even a well-thought-out privilege system does not automatically dispense with the numerous clinical problems that fall outside its domain or contradict the very premises of the levers employed. Although clinicians already know a good deal about treatment levers and could get much better results if they applied this knowledge in the design of treatment programs, it also is apparent that far less is known than is ordinarily assumed. Because more knowledge about these matters is so vital for the nonsomatic treatment of chronic schizophrenics, it is essential that more formal and informal research be conducted to discover more powerful levers which are both practical and ethical to employ and to resolve such seeming contradictions of the theory underlying privilege systems as the reverse polarity of reinforcers, the shifting valences of reinforcers, and the problem of adaptation.

chapter 10

Exploiting Nonspecific Influences

The importance of the potential influence of nonspecific factors on treatment outcome has been commented on by others (Frank, 1961; Sargant, 1957; Kiev, 1964). In a recent conference on schizophrenia (Solomon and Glueck, 1964), one of the participants stated the problem in a very apt and succinct manner.

> After hearing thoughtfully written and well-presented papers and discussions on the psychotherapy of schizophrenia, one is impressed, in spite of the dearth of objective or controlled data, with the favorable results and plausible rationale offered in explanation and support of these results. Yet one naturally wonders how these results can be specific in any sense when they seem to be about equally obtainable through the utilization of a number of different psychotherapeutic theories. The operation of nonspecific factors suggests itself, such as subtle suggestion, persuasion, coercion, or other transference elements.

Although most clinicians are willing to acknowledge the existence of these nonspecific factors, there has been little systematic investigation into their nature and the extent of their influence, especially in the area of psychotherapy. Yet if these factors do exist and contribute to the effects of various therapeutic techniques, it seems essential that more research be done in this area. Unless it can be established that the specific programs or procedures employed to treat chronic schizophrenics or psychiatric patients in general contribute something to the ultimate treatment outcome above and beyond that of the nonspecific factors, the use of these specific approaches may be superfluous. Instead, it may become possible to treat psychiatric patients with nonspecific approaches alone. Although many clinicians may balk at this prospect, mainly because the conscious use of nonspecific factors is associated with the deliberate use of placebos or even the practice of charlatanry, this concern is more ethical than practical. From a practical standpoint, the critical concern should be whether these nonspecific approaches work as well as if not better than existing specific approaches. If they do work, then the question can be raised whether they can be applied in some intelligent, consistent, reproducible, systematic manner in order to obtain the best therapeutic results with patients. It seems far better to employ a placebo or even wave a magic wand that, because of its dramatic qualities, permits some patients to get well, if only briefly, than to employ a respectable, highly specific scientific procedure devoid of nonspecific contaminants that produces absolutely no improvement.

To determine the nature and influence of nonspecific factors, it is far too constricting to study only current psychotherapeutic procedures. Modern, formal psychotherapy represents only a recent development in the history of the healing arts and, even at present, represents only a relatively insignificant proportion of the healing procedures used throughout different societies for coping with and treating deviant behavior. Although modern psychotherapy has advanced considerably, it has failed to pay attention to potential sources of knowledge and useful techniques that other societies and groups, both past and present, have employed to deal with similar types of problems. These techniques pertain to a variety of mental healing and behavior modification practices, such as faith healing, religious or ideological conversion, religious instruction, exorcism rites, rites de passage, spirit possession, indoctrination programs, moral suasion, self-help and suggestion therapies, abreaction procedures, and propaganda techniques.

A Therapeutic Smorgasbord

It is one matter to speculate and theorize about the potential contribution of nonspecific factors to treatment success and another to investigate their actual contribution. Fortunately, during the course of our various studies, we were able to acquire considerable information relevant to this issue.

Interestingly enough, the *total push treatment program* of Myerson (1939), which has had such an enormous impact on all subsequent psychiatric hospital treatment programs, incorporates many elements similar to those in the program to be described. The major differences pertain to the labeling of these elements in the total push program as specific rather than nonspecific and in the rationale offered for their use. For example, in the total push program, patients receive a variety of tonics, such as showers, douches, massage, rubdowns, and ultraviolet radiation, participate in much exercise and games, and are exposed to the constant psychological push of moral suasion and the liberal use of praise, blame, reward, and punishment. As shall be seen, it is easy to translate these activities into nonspecific terms.

For the first of these studies (Ludwig, 1968), I started with assumption that a number of common denominators could be found in all healing and behavior modification practices, including formal psychotherapy. Rather than regard these nonspecific common denominators as contaminants of pure psychotherapy, I operationally speculated that these nonspecific factors might represent, in fact, the specific influences responsible for most forms of mental healing. To this end, a treatment program was designed to exploit whatever therapeutic potential might be inherent in these nonspecific influences. It was my thesis that if these nonspecific factors, representing common denominators of all healing practices, could be defined and applied in a systematic, intensive, and concentrated manner to chronic schizopnrenics that substantial improvement in their behavior might result.

A Latin square experimental design was employed to conduct the program. For the first ten-week block of time, fifteen patients were assigned to the experimental treatment (pertaining to the application of nonspecific factors) and fifteen patients to the control treatment group. At the end of this period, the initial experimental group received the control treatment and the initial control group received the experimental treatment for a comparable time period.

The treatment program for the control group consisted of three general ward meetings per week, as well as exposure to the usual, hospital acitivities. The experimental group, in contrast, was exposed to a variety of different procedures. A description of the specific ingredients of the experimental treatment and the rationale for their use are given below.

Emotional Arousal Meeting

It has become almost a therapeutic truism that before patients can benefit from or be motivated for treatment they must experience some type of distress, admit to sickness, and seek relief from discomfort. Such is not the case for many chronic schizophrenic patients who have adapted to long years of hospitalization and have also developed a psychologic stimulus barrier, relatively impervious to unwanted outside stimulation. Therefore, because of the therapeutic immunity that emotional apathy confers, healers have intuitively or empirically resorted to a variety of techniques to induce emotional arousal, thereby making the supplicant or patient more susceptible to their therapeutic ministrations.

As illustrations of these practices, we find shamans, medicine men, hungans, curanderos, and tribal priests employing numerous techniques to produce fear, awe, mystery, and anxiety in their subjects prior to inducing spirit possession fits, trance, and hypersuggestible states. A number of these techniques have been described for the faith cure. For example, after supplicants made a long arduous trek to the religious healing shrines, such as the ancient Egyptian and Grecian sleep temples and Lourdes, the priestly guardians would prescribe cold water baths, prayer, confession, and offerings prior to temple sleep (incubation) or the healing experience (Ludwig, 1964). The elements of sacrifice, propitiatory rites, and hardship appeared to be crucial ingredients for producing the desired abject and humble state of mind. Somewhat similar practices have presumably been employed for initiates during tribal puberty rites (Sargant, 1957) or introduction to the lesser and greater Eleusinian mysteries.

In addition to the above, healers may employ other techniques—coercive, exhortative, etc.—to induce a receptive state of mind in their audience. Such famous revivalistic preachers as Jonathan Edwards, John Wesley, and Billy Sunday have converted countless people by threatening them with "hell, fire, and brimstone" if they failed to heed "the word of God." Other fundamentalist preachers among the Holy Rollers or snake-handling cults use similar techniques, in addition to emotionally rousing music or chants, to increase the susceptibility of members in their congregations to visitations by the Holy Spirit (LaBarre, 1962).

Although brainwashing procedures at first appear alien to healing practices, they are indeed often similar in terms of techniques and desired goals (Sargant, 1957; Frank, 1961). The interrogator attempts to achieve in his victims a suggestible mental state, characterized by apprehension, confusion, doubt, and emotional distress, through such techniques as verbal badgering, sleep deprivation, fatigue, drugs, humiliation, and physical discomfort. The goal of thought reform is to align the victim's attitudes and behavior with those in authority.

These practices differ only in degree from those employed by the modern-day psychotherapist. Fully convinced that the patient must hurt if he is to benefit from treatment, the therapist often uses a variety of techniques to shake up the emotionally complacent or resistive patient. It has almost become dictum for most insight-oriented psychotherapists that the patient's motivation for help is, roughly, directly proportional to his discomfort. Moreover, therapeutic insight most likely will occur following the reliving and verbalization of certain past traumatic events.

Given these considerations, one component of the experimental treatment included a group meeting—one hour per day, five times a week—designed to produce the maximal amount of emotional response and arousal in patients. In general, the group leader openly confronted patients with taboo topics and voiced criticisms of an unsympathetic society toward their deviant attitudes and behaviors. The crazy behaviors of patients were parodied and caricatured. Patients were badgered, pestered, confronted, challenged, derogated, ridiculed, and belittled in an effort to provoke protest, anger, irritation, discomfort, and self-assertion.

Because the purpose of these meetings was to stimulate all forms of emotional arousal, the expression of pleasurable emotion was likewise encouraged. The group leader frequently used humor, satire, mimicry, and comic expression to induce laughter in patients. Exaggerations, hyperboles, and inanities were also used to provoke denial or argument. In short, the primary focus of these sessions was on emotional rather than intellectual response.

Suggestion-Inspiration Meeting

Almost all therapeutic and behavior modification procedures utilize suggestion either implicitly or explicitly to achieve their goals. The use of suggestion and autosuggestion techniques dates back to antiquity. The cupping and sucking rituals of shamans, the potency attributed to incantations, spells, amulets, talismans, and prayer, the healings that occurred in the ancient Egyptian and Greek sleep temples, cures attributed to the healing touch of kings, the miraculous cures produced by faith healers, magnetizers, and even charlatans probably owe their efficacy to the effects of suggestion (Ludwig, 1964). In more recent times, the autosuggestion techniques of Coué (1922), autogenic training (Jacobson, 1938), hypnotherapy, and many self-help techniques (Carnegie, 1965; Peale, 1952; Schindler, 1954) have made explicit use of the power of suggestion for treatment purposes. Although the placebo effect of pharmacologic and other somatic agents has received much attention, some influential clinicians (Lesse, 1962) believe that a similar effect operates in psychotherapy and may be responsible for much of its efficacy.

According to Sargant (1957), persons are more susceptible to suggestion during altered states of consciousness, which, incidentally, may be induced through the arousal of strong emotions (Ludwig, 1966a). Therefore, in an effort to capitalize on the presumed heightened emotions of patients produced during the emotional arousal meeting, patients met again for daily suggestion and inspiration sessions. By emotionally priming the patients beforehand, we hoped they would prove more receptive and susceptible to the various suggestions given them.

During each morning session—one-half hour per day, six days a week—a different standard tape was played (Powers, n.d.). The primary emphasis in these tapes was on will power, placing the responsibility for mental health directly on the shoulders of the patients. These tapes stressed a variety of self-help and autosuggestion techniques that might be employed by patients to overcome many of their problems. The topics covered included self-confidence, self-mastery, will power, magnetic personality, financial success, and deep relaxation. The subject matter for each of these tapes took ten minutes and the same topic was played three times. Therefore, during the ten-week period, patients would hear each tape thirty times. We hoped that the effectiveness of these tapes would be increased through sheer repetition—a favorite practice in propaganda and advertising.

Moral Suasion and Reeducation Meeting

Moral suasion, education, and reeducation are old and widely used methods, employed by almost all agencies concerned with healing or, in a general sense, the modification of behavior. There appears to be consensus among modern therapists that one of the major goals of psychotherapy is to learn new and more adaptive ways to cope with problems and to unlearn maladaptive habits or patterns of behavior. Within the framework of this model, the role of the therapist may be likened to that of a parent, teacher, confessor, tutor, counselor, preacher, inquisitor, supervisor, or political demagogue who provides guidelines for desirable and appropriate behavior. Likewise, it is generally assumed that the patient, novitiate, child, apprentice, heretic, supplicant, or potential convert must be instructed or indoctrinated concerning future behavior by those who hold socially or professionally sanctioned positions of authority.

It is my conviction that if the chronic schizophrenic is to be successfully treated, he must have a clear conception of the nature of psychologic and social health. Not only have many patients received faulty or distorted instructions during their upbringing concerning appropriate personal and group behavior, but many patients with lengthy hospitalizations either have forgotten how to behave normally or acquired bad habits and attitudes that tend to be maladaptive once they leave the protective setting of the hospital. Therefore, in formulating this group, I have started with the assumption that patients need to learn or relearn certain very basic personal and social attitudes, skills, and behaviors in order to make a healthy social adjustment.

Almost all members of the staff participated in presenting the course material to patients. The subjects covered included such areas as etiquette, eating habits, appearance, personal hygiene, social conversation, dating, normal sexual behavior, perversions, applying for jobs, work attitudes, self-help techniques for coping with difficulties, and basic ethics and morals. The sessions occurred for one hour per day, five times a week. During the last session of the week all patients were given a twenty-item choice questionnaire based on the material presented during the week. The patients' answers were graded immediately, and they were told the correct answers. To increase patient motivation for taking these quizzes seriously, half the number of questions answered wrong was deducted from the weekly behavior rating score that determined their level of privileges.

Dynamic Interpretive Meeting

Almost all systems of healing provide supplicants with some type of theoretical framework to account for the nature of illness and cure. Primitive man may have explained his distress on the basis of withcraft or the anger of tribal deities; the devout mystic seeks to overcome his presumed alienation with God; the spiritualist attempts to salve his grief by establishing contact with departed spirits; and the modern-day analysand or psychotherapeutic candidate expects to overcome his difficulties through insight into the origins and nature of his conflicts.

Without such theoretical explanations, persons would feel helpless and frightened about their illness. If they can make sense out of their predicaments, or if the socially designated healer can diagnose the cause of their problems, they need not feel so impotent in the face of adversity. To quote Frank (1961, p. 63), "The ideology and ritual supply the patient with a conceptual framework for organizing his chaotic, mysterious, and vague distress and give him a plan of action, helping him to regain a sense of direction and mastery and resolve his inner conflicts."

In order to meet this need, we established a group in which patient behaviors were discussed and interpreted within the framework of psycho-analytic theory. Generally, the sessions—which met for one hour per week—were both didactic and directive. As stated in a previous publication (Ludwig, 1966b), I feel that almost any comprehensive theoretical system probably would prove as effective and valid as psychoanalysis provided that it be internally consistent and make sense both to the patient and therapist. For this particular group, the psychoanalytic framework was selected because it was best known to the psychiatrist conducting the sessions.

Behavior and Privilege Clinic

In every society, organization, and total institution, there are relatively well-defined roles and ranks for the constituent members. The rank accorded to any member generally determines both his privileges and responsibilities.

In the mental hospital, the definition of roles is mainly limited to staff. The role of the patient, however, often is ill defined and ambiguous. Although there is little question that patients establish an informal social structure of their own, the formation of their social hierarchy tends to be haphazard, without explicit rationale, and serves little constructive purpose in terms of rehabilitation. Rather than settle for the unhealthy and unstructured social system of patients, we decided to create a new, artificial system based on certain rational principles of responsibility and sanity. Within the framework of this artificial patient society, we wanted to minimize reinforcement for crazy and maladaptive behavior and to maximize the rewards for responsible, healthy behavior. Because we felt it would be helpful for patients to gain a clear conception of where they stood in relation to other patients in terms of sanity, we constructed a social caste and class hierarchy consisting of seven separate levels. This artificial social system was designed to encourage vertical mobility, whereby patients could move up or down the levels depending on scores they received on their weekly behavior rating. (Sessions pertaining to this behavior rating met for three hours per week.) The privileges and responsibilities of patients were strictly contingent on their weekly social level. A simplified schema for the daily activities of all experimental group patients is presented in Chart 10-1.

Chart 10-1. WEEKLY ACTIVITIES FOR EXPERIMENTAL TREATMENT PROGRAM

	Monday	Tuesday	Wednesday	Thursday	Friday
7:00	Breakfast, Clean-up and Chores				
8:30	Emotional Arousal				
9:45	Suggestion Inspiration				
10:15	Free Period				
11:00	Lunch, Clean-up and Rest Period				
1:00	Moral Suasion and Reeducation				
2:15	BPC	BPC	D-I	BPC	Open (BPC?)
3:15	Free Period				
4:15	Supper, Clean-up and Rest Period				
6:00	Free Period				
7:00	GWM	GWM	Free	GWM	Free
7:45	Free to Bedtime				

Key: BPC = Behavior privilege clinic
      D-I = Dynamic interpretive
      GWM = General ward meeting

An elaborate presentation of the results seems unnecessary. Basically, statistical analyses indicated significantly greater improvement in patient when exposed to the experimental compared to the control treatment conditions. Figure 10-1 illustrates the weekly progress made by the entire group of chronic schizophrenic patients during the experimental program.

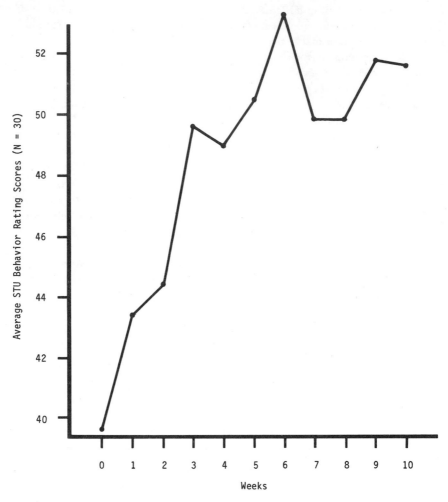

Figure 10-1: Group progress chart during experimental treatment program.

    Although these results indicate that the systematic, concentrated and intensive application of nonspecific healing influences could produce substantial changes in patient behavior—i.e., reducing psychopathology and increasing constructive behavior—it must be emphasized that this neither derogates the effectiveness of other types of treatment programs nor argues for the establishment of similar programs in other hospital settings. These results mainly indicate that there are potent healing forces in the so-called unintentional or nonspecific factors representing common denominators of most psycho-therapeutic or modification practices. There is the additional implication that when modern investigators become concerned about eliminating the nonspecific contaminants of therapy from their treatment programs, they may well become guilty of eliminating the very forces that make psychotherapy effective. By ridding their therapies of these unintentional influences, they may, metaphorically speaking, be throwing out the baby with the bath water.

Attention and Structure

Although a number of important theoretical or conceptual issues can be raised about the interpretation of results of the above study (see Ludwig, 1968), perhaps the most relevant one pertains to whether the increased attention and/or structure per se, both representing even more basic elements of the nonspecific factors employed, could have been largely responsible for the relatively successful results obtained. It is quite possible that the large variety of nonspecific activities are really superfluous and that, more parsimoniously, the even more critical therapeutic ingredients pertain to the greater amount of attention and/or structure received by patients in the experimental compared to the control treatment conditions. Although we have not conducted a treatment study to compare the effects of an experimental program, such as the one described, with one balanced equally for the amount of attention and structure given, we nevertheless are in a position to provide a partial answer to this issue.

In a subsequent study (Ludwig and Marx, 1971), we decided to evaluate the effects of the following four treatment conditions: attention, structure, attention-structure, and unstructured. Twenty-eight chronic schizophrenic patients (fourteen males and fourteen females) served as subjects. For the first treatment period, patients were randomly assigned to one of these treatment conditions, thereby creating four groups of seven patients each. There were four successive treatment periods, each period lasting six weeks. The nature of the design was such that each group was exposed to each of the four treatment conditions sometime during the twenty-four-week program. The order of administration of treatments differed for each patient group. In this manner each patient served as his own control under the four different treatment conditions. (See Figure 10-2 for the experimental design.) A description of each of the four treatment conditions follows:

1. Attention was operationally defined as any interpersonal contact, exposure or interaction patients have with hospital staff in both formal and informal situations. For this condition, patients in small groups of three or four were scheduled to meet with assigned staff (essentially nurses and aides) for one hour per day, six days per week. The assigned staff would change from day to day in order to discourage any continuity of theme or specific psychotherapeutic orientation. In addition, staff were also assigned to meet with

Period

	1	2	3	4
Group 1	A	S	US	AS
Group 2	S	AS	A	US
Group 3	AS	US	S	A
Group 4	US	A	AS	U

Figure 10-2: Balanced latin square design. (A=attention; S=structure; AS=attention-structure; US=unstructured.)

patients, in individual sessions, for fifteen minutes per day, six days a week. As with the group sessions, there were no specific therapeutic goals established for these meetings. All patients assigned to this condition received the usual hospital privileges, which were dispensed in a liberal manner and not made contingent on their performance.

2. Structure referred to a general ward situation in which clearly defined staff expectations regarding standards of acceptable behavior would be transmitted to patients concerning the parameters of constructive behavior. In addition, patient privileges were made contingent on performance. For this condition, the only formal contact the patients had with the staff was on an individual basis for ten minutes twice a day (approximately between the hours of 2-3 P.M. and 9-10 P.M.). During these contacts, an assigned staff member provided direct verbal feedback about the prior seven to eight hours of patient behavior. A standardized, brief evaluation form, emphasizing socially adaptive, responsible behavior, was used for rating patient performance. On the basis of the combined total score of these two ratings, patients were assigned to one of four privilege levels for the following day.

3. Attention-structure represented a combination of both the attention and structure conditions. Patients assigned to this condition received the same amount of exposure to staff as in the attention condition as well as the systematic feedback (daily behavior ratings with privileges contingent on performance) associated with the structure condition.

4. In the unstructured treatment condition patients were treated in a custodial fashion. Aside from the necessary informal encounters concerning meals, housekeeping, etc. staff spent no formal time with patients and provided them with no systematic feedback about their behavior. Privileges were awarded in the same manner as for the attention condition.

Although the results of this particular study were not so impressive as the one employing the smorgasbord of nonspecific factors, a number of clinically intriguing findings did arise: (1) Of the three global behavior rating instruments employed, statistically significant results were obtained on one, with attention-structure producing the greatest improvement and unstructured the least; the attention and structure conditions fell between these extremes. Although significant results were not found for the other two rating instruments, the mean scores reflected the same direction of treatment effects, thereby offering some corroboration to the one significant finding. (2) Highly significant period effects were found on all measures. Regardless of the treatment condition, the global behavior rating scores indicated that patients got progressively worse following exposure to each of the four successive treatment periods. It was our clinical impression that these adverse period effects were largely a reflection of the decrease in staff enthusiasm over the course of the study as they repetitively had to implement the same treatment formats regardless of patient response. These unanticipated findings indicated that the dimension of time, representing another nonspecific factor, must be reckoned with in the construction and assessment of any treatment program. (3) Finally, and perhaps of most clinical significance, the results of the study indicated that different subtypes of chronic schizophrenics responded differentially to the various nonspecific factors employed (see Figure 10-3). Although both the socially responsive and withdrawn patients responded best to the combination of attention and structure, their response to the other treatment conditions differed considerably. The socially responsive patients, who were composed largely of the more overtly paranoid, active patients, seemed to tolerate a situation where no demands were made of them and no particular attention granted (unstructured) much better than one where they were provided feedback and held accountable (in terms of assigned privileges) for their behavior. In contrast, the socially withdrawn patients seemed to respond to attention or structure about equally well, but did much worse in the custodial type unstructured setting.

The results of this study receive some confirmation from other independent sources, as well as other informal studies of our own. O'Conner and Rawnsley (1959), for example, studying the effects of a sheltered workshop situation, found that the work output in paranoid patients may be diminished under an incentive system (similar to the structure condition). Wing and Freudenberg (1961) investigated the performance of chronic schizophrenics under similar circumstances, the experimental variable being active supervision

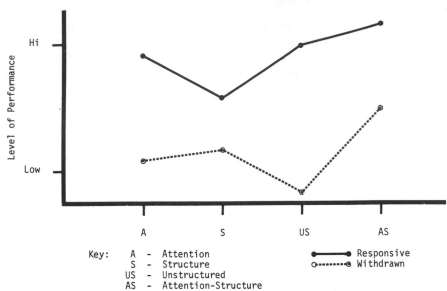

Figure 10-3: Differential response of patients to treatment conditions.

(similar to the attention-structure condition) and the control variable being passive supervision (similar to the attention condition). The findings indicated that active supervision produced the best results. However, their observations revealed the existence of two subgroups of patients, comparable to our active and withdrawn samples, in terms of response to supervision. About one half the patient sample accounted for 90 percent of the initial work output of the group and all of the improvement due to practice but only 40 percent of the increase in work output due to increased social stimulation. The remaining patients, who resembled our withdrawn sample, accounted for 60 percent of the increased output under active supervision.

The importance of the attention variable also receives confirmation in the study by Kellam, and co-workers (1967) on acute schizophrenics. These authors, who participated in the nine-hospital National Institute of Mental Health collaborative study on the effects of phenothiazine medication, attempted to assess the influence of ward atmosphere on treatment response. Their results showed that the amount of social contact provided on a ward bore a direct, significant relationship to treatment outcome. The less patients had an opportunity to remain alone, the more patients participated in groups, and the higher the staff-patient ratio, the better the treatment response, regardless of the drugs administered.

The importance of attention and structure for certain subgroups of patients was also revealed in a modest clinical study on social deprivation conducted primarily by E. Seidman on our Unit (data not written up or published). Five of our most socially withdrawn nonverbal patients were placed together in one room throughout the day, served meals there, and had virtually no verbal communication with the staff. The rationale for this program was to induce a state of social hunger in these patients which, in turn, should induce them to relate more with one another over the course of time. The supposition was that these types of patients ordinarily could achieve satisfaction of most social needs simply by watching the interaction of others, both staff and fellow patients, on the ward, thereby relieving them of the need to communicate. Therefore, removing them from the ward situation and isolating them together, we hoped to encourage greater social interaction by enhancing their need for social stimulation.

Although the program was scheduled to run for a minimum of six weeks, the response of these patients forced us to terminate it within two weeks. Exposed to this highly unstructured situation, patients rapidly began to deteriorate in their behavior and to act in a number of very primitive ways, such as becoming highly aggressive toward one another, displaying urinary incontinency, and losing all interest in personal appearance. Although we could not have foreseen these results, this experience dramatically illustrated the tendency of socially withdrawn patients to fall apart under unstructured conditions—a situation partially comparable to a strictly custodial setting.

As our findings and those reported in the literature indicate, the variables of attention and structure can exert powerful therapeutic effects or affect certain subgroups of patients differentially. Socially active, paranoid patients do not seem able to tolerate a highly structured ward environment without the addition of attention, and socially withdrawn patients show marked deterioration when structure and attention are absent. These results would argue for the need either to devise different types of therapy programs for these different types of patients or, because both of these subtypes of patients respond well to the combination of attention and structure, to exploit the influence of these variables by including them in any treatment program for general population of chronic schizophrenics.

A Nonspecific Overview

There are several general matters yet to be discussed:

1. It is essential to determine to what extent the relatively successful results noted with the study employing a smorgasbord of nonspecific factors (i.e., emotional arousal, suggestion, moral suasion, etc.) could be accounted for solely on the basis of attention and structure. If it is determined that attention and structure represent the critical ingredients, the variety of other nonspecific factors employed can be regarded as superfluous. Because a direct, comparative

study was not performed, there is no way to resolve this matter definitively except by clinical impression. Although the more basic variables of attention and structure contributed to the successful treatment outcome in the former study, they could not entirely account for all the findings. This conclusion is based on the fact that in the second study the combination of attention and structure only produced moderate and somewhat inconsistent improvement in patients whereas in the first study the smorgasbord of nonspecific factors produced a much more dramatic and consistent response. It therefore appears that certain nonspecific factors or combination of factors, other than those of attention and structure, must be present in order to obtain a maximum response to nonspecific factors.

2. It should also be apparent that the use of nonspecific treatment factors does not guarantee that behavioral change will occur or that, if it does, the change will be clinically meaningful. Statistical significance need not be regarded as synonymous with clinical significance. For example, with the smorgasbord program, about one third of the patients seemed relatively unaffected, whereas with the attention-structure program the overall amount of change was even less. Obviously, to be regarded as highly successful and clinically relevant, the treatment program should make some provision for dealing with the psychologically unreachable or socially unresponsive patients as well as inducing even greater improvement in patients.

3. Perhaps most crucial, if nonspecific factors are to be deliberately exploited in the conduct of a treatment program, clinicians must address themselves to the issues of quantity and quality. For instance, it is simply insufficient to talk in terms of applying attention and/or structure without operationally defining their parameters and to what extent they are used. Many different amounts and kinds of attention and structure can be employed; some may prove therapeutically helpful, others will have no effect, and still others will have detrimental effects. The issue, then, should not be one of whether to use nonspecific factors but rather one of explicitly using them in specific ways designed to obtain effects.

Given these considerations, what then are the implications for interpreting the results of treatment programs in which specific techniques and procedures are employed? Actually, all that these nonspecific treatment studies indicate is the likelihood that a certain portion of the improvement noted in patients exposed to such successful programs as the buddy or double-conditioning model can be attributed to nonspecific influences. However, it is equally likely that these results do not account for all the improvement noted. For example, it is difficult to imagine that any of the nonspecific factors mentioned could explain adequately the development of a mutually helpful relationship between buddies or the learning of certain interpersonal influencing techniques on the part of guardian patients or many other of the phenomena observed. It seems more reasonable to attribute the realization of these goals to the specific treatment models or techniques designed explicitly for this purpose.

In this regard, it appears that if a therapeutic program is to prove maximally effective in improving patient behavior, it not only will capitalize on the presence of nonspecific factors but will also compensate for their limitations by employing a variety of specific techniques designed to achieve certain designated goals. The simultaneous use of specific and nonspecific factors is not contradictory but rather complementary. It is my contention that only when both are employed in concert will optimal and more lasting improvement be noted in patients.

part four

The Outside World

chapter 11

The Transition from In to Out

There are three major phases to any comprehensive treatment program for chronic schizophrenics: (1) the modification of patient behavior within the hospital setting; (2) the preparation of patients for discharge; and (3) the provision for maintaining and rehabilitating discharged patients in the community. All three phases may be regarded as mutually complementary, of relatively equal clinical importance, and of comparable difficulty. So far, there has been extensive discussion of the first of these phases. It is now necessary to move on to an entirely different set of problems associated with the second of these phases. These problems pertain to many theoretical and practical issues about the best way of preparing patients to emerge from their institutional cocoons and venture forth into the outside world.

Aside from dealing with the residual psychopathology present in pre-discharge patients, the clinician must come to grips with many artifactual and superimposed difficulties resulting from their prolonged hospitalization. Most of these difficulties may be conceptualized as part of the Rip Van Winkle

191

syndrome. The patient, awakening from his long emotional and intellectual slumber, finds that the world outside the hospital is vastly different than when he was first hospitalized. During the years, there have been vast technological changes, prices have risen, new products are available, well-known landmarks have disappeared, new buildings have been erected, changes in the social philosophy have occurred, transportation facilities have changed, and a myriad of other things have happened. The net result of this societal change and flux is that the world outside, in contrast to the relatively stable hospital environment, becomes a confusing, scary, and frightening place to explore for many patients. To borrow an analogy from the science fiction writers, it is as though patients were teleported by a time machine into an advanced, foreign civilization without possessing the necessary social skills or language for survival.

This situation is complicated further by the fact that during the course of prolonged hospitalization many patients experience a deterioration in work habits, a diminution in self-discipline, an atrophy in social skills, the avoidance of competetive situations, a passive rather than active orientation toward the satisfaction of their needs, and long exposure to an environment that places minimal demands and stresses on them. There is also a tendency for their value system to change. Ambition, success, and the dreams of youth begin to vanish and are supplanted by a resignation to the status quo and a nagging insecurity about their ability to cope outside the familiar hospital setting. To accentuate this feeling of social alienation even further, friendships evaporate over the years, family members die, family ties weaken, and numerous other roots to original community begin to wither. In effect, the patients' emotional and intellectual life lines to the outside world becomes progressively closed off.

With all these factors operating, it is little wonder that many chronic schizophrenics, even those responding well to hospital treatment, show little motivation for leaving and cling tenaciously to their relatively secure hospital existence. It also is not surprising to find the readmission rates of these patients so high because of their failure to cope in society. The longer patients have been hospitalized, the more frightening and alien the outside world. If we can grant the relevance of these observations, it becomes apparent that this second phase of treatment is enormously important. The quality and effectiveness of a predischarge program may make the difference between successful discharge and rehabilitation or not. It is simply insufficient and therapeutically negligent to discharge the vast majority of these patients into the community without extensive preparation and planning even though their behavior within the hospital seems adequate. To do so would be to permit patients to enter the world socially naked and emotionally vulnerable.

In any adequate predischarge program, some provision must be made for enhancing the patients' social and work skills, increasing their self-confidence in their ability to cope with novel and frustrating situations, and helping them to feel a part of the community at large. These are indeed formidable goals. To accomplish them in some degree, many innovative procedures will have to be employed, some conceptual revisions will be necessary, and certain practical considerations met.

The Areas of Deficit

One of the first postulates for a predischarge program is the recognition that nothing can be taken for granted about the minimal knowledge, skills, or abilities possessed by patients. The clinical truth of this has been confirmed time and time again when we have attributed to patients certain coping abilities that they did not have. In the process of teaching patients a social language, it often is easy to overlook the fact that they have not yet mastered the abc's.

To illustrate this, we have observed numerous instances when patients have received serious setbacks after discharge in situations of not knowing how to operate a laundromat, to fill out a job application, to shop, to make social conversation, to take public transportation, to find their way around the city, to prepare a meal, to make a phone call, and not knowing whom to contact in emergencies. These are only a few of innumerable examples that can be given. These particular patients cannot be regarded as stupid or psychologically disorganized. They simply do not know or have forgotten how to do these simple tasks. It soon becomes apparent that a predischarge program focused primarily on resolving the existential or intrapsychic conflicts and anxieties of patients pertaining to the prospects of hospital discharge is an irrelevant luxury compared to the necessity of teaching them certain elemental knowledge and skills about coping in the outside world. This does not mean that a complete reprogramming of social behavior is necessary; rather, the clinician should become acutely aware of the possibility that hospitalized, well-functioning patients do not necessarily possess all the requisite, practical knowledge for functioning in society once their intrapsychic problems seem resolved.

In a brilliant theoretical paper, Mechanic (1967) points out how psychiatrists traditionally have focused their treatment programs on the defensive rather than coping aspects of patient behavior. The concept of defense refers to the ways patients manage their emotional life when discomfort is aroused or anticipated. With the psychodynamic or defense approach to rehabilitation, therapy often is undertaken without a careful appraisal of the situation and problems to which the patient will return, the skills he will need, and the attitudes and feelings about his disabilities among significant others in the community. On the other hand, coping refers to the instrumental behavior and problem-solving capacities of patients in response to realistic life stresses. It pertains to the application of skills, techniques, and knowledge that patients have acquired. The discomfort and anxieties that patients experience, according to the coping concept, can be regarded as directly related to the inadequacies and limitations of their repertoire of such skills.

It is Mechanic's thesis (and one to which I fully adhere) that most traditional treatment rehabilitation programs have made no provision for assessing the work skills and habits of patients or developing effective procedures for improving them. Unless such skills and habits prove adequate, it is unlikely that patients will ever become self-supporting in the outside world—or develop, as well, the sense of self-confidence associated with this type of independence. Yet it is rare to find clinicians addressing themselves to such vital issues as how patients organize their activities, the extent of planning, preparation, and rehearsal they use in a psychological and social sense, the ways they test problem solutions, the manner in which they choose alternative courses of action, and the way they allocate their time and effort.

Another area of neglect has been the failure of treatment-rehabilitation programs to train patients in necessary interpersonal skills. Such techniques or skills pertain to initiating new relationships, distributing interpersonal invest- ments as a safeguard against the threat of loss, interpersonal influencing techniques, the handling of anger through humor or other constructive means, interpersonal compromise, learning how to withdraw gracefully from difficult situations and how to produce friendly, interested responses in others. It is assumed that the degree to which patients develop competence and mastery in these areas will determine the degree to which they can be successfully rehabilitated.

The chief practical advantage of this educational rather than medical approach to rehabilitation is that the source of the patient's deficiencies is not regarded so important as the possibility of remedying them through specialized training procedures. It makes little difference whether these deficits are a result of genetic influences, abnormal brain dysfunction, emotionally traumatic childhood, or other possible determinants. The prime issue is whether these disabilities can be overcome through education, training, or retraining. Needless to say, theorizing is no substitute for clinical trials and experimentation in resolving this issue.

It may not be possible to devise or conduct an ideal rehabilitation program that can remedy all the social deficiencies and coping handicaps of patients, but this need not prevent clinicians from adopting this goal and attempting to realize it, at least in part.

Various Teaching Approaches

Once it is accepted that patients require instruction in a variety of essential areas, the techniques for accomplishing this should be considered. The teaching of coping techniques and requisite information for patients need not be confined to the predischarge period alone but may also be incorporated into an ongoing inpatient treatment or aftercare program. The problem for any formal, comprehensive treatment program, then, is both whether and how it is possible to teach or impart potentially useful information to relatively unmotivated patients with the assurance that this information will not only be learned and retained but, also, hopefully applied. Because there is a sizable gap between what is taught and what is learned and an even larger gap between what is learned and what is used, any effective clinical teaching procedures must take measures to close these gaps.

It is not my intention to present an exhaustive or even sophisticated presentation of the range of educational technique theoretically available for schizophrenic patients. Although there have been innumerable experimental studies investigating the variables influencing the performance of chronic schizophrenics in task-learning situations (see Garmezy, 1966, and Lang and Buss, 1965, for reviews), little has been done to evaluate the practical, applied use of innovative teaching techniques within the context of a ward treatment program. Because we have had the first-hand opportunity to employ several different types of teaching and training formats, it seems more appropriate to present our experiences with them than to deal in a second-hand way with the writings of others. Essentially, these experiences include three types of teaching situations—passive, didactic, and active participatory.

Passive Teaching

During one of the experimental treatment programs (Ludwig, 1968), we investigated the efficacy of employing suggestion and self-help inspirational techniques as a means of directly combatting the psychological insecurity and lack of self-confidence in patients. It was our belief that professionals have long ignored the potential wisdom in the various self-help manuals available to the general public and effectively utilized by a large proportion of this public. The self-help techniques advocated bore a close resemblance to those employed by numerous self-help groups, such as Recovery, Inc., Christian Science, Alcoholics Anonymous, Encounter, and Synanon. These techniques stressed the importance of believing in oneself, the use of positive, visual imagery while thinking of the future, the systematic negation of unpleasant or undesirable thoughts, the minimizing of difficulties and obstacles, the power of constructive thought, the belief in a solution to every problem, the necessity for calmness and reflection, the belief in a higher power through which greater emotional strength could be gathered, and the continued self-affirmation of one's abilities.

All this material was incorporated on tapes and played to patients once a day for about forty-five minutes, six days a week, for a ten-week period. The inspirational taped material, which could be regarded as a type of therapeutic propaganda, was presented in a didactic, authoritative way. Patients not only were instructed to believe the material but also were encouraged to repeat certain key inspirational statements to themselves, much in the manner of autohypnotic procedures.

The following features characterized these sessions: The material on the tapes was stereotyped, relatively boring, monotonous, repetitious, and contained numerous variations on the theme of self-help. This therapeutic propaganda was presented in an impersonal manner designed to obviate doubts and questioning on the part of patients. The learning situation was basically a passive one with no direct incentive or rewards given to patients for mastering this material except for the nebulous promise of happiness and success.

In order to determine the degree to which learning would occur with this type of teaching approach, we constructed a multiple choice questionnaire based solely on the material on these tapes. The questionnaire was administered before and after the sessions and given to a control group at comparable intervals as well. In brief, the results indicated that patients completing these tape sessions displayed a statistically significant greater increment in knowledge pertaining to the presented material than when exposed to a comparable control period. It would appear, then, that despite the passive, boring, repetitive, impersonal nature of these sessions, the learning situation was conducive for some of the taped therapeutic propaganda to register and stick in their memories, at least until the time of testing. I shall have more to say about these and other matters shortly.

Didactic Teaching

During the same treatment program, we also conducted sessions with a somewhat different orientation. The format of these sessions resembled that of a traditional classroom with time allotted both during and after the lectures or films for questions and discussion. The operating rationale for these sessions, based on previous clinical experience, was that these patients had difficulty handling even seemingly trivial personal and social problems and situations. Many of these patients had received faulty training during their youths regarding personal and social behavior; others, who apparently had learned the requisite social skills, appeared to have forgotten them during their prolonged hospitalizations. Therefore, it seemed essential to establish a type of teaching program aimed at teaching or reteaching such basic information to patients.

Almost all members of the staff participated in presenting the course material to patients. The topics covered in these lectures included personal hygiene, etiquette, eating habits, appearance, housekeeping, human physiology, social conversation, dating, sexual behavior, work attitudes, filling out job applications, budgeting, self-help techniques, ethics, and morals. Following certain lectures, such as those concerning social conversation and applying for jobs, some role-playing with patients was attempted. Patients were also given limited homework assignments and referred to additional reading sources. These sessions were held for one hour, four times per week over a period of ten weeks.

In contrast to the taped sessions, these teaching sessions possessed an entirely different format. The material presented could be regarded as diversified, nonrepetitious, and colorful. The interpersonal element was present throughout, and patients were provided with an opportunity for interaction through questions and discussion. Not only was it a more active learning situation, but an attempt was made to increase motivation for learning through weekly quizzes, the scores of which bore some relationship to the privileges received.

The patients responded to the content material in a predictable but rather normal manner. More neutral material, pertaining to body hygiene, manners, etc., generally elicited blander responses from the patient group, whereas more emotionally laden material, such as in the areas of sex or ethics, evoked more interest and produced more lively discussion. With all the subject matter presented, there was ample corroboration of our prior clinical impressions concerning the relative unsophistication and naiveté of patients about basic, taken-for-granted knowledge. To illustrate the tone of these meetings, the appropriateness of the content, and the responsiveness of patients, I should like to present a selected discussion in response to a lecture on personal hygiene and menstruation.

> CM: "My folks never told me about sex. The only damn answer I got was I came by the stork"...
> WM: "No one has to be told."...
> MF: "I've always been told sex is a sin." [*Relates old wives' tales about not taking baths during menstruation.*] "I don't understand what I don't see. I can't see my insides... [*Angrily*] "Men are proud of their bodies... How do you know a baby is your own?"
> BF [*asks about hysterectomies and clots in menstruation*]
> MM: "You were saying something about the glands [*in a woman*]
> T [*explains*]
> MM: "So the ovary isn't really connected with the tubes?"
> MF: "Is that where a man's vagina goes in?"
> BF: "It's a penis."...
> MF: "What's the uterus? Is it true that all women don't have their period when they get married? Can they still get pregnant? I heard some do."
> BF: "How many hours a month are you fertile?"
> MF: "Don't you have to know what you are doing in order to have a baby?"
> WM: "Nope!"
> BF: "My husband read a book for a week on the art of love-making on our honeymoon. He's a jack rabbit. Excuse the expression."
> WM: "What's that? I've got a good idea [*laughs*]."

T [*goes on to answer some questions*]
RM: "Can you tell me if they [*babies*] come feet first or head first? Do they pat them on the back?"
WM: "From where do they get their nourishment?". . .
MM: "What causes some of the irregularity? Pregnancy is probably one of the most obvious."
CM: "What causes a long period?". . .
MF: "Do men have a menstruation cycle too? I've heard that." [*gets very upset and starts crying*] "Why do we have to know all this?"
BF: "It's a function of your body. You should know about it.". . .
MF: "What effect do birth control pills have on a woman's cycle?". . .
BF: "Do you go into a change of life sooner if you menstruate earlier in life?". . .
CM: "Is menstruation a painful time? Can they have intercourse during that time?". . .

Surprisingly, the type of naiveté displayed in the questions of patients could be considered characteristic of the bulk of our patients for a variety of topics, even those less emotionally charged. As one patient stated after a session on elementary ethical principles, "I grasp a little bit of what you say but it's the first time I ever heard of some of these things."

With such a diversification of material presented to patients, an evaluation of the degree to which they learned and retained this material seemed indicated. For this purpose, a 177-item multiple choice questionnaire was used and given to patients after completion of the ten-week program as well as to patients exposed to a control program. Statistical analyses revealed that patients displayed a much greater fund of knowledge on completion of these sessions than after a comparable control period. At the end of the control period, the mean number of errors was approximately 51 percent compared to 44 percent at the end of the didactic teaching sessions. For the type of elementary material presented in these sessions, the average percentage of incorrect answers was still far too high. However, given the wide variability in patient scores, these sessions did seem capable of filling in some crucial gaps in basic knowledge and clarifying important misconceptions for most of the patient group.

At this point, it seems appropriate to take stock of both the advantages and limitations of the passive and didactic teaching formats. Despite the radically different formats of both approaches, the results indicated that both were capable of increasing the patients' fund of knowledge pertaining to predetermined course material. Although these results may simply seem an elucidation of the obvious, they do have certain practical implications: (1) It seems necessary to point out that very little work has been done to establish in an experimental way that chronic schizophrenics can effectively learn diversified types of material. (2) Even less work has been done on describing and evaluating different types of teaching approaches, especially on a programmatic basis. (3) The results illustrate the fact that regardless of the patients' initial level of knowledge regarding certain basic, essential kinds of information, there is considerable room for improvement. Patients simply do not automatically gain this important information while exposed to the more traditional types of hospital activities and programs.

From a practical standpoint, these findings have some relevance for treatment programs employing or planning to employ teaching techniques for chronic schizophrenics. For example, a well-staffed ward can afford to present the desired material in a lecture-discussion format with some assurance that most patients will learn some of what is taught them. If the ward is understaffed, it seems economically feasible in terms of staff time to standardize the material to be taught, transcribe it on to tapes, and present it to patients in a repetitive manner over a specified period of time.

One of the major problems still to be resolved in most teaching programs involves the retention of the material learned. Because both the teaching formats described above were administered during the course of an ongoing experimental treatment program and not immediately preceding discharge, we had an opportunity to measure the amount of material retained ten weeks after completion of these teaching programs. The data obtained revealed a progressive loss of the learned material acquired from both teaching formats. Certainly, the loss of large portions of learned material would follow exposure to almost any type of teaching situation for most people, chronic schizophrenics as well as normals. However, the realization that the acquisition of learned material does not preclude its retention should hold certain implications for treating these patients. Perhaps the most obvious implication is that patients will be unlikely to retain learned material unless they have ample opportunity to apply it in some direct way and to discover its value for helping them to cope with real-life situations. The learning and retention of this basic information solely within a hospital setting holds only academic interest for patients; this information is really inessential for their functioning as hospital patients. For this information to assume gut level importance, it must be practiced, applied, and utilized in preparing patients to make the transition from inside to outside the hospital.

Active, Participatory Teaching

The third type of teaching format attempts to compensate for the failings of either a passive or didactic approach to learning. We have come to adopt it only after much trial and error and it has become an integral part of all our predischarge activities. It is streamlined, economical regarding staff time, and permits a standardized way of measuring patient progress. Its chief advantage is that it has been designed to remedy certain obvious social deficits apparent in many patients and involve patients actively in their own discharge. Patients not only receive instruction in a number of vital areas, but are also expected to become proficient in the application of this knowledge through practice and the opportunity of receiving corrective feedback from the staff. Mrs. Barbara Lontz deserves credit for the formulation of much of this program. It is presented as only one example of numerous approaches that may be used (see Weinstein, 1967).

The program to be described presupposes that the patient has achieved a sufficiently high level of adjustment within the hospital in order to be eligible for discharge. Although this program has been established to handle groups of discharge-ready patients, each individual patient can progress at his or her own rate and receives instructions on an individual basis. A necessary precondition for participating in this *community adjustment group* is that all eligible patients (1) do their own washing and ironing, (2) maintain good grooming, (3) watch the news on television every day, (4) keep their clothes in good repair, and (5) keep up on current events. Once patients show themselves capable of this behavior, they enter the first of four phases. On completion of each phase, they progress to the next higher one. An outline of the activities associated with each phase is given as Chart 11-1.

Chart 11-1. THE COMMUNITY ADJUSTMENT GROUP PROGRAM

Phase 1. General Information
1. Instructions on reading a map of city, followed by a quiz
2. Demonstration on correct use of washer and dryer; instructions on how to wash clothing, etc.; quiz
3. Instructions on use of telephone book; quiz
4. Instructions on reading of bus schedules, fares, transfers, etc.; quiz
5. Completion of Division of Vocational Rehabilitation forms, if not already completed by this time
6. Two outfits of clothing in good repair before progressing to next stage

Phase 2. Use of Telephones
1. Completion to the staff's satisfaction of three interhospital calls; role-playing three different situations
   A. Social conversation with staff
   B. Answering a want ad from the paper
   C. Calling the bus company for information about certain route
2. Completion to staff's satisfaction of three extrahospital calls to "real" people in the community:
   A. Movie theater, requesting information on time, feature, shorts, etc.
   B. Calling "O" for information
   C. Answering a want ad (not for jobs)—have list of questions ready
   D. Bus depot
   E. Airport
   F. Cab company
3. Completion to the staff's satisfaction of several calls from a pay phone

Phase 3. Escorted Groups into Town
1.	Learning to use the bus system (except for transfers, remain on bus entire trip)
	A.	Preplan the trip on the ward to include seeing

(1) State employment office	(9) Local hospitals
(2) Public library	(10) YMCA/YWCA
(3) Rescue Mission	(11) Bus depots
(4) Halfway houses	(12) Airport
(5) Neighborhood house	(13) Downtown
(6) State offices	(14) Beltline
(7) City/county building	(15) University campus
(8) Opportunity center	(16) Capitol

(17) Vocational school
	B.	Use of transfers
	C.	Change zones
	D.	Compare cost of trip with cost of cab over same route
2.	Trip to laundromat, combined with trip to shopping center
	A.	Use change machines
	B.	Use washer and dryer
	C.	Have preplanned list of items (e.g., grooming aides, clothing, etc.) before going shopping
	D.	Ask people for directions
	(These escorted groups will be small, consisting of two patients and one staff member and will probably take all afternoon.)

Phase 4. Trips to Town Alone or in Buddy Pairs
1.	Scavenger hunt. An all-day trip into town with no schedules to meet, but specific places to go. Patient must bring back proof of his visits to the various places.
2.	Barber shop/beauty shop
	A.	Call for an appointment
	B.	Arrange bus schedules and finances accordingly
	C.	Go for appointment
3.	Apply for an identification card

A program such as this, though seemingly simple and straightforward, will possess many inherent shortcomings. It is one matter to expect that patients will progress in a smooth, orderly fashion through the four phases and another matter for this to happen. Often, patients will get stuck at one phase and find it difficult to proceed to the next. Although provision has been made to teach patients certain basic, requisite skills in a comprehensive manner, there are many situations where crucial patient deficits have been overlooked, thereby demanding special improvisation. Moreover, the most critical ingredient necessary to make this phase program work—and one that is difficult to define—is the ingenuity and patience required of the staff to help patients master one hurdle after another.

It also should be apparent that the effectiveness of this type of predischarge program cannot be measured by questionnaire techniques or behavior rating procedures. The ultimate test of these procedures must be in terms of their success in facilitating discharge and providing the necessary social tools for patients to make an adequate adjustment outside the hospital. Unfortunately, because this program is of relatively recent origin, we have not collected sufficient data to substantiate its long-term effectiveness or to compare it to other types of predischarge procedures. Nevertheless, it does seem to possess an inherent face validity in that it has been designed to compensate for certain obvious patient deficits as well as the defects apparent in the more perfunctory discharge procedures practiced in many mental hospitals. At this point in time, it makes good clinical sense that a program geared to help patients overcome their basic lacks through active, participatory learning and, most important, to desensitize them to the scary world outside the hospital will be headed, at least, in the right direction.

The Patient and His Family

There currently is considerable interest within psychiatric circles in the potential contribution of the family of schizophrenic patients to their original illness. Terms, such as *double-binding mother, schizophrenogenic mother, pseudomutuality of parental roles, familial scapegoating of patient,* have all become a part of the standard psychiatric parlance and reflect a growing trend to incriminate the family, especially during the early formative years of patients, as an important etiologic determinant for the development of schizophrenia. As a result of such theorizing, it follows clinically that an adequate treatment program for schizophrenic patients should attempt to get the families actively involved in the treatment and rehabilitation process. Once family therapy is begun, it becomes the task of the clinician to unravel the intrafamilial psychodynamics responsible for the patient's plight and, hopefully, to resolve certain areas of family conflict so that the patient can return to a healthier, emotionally more salubrious family environment. Because of the clinical appeal and cogency of these assumptions, family therapy for these patients is becoming a greater part of the psychiatric scene.

In a series of clinical studies (Marx and Ludwig, 1969; Marx and Lontz, n.d.), we described our impressions of the characteristics of the families of chronic schizophrenic and the peculiar problems of getting them involved in the treatment and rehabilitation process with their patient relatives. Prior to our intervention, most of these families assumed a role that they naturally drifted into over time, namely, either gradually severing all contact with patients over the years or periodically making perfunctory visits to the hospital on special visiting days and providing canteen money, treats, similar goodies, and an occasional outing into town for their patient relatives. These families showed little interest in the psychiatric treatment administered to their kin or in encouraging the hospital staff to explore new treatment modalities to enhance the prospects of their kin for improving and eventually leaving the hospital. Instead, they seemed to display a tenacious emotional investment in keeping their kin institutionalized for the remainder of his or her days. When concern was shown, it was mainly for the creature comforts of the patients: e.g., "Is Joe getting enough to eat?" "Don't you think it would be nice if Mary had some more things to do to occupy her time?" "Bill should be allowed to go outside more."

This description of these families is not meant to be derogatory. Their attitudes and behavior are quite understandable and justifiable. Over a period of years, they have experienced many aggravations, much emotional turmoil, embarrassments, fears, and guilt prior to hospitalization of their patient kin or during his multiple discharges or home visits. With time, they have come to some resolution of their feelings, established a new familial homeostasis, and have adapted to the loss of their patient relative in a manner producing the least emotional distress. Whatever optimism they originally harbored concerning the patient's prospects for improvement and successful rehabilitation has long dissipated and been supplanted by a sense of resignation and pessimism. To hope again is to reopen the healed emotional wound and make themselves vulnerable to more pain. This may account for the propensity of these families to ignore letters and phone calls inviting them to participate in family therapy sessions, as well as to become panicky and write letters to the hospital administrator or ward psychiatrists requesting transfer of their kin to less active treatment wards or to seek assurance that their relative will not be discharged.

The necessity of getting families involved in the predischarge and aftercare programs for patients could be easily ignored were it not for the paradoxical problem that these same families tend to become overly involved in many unhealthy ways with their patient relatives once they are discharged. This involvement is initiated either by the families themselves or by the patients. In any event, it tends to create all types of troubles for the patient and lessens the prospects of his making a satisfactory adjustment on the outside.

As a result of our experiences, we have come to feel very strongly that it is therapeutically contraindicated for a discharged chronic schizophrenic to return permanently to his original family home. This opinion is based on one main theoretical assumption and one main clinical fact. The theoretical assumption is that all these patients may be regarded as grown, responsible adults, despite their long seige of hospitalization, and the place for such persons is not with their family but in a relatively independent living and work situation that provides them the opportunity of making it on their own. To return to the family is to encourage their sense of inferiority and to diminish whatever sense of self-confidence they possess. The clinical fact is that these patients already have demonstrated on numerous previous occasions their inability to function within the family setting. Although it may be more convenient and economically feasible to place the patient with his family when he first enters the community, the long-term price seems far too high. Aside from the problem of sending a patient back to a familial environment that presumably contributed to his original psychopathology, even in the best family environments the family is so sensitized to the behavior of its patient kin that the patient is forever treading on thin ice. The pressures the patient faces to behave properly, the pressures the family feels to treat the patient gingerly, and the latent but ever-present family dynamics all conspire toward the reactivation of deviant behavior and psychopathology on the part of the patient—the end result of which is rehospitalization.

Obviously, then, the task of an adequate predischarge program is twofold: (1) The patient must be convinced that it is inappropriate and even harmful to his emotional welfare to return to the family. (2) The family must be convinced that close involvement with the patient would be damaging to all persons concerned. Although this task appears simple, it is extremely difficult to accomplish. There is a perverse emotional bond existing between patient and family (especially with parents) that draws them closer and closer together despite their intellectual appreciation of the potential dangers of this relationship. It is not sufficient for clinicians to rest content with keeping family and patient apart at the time of discharge. Continued efforts are required to keep the family from meddling in the affairs of the patient and to keep the patient from returning permanently to the family womb even after he has been functioning well in the community.

The Question of Motivation

Another factor to be taken into account in discharge programs for chronic schizophrenics is their degree of motivation for leaving. There is no need to describe again the apprehension that most of these patients experience at the prospects of leaving their secure hospital homes. At best, even the patients most eager to leave the hospital display considerable ambivalence, either verbally or behaviorally expressed, about preparing to enter the community. From a traditional clinical viewpoint, it can be expected that the best rehabilitation results will be seen in patients highly motivated to be discharged. Although this expectation may play an important role in the discharge plans for more acute mental hospital patients, it cannot be given too much weight in determining whether chronic schizophrenics should or should not enter a predischarge program. To reach a decision concerning the feasibility of discharge of these patients solely on the basis of their professed motivation for leaving would be to eliminate a large majority of patients from consideration. In planning a predischarge program for these patients, the clinician must work within the framework of clinical reality. The clinical reality is that the motivation of chronic schizophrenics for leaving is not all it ideally should be.

One of the most interesting but frustrating situations we have encountered in our predischarge programs pertains to the paradoxical practice of several patients to elope from the hospital to avoid being discharged. In all instances in which this had occurred, the covert meaning of this behavior seemed clear because these same patients soon engaged in certain activities in the community that gave them high visibility and ensured their return to the hospital. In essence, the implicit message they conveyed by this behavior might be stated as "I am proving to you [the staff] that I am not ready to go out into the world by going out into the world and demonstrating I can't make it."

Although many patients actively cooperate with the predischarge and discharge programs, it has been our impression that the greatest proportion of patients passively cooperate. This attitude and behavior may reflect a docility acquired over long years of institutionalization or a long-standing personality characteristic preceding institutionalization, but it need not be regarded as a deterrent to discharge. There are yet other patients whose level of functioning within the hospital is sufficiently high to warrant consideration for discharge but who are actively uncooperative and make every attempt to thwart all discharge planning on their behalf. In many instances, these patients literally may have to be pushed out the door.

An elaborate description of the varied patterns of cooperation and expressed motivation for leaving the hospital is unnecessary because there is one guiding principle that pertains to formulating discharge plans for all patients. This principle is that the staff must explicitly and implicitly convey the message to all discharge-ready patients that they will not be abandoned once they leave the hospital and that the staff will do everything humanly possible to help them succeed in the community. As a corollary to this message, it is essential to indicate to patients that the mental hospital can no longer be viewed as a rescue mission or retreat to which they can easily return any time the going gets rough. If patients know that whenever they get upset they can use the hospital as a crutch, there is little incentive for them to learn to stand on their own two feet.

These, then, represent some of the necessary considerations in the formulation of any clinically relevant predischarge and discharge program. From this discussion, we may assume that a perfunctory predischarge program may prove a disservice to patients and that considerable forethought, planning, and effort are necessary to increase the patient's chances for successful rehabilitation.

It should also be mentioned that the specific teaching formats described have not been presented as ideal paradigms but rather as some examples of what can be done. Because the teaching of coping and social skills to patients represents a relatively new area for psychiatric investigation, we can anticipate that future clinical research will uncover ways of increasing the effectiveness of existing training techniques and for the development of new ones.

This still is not the whole treatment story. The clinician's responsibility is far from over. Even when patients successfully complete an adequate pre-discharge program, the clinician must be prepared to deal with another set of problems, namely, those related to maintaining the patient in the community.

chapter 12

The Price of Discharge

It has become a common practice to judge the success of a treatment program for chronic schizophrenics by the percentage of these patients discharged, as well as by the proportion of this percentage subsequently readmitted to the hospital. For the clinically unsophisticated, discharge tends to become equated with cure and not being readmitted tends to become equated with functioning well in the community. Although these kinds of statistics and their implications hold great appeal for many hospital administrators and mental health personnel, they cannot be accepted at face value by knowledgeable clinicians. This is largely because many of the criteria for hospital discharge and readmission are far from objective. Such "soft" criteria as the discharge philosophy of the clinician, the availability of community resources, the feasibility of aftercare services, the tolerance of the local community toward mental illness or deviancy, and the extent to which hospital administrators are willing to resist community pressures to confine patients enter into decisions about discharge and readmission.

To demonstrate the inherent fallibility of these statistics, I should like to pose an extreme, probably ridiculous possibility. If the clinician in charge is so predisposed and has the necessary administrative backing, he may achieve completely successful results, regardless of the specific nature of his treatment program, by discharging 100 percent of all chronic schizophrenics and refusing them readmission to the hospital. This, indeed, would prove an impressive testimonial to the efficacy of his treatment program according to these traditional assessment criteria. However, what this type of policy ignores are the consequences of its implementation. The discharge of patients not capable of fending for themselves may seriously jeopardize their physical welfare while the refusal to readmit them may place a terrible emotional and financial burden on the patients' families and community.

Although such a hypothetical discharge policy may seem absurd, it does highlight a vital issue seldom considered in rehabilitation studies—namely, whether the social cost of maintaining certain patients in the community is worth the potential value for these patients and society. It is also important to note that this type of policy is not so hypothetical as it may first seem; it reflects a growing trend in the field of psychiatry that regards the mental hospital with opprobrium and places a premium on the treatment of patients in the community. As a result, it has now become professionally fashionable for superintendents to expend considerable effort to reduce the population of chronic patients in their hospitals or for clinicians to employ much stricter criteria before admitting patients to their hospitals. There can be no question that this trend is therapeutically enlightened, for it has arisen out of an increased awareness of the potentially noxious effects of institutionalization. It does, however, mask certain important qualifications pertaining to an assessment of its real value. For example, often a reduction in the population of a large state hospital is merely a reflection of transferring these patients to nursing homes or other completely sheltered settings, which serve as surrogate institutions, while the practice of trying to treat all patients in the community may indicate only the redistribution of responsibility for treatment and its associated headaches from the mental hospital to the family and community.

What is most important in appraising this new trend is the recognition that the clinical course of chronic schizophrenia need no longer be regarded as synonymous with its social course. In the past, there was more of a tendency to view these courses as directly related. If a patient failed to improve within the mental hospital or showed only a marginal adjustment there, the prospects for his being discharged or placed in the community were small. Nowadays, the professional and social climate has changed sufficiently so that discharge from the hospital need not be completely contingent on the behavior of patients within the hospital. Although this divergence of the clinical and social course of chronic schizophrenia has opened up many new treatment-rehabilitation vistas, it likewise has created a new set of problems for clinicians and society.

This does not mean that an aggressive and active discharge and rehabilitation policy is undesirable. It does imply, however, that the implementation of such a policy will not lead to a therapeutic millennium and that the clinician should not be lulled into therapeutic complacency by impressive discharge and readmission statistics. These statistics often cover up a potpourri of patient problems which are compounded by complementary familial and societal ones. If the clinician is to fulfill his entire therapeutic obligation, he not only must be aware of the nature and extent of these problems but must be prepared to deal with and hopefully resolve them when they arise.

The Social Cost

Surprisingly, there have been only few clinical and/or research reports focused on the social cost of maintaining discharged chronic schizophrenics in the community. Although there have been numerous reports on the treatment of these patients on an outpatient basis or by visiting nurses, descriptions of the problems encountered tend to deal primarily with the behavior of the patients themselves. Seldom is any mention made of the ripple wave produced by this behavior, which extends the sphere of influence of patients far beyond the boundaries of the traditional therapist-patient relationship. The clinical difficulties encountered by the therapist may be nothing compared to what others, both related and unrelated to the patient, may experience.

Because the concept of social cost looms so large in the implementation of any rehabilitation program for mental patients, it is essential that we read between the lines of discharge and readmission statistics and examine their implications. In this regard, Grad and Sainsbury (1966) were among the first to draw attention to the burdens placed on the families of schizophrenic patients by an active community-care service. A large percentage of the families studied displayed considerable concern and worry over a variety of troublesome patient behaviors. The type of behavior most frequently referred to as worrisome was the patient's excessive preoccupation with and harping on bodily complaints. Second in importance was the family's fear that the patient might seriously harm himself either through suicide, a traffic accident, or an accident at home. Another group of patients remained bedfast or housebound and seemed to need constant nursing care or supervision at home. Many of these patients were importunate and demanding, uncooperative and contrary, restless or overtalkative, troublesome at night, and objectionable or rude. Many families were also embarrassed by the odd and peculiar behavior shown by patients or frightened by the possibility that these patients might constitute a danger to others.

As a result of these worries, many families reported that the mental and/or physical health of the closest relative was affected, that the social and leisure activities of the family were disrupted, that the children were affected, and that the domestic routine and income of the family suffered. Still other families reported the loss of employment of one or more members or difficulties and quarrels with neighbors brought on by certain behaviors of the patient.

In summarizing their findings, Grad and Sainsbury (1966, p. 277) state that "for certain types of patients and in certain social circumstances home care . . . leaves the family with more problems than mental hospital care does." This would indicate that

> any schemes for home care and the treatment of patients outside the mental hospital will need to make some provision in the community for those social, health, and economic peculiarities of families shown to be especially liable to hardship when they have a patient at home. Similarly, allowances need to be made for interpersonal stresses within a family in deciding whether treatment within or out of a hospital is to be preferred (Grad and Sainsbury, 1966, p. 273).

In another study of the effects of early discharge practices on the families of acute and chronic schizophrenics, Brown and his colleagues (1966, p. 209) raise other but related issues:

> Our conclusion is that the present early discharge practices can continue even if extra services are not provided, without undue complaint from four-fifths of relatives. Relatives are not in a strong position to complain—they are not experts, they may be ashamed to talk about their problems, and they may have come to the conclusion that no help can be offered which will substantially reduce their difficulties. No "consumer" association exists which can express their discontents and they must sometimes feel that doctors and social workers are biased towards taking the patient's point of view. At the same time a strong feeling of duty and humanity makes many relatives accept the burden of caring for a handicapped patient.
>
> It is not necessarily good clinical practice to accept this situation as a justification of "community care." If relatives were told that handicapped patients would be better off in hospital, they might well agree to that as well (perhaps in many cases with relief). . . . In accepting the present situation the clinician is tacitly assuming that it is better for the patient to be at home, and there may be a built-in tendency, therefore, not to inquire too closely into the social circumstances of the family in case evidence to the contrary is found.

Although the above observations pertain primarily to difficulties encountered when patients have been returned to their families, the problem of social cost is far more extensive. Not all families are willing or able to take patient relatives back into their fold, and not all patients are willing to return to their families or even have families to return to. In these instances, the slack of social cost is taken up by the community at large in a variety of ways.

From the financial standpoint, the discharged chronic schizophrenic still requires considerable support. Although the direct costs of hospitalization have disappeared, a number of indirect, or hidden, costs emerge; these are diluted or distributed among many social agencies. For example, society must still foot the bill to maintain patients in semisheltered settings as halfway houses or family care, to pay professionals to administer aftercare services, or to offer more direct financial aid through vocational rehabilitation, aid to the permanently disabled, city welfare, social security, etc. These patients are also predisposed to avail themselves of a variety of medical-psychiatric services, taking up countless hours of medical staff time in emergency rooms and psychiatric clinics. The costs for the provision of these services are most often absorbed by state or private agencies.

There is another small proportion of patients who are of a more legalistic bent, either voluntarily seeking out legal authorities or getting in difficulties with the law. We have had several patients contact the local legal aid society or local judges to inform them of the injustices taking place in the mental hospital or the unfairness of their conditional release status. Other patients have encounters with the law in a number of areas, such as stealing, making obscene phone calls, disorderly conduct, vagrancy, lewd and lascivious behavior, writing bad checks, or multiple traffic violations. Still other patients plague the police nightly with phone calls about people supposedly trying to break in the apartment to rape or harm them. In our own experience, perhaps the most creative use of the police by patients involved calling the police station, informing the desk sergeant that they were mental patients and had to return to the hospital. Within a short while, a police car would arrive and provide them with free taxi service to the hospital to attend ward meetings or present complaints to the ward staff.

For those patients living in relatively independent accommodations, another type of social cost involves the emotional wear and tear on landlords, houseparents, or fellow roomers. The complaints made by these sources vary from accusing patients of not following house rules, not paying their rent, sleeping all day and staying up all night, having a bad influence on others to talking "loud, vulgar, and mean."

For anyone not directly affected by these patients, many of the complaints could be regarded as amusing. For example, one landlady tried to get us to readmit a patient because he didn't wash his hands after toileting or before eating, ate without manners, did not change his underwear, and put gum on the bedpost. In another instance, a male boarder at a rooming house locked himself in his room at night because the female patient was always talking about "sex, rape, and babies." Another patient, who was discharged after being hospitalized for more than twenty years, caused untold horrors for the resident manager of the apartment building and a male roomer on the same hall who shared a bathroom with her. The resident manager complained that she always flushed the toilet six or seven times, ran water constantly for no reason, left the bathroom door open while tending to her excretory functions, and would come to his apartment for a visit and then not leave. Her bathroom mate was upset because she used the bathroom for forty-five minutes every morning and would not let him in, used the toilet paper to excess, used up all the hot water, and occasionally would tear little pieces of paper up and burn them individually. It is largely because of living difficulties such as these that many discharged chronic schizophrenics display a house-hopping pattern, either leaving their domiciles at their own initiative or under pressure by the landlord.

Many of the difficulties encountered at work parallel those found in the living situations. Difficulties with supervisors and fellow employees are rife with many patients, and their work pattern is characterized by numerous short periods of employment intermixed with collections of unemployment compensation or welfare payments. Aside from the limited output of patients employed in sheltered workshops, such as Goodwill Industries, Opportunity Centers, and other programs supported by the Division of Vocational Rehabilitation, the working habits and behaviors of many patients regarded as independent produce a substantial economic loss to the organizations willing to hire them. A number of these patients keep showing up late for work, frequently call in sick, are inefficient at their jobs, and take supervision poorly. These patients engage in other behaviors that tax the sincere good will of employers willing to give handicapped persons a chance. For example, one employer complained about a male patient who would always masturbate in the ladies room with the door open. Another patient always wanted to talk about sex with his supervisor. Another female patient apparently kept upsetting the girls at work by her constant "radical talk about sex, babies, and marriage."

Many innocent bystanders in the community also tend to be drawn into the network of the patient's activities as well. Some patients harass neighbors with phone calls, sometimes during the early hours of the morning, or accost them in the streets to discuss their somatic complaints at length. Other patients innocently wander about the streets late at night inadvertently frightening people by their suspicious behavior. Others plague the Suicide Prevention Center with frequent calls. There are also more idiosyncratic types of nuisance behavior. For example, one of our former patients kept calling Sears and inquiring about "fuzz boxes" (Kotex) and jock straps. Again, from a humorous standpoint, we even had one patient who regarded himself a war hero and wrote to the governor, various senators, congressmen, and even the President informing them of his exploits. Although these honorable gentlemen probably could not know the true situation, all of them reinforced this rather circumscribed idiosyncracy by sending him letters of commendation. These examples go on and on.

The main purpose in presenting the foregoing varieties of social cost is simply to document their existence and to dramatize the fact that hospital discharge cannot be regarded as synonymous with smooth functioning in the community. Although many mental hospital clincians are willing to settle for discharge as a termination of their therapeutic obligation to patients, the very presence of these types of social cost should indicate the necessity for the extension of treatment services into the community—if clinicians are interested in preventing the high hospital readmission rates associated with chronic schizophrenics. Unless measures are employed to reduce the ensuing social friction and costs, patients are apt to accumulate a variety of failure experiences in the community, thereby reducing their self-confidence, and the community is apt to become increasingly intolerant of these patients, thereby resorting to the convenient solution of rehospitalization.

Cost versus Value

So far, we have directed attention to the problems caused by patients in the community. This focus, however, is far too limited and biased a one on which to form judgments about the value of an active and aggressive rehabilitation program. To assess the issue of social cost fairly, several other important factors must be taken into consideration.

1. It is essential to realize that a substantial proportion of these patients do not create any serious social problems after discharge and, in fact, manage to achieve relatively independent living and work situations. In other words, not all discharged patients make trouble. For some who do, the trouble may be too trivial to warrant clinical concern.

2. It is unfair to base opinions about the worth or functioning of patients solely on the basis of handicaps, deficits, or nuisance behavior. To balance the ledger, their assets, abilities, and positive attributes must also be taken into account. Lacks in certain areas may be more than compensated for by skills in other areas. Naturally, these lacks may allow patients to achieve only a limited social adjustment, but this limited social adjustment may be preferable to no social adjustment at all.

3. It is essential to realize that these examples of social cost do not represent continuous, perpetual behaviors on the part of patients. Patients do not spend every waking moment wreaking havoc in the community or draining off its emotional or financial resources. Most of the troublesome patient behaviors mentioned are periodic, sporadic, or transient in nature and are most likely to appear during situations of stress.

4. There is the matter of both the extent and kind of social cost. Obviously, the more instances of troublesome behavior on the part of a particular patient over a given period of time, the greater the social cost; the fewer instances over a comparable time period, the less the social cost. This quantitative relationship must be qualified somewhat by the nature of the social

cost. Nuisance, pesty, idiosyncratic, or weird behaviors are of different order of seriousness than illegal, self-destructive, assaultive, threatening, or sexually taboo behaviors. Whereas it may be reasonable to expect the family and community to tolerate a greater number of these former behaviors, the social cost for even one incident of the more serious behaviors may be far too high a price to pay.

All these considerations naturally lead to the issue of whether the social price of maintaining chronic schizophrenics in the community is worth the value to patient and society. Again, this is another one of those issues that cannot be settled by mathematical formulae or logic; rather, some philosophical stance seems required. The only legitimate resolution to this issue is that a balancing process must be established whereby decisions about the cost-value dilemma are reached for each individual patient. In the process of balancing, the clinician must weigh the potential gains of having the patient live and learn in the community against the burden that this may impose on the community.

In this regard, it is impossible to guarantee a patient the opportunity to grow humanly in the real world if hospital clinicians and society are not willing to take some risks. Because of the likelihood that patients will encounter innumerable stresses outside the hospital, it must be expected that periodic difficulties will arise. During these times, patients may resort to old, maladaptive, deviant behaviors or momentarily give up in response to stress. Part and parcel of any sensible rehabilitation program involves clinicians dealing with these difficulties *in situ* rather than resorting to the easy convenience of automatic rehospitalization the first time patients falter. Only by learning to cope with and live through these stresses in the real world can patients mature. If they are returned to the hospital at the first indications of trouble or inconvenience to family members or community, assuming that this trouble does not represent a serious threat to others, patients may never achieve any constructive resolution to their problems.

Certainly in the balancing process, there will be many instances in which the price that society or even the patient himself may pay will prove far too exorbitant compared to the potential value for the patient of residing in the community. Some patients will prove so continually pesty to others that it would be unfair to expect these people to have to put up with this behavior. Some patients will prove so inadequate in their social functioning or ability to care for themselves even in fairly sheltered settings that it would be clinically negligent not to readmit them to the more controlled, supervised setting of a mental hospital. Still other patients will engage in such socially taboo, dangerous, illegal behavior, if only on one or several occasions, that it is necessary to protect society from them. For these particular behaviors, one time may be one time too many.

The above examples, however, represent only one end of the spectrum of social cost. At the other end are those patients who require only minimal aftercare services and who come to lead relatively independent and socially productive lives. In these instances, the social cost is obviously negligible. Even if some social cost does occur shortly after discharge, there can be no question that the ultimate clinical outcome is well worth the price.

Between these extremes are the bulk of patients with whom the issues of social cost in terms of rehospitalization versus maintenance in the community are less clear cut. However, inasmuch as it can be taken as axiomatic that these patients will have no chance to mature and to acquire new coping and social skills unless they are granted the maximal opportunity to live and learn in real life settings, they deserve the benefit of doubt in all instances. In other words, unless the social cost should become extreme, every effort should be expended to treat patients in the actual settings in which difficulties arise and in the presence of those disturbed or concerned about the behavior of these patients.

The Community and Feedback

Once patients leave the mental hospital, the influence of the ward clinician becomes greatly reduced; the behavior of patients is no longer under his direct aegis, supervision, and control. On entering society at large, patients are exposed to countless stresses and dilemmas, which, for the most part, they must resolve on their own. No matter what degree of freedom and latitude in decision-making is permitted patients within the hospital prior to discharge, this represents an artificial situation; patients are still protected by the knowledge that therapeutic intervention is immediately available and, if worse comes to worse, they need not leave the hospital. The risk of real failure can only come once they have taken the gamble of rehabilitation. The critical therapeutic paradox is that patients often receive the least structure, guidance, and attention at a time when they require these the most, namely, after they leave the hospital.

Obviously, if patients are to be given the best chance for successful social rehabilitation, it is essential that provision be made for continuity of care during this crucial transitional period. So much has been written about the value of coordinated aftercare programs and utilization of all appropriate community agencies that there is no need to belabor the obvious. The necessity for offering services of this sort to all discharged patients should be taken as axiomatic. What does require discussion, however, is a special aspect of these aftercare services. This aspect does not pertain to the patient's relationships with professional or paraprofessional agencies but with his relationships with key laymen who may play a decisive role in the success or failure of his rehabilitation in the community. The laymen referred to are landlords, employers, etc. Although most mental hospitals make some provision for professional aftercare services, direct work with these types of laymen is often neglected. Yet it is these very people who are involved in the stability of the patient's living and work situations and with whom he will have most contact.

In our own rehabilitation programs, the difficulties encountered with these people are not related to their disinterest in the patient's welfare but rather to their many misunderstandings about dealing with mental patients. The essential problem is getting them to treat mental patients as people and not as fragile creatures who must always be handled with care. In a desire to be helpful, these laymen are apt to be extremely cautious in most of their communications with patients and, hence, deprive them of the benefit of honest human feedback—an ingredient necessary for any normal person to become socially mature.

We have encountered many situations where otherwise well-meaning landlords or work supervisors, who are knowledgeable about the former hospitalization of patients, refuse to confront them about what they are doing wrong for fear of upsetting them or eliciting some unpredictable response. Instead, they permit the patient to continue in his erroneous or annoying behavior to the point where they can no longer tolerate it and then precipitously either ask him to leave the premises, fire him, or make a frantic call to the police or hospital requesting that the patient be returned. In many of these instances, this situation could easily have been prevented simply by giving the patient some direct, constructive feedback about the social impact of his behavior and setting some reasonable limits—in other words, treating patients like anyone else. What is often forgotten is that these patients have been out of social commission for a long time and that they simply require lots of corrective feedback if they are to acquire some degree of social perceptiveness and adaptiveness. If no one tells them exactly what they are doing wrong, they simply have no way of rectifying their behavior. In any event, this very important point must be borne in mind in the implementation of any rehabilitation program. It is not sufficient to refer patients to other agencies; some effort must be expended to reach, educate, and help the key laymen who will inadvertently play the most vital role in the potential rehabilitation of patients.

Another aspect of this problem has to do with the legal authorities. There undoubtedly will be occasions when a number of these patients will have encounters with local police or judges for either minor transgressions (e.g., vagrancy, suspicious behavior, creating a public nuisance) or more major legal infractions. Unfortunately, the legal authorities have become so sensitized to mental patients and the legal issues surrounding competency to stand trial that there tends to be the automatic assumption that patients are exempt from legal sanctions and belong back in the hospital if any infraction, no matter how minor, is committed. It is as though people with a prior history of mental hospitalization are forever tainted even though they may have subsequently demonstrated some degree of competency. One example typifying this attitude involves a former patient who was put in jail for a few days after a minor scuffle with the police. Outside the jail cell, the police had placed the following sign: "This prisoner is a mental patient. Do not rile him up!" Attitudes such as this tend to be self-fulfilling prophesies. As long as patients are treated differently than normal people and permitted to escape the consequences of their behavior largely because they have a history of mental illness or behave somewhat peculiarly, they will never have the chance to become responsible and, hence, accountable human beings. Each time they commit some minor offense and are exonerated by the special dispensation of presumed insanity, they are taught to accept themselves as alien creatures with prerogatives different from those of the rest of mankind. The difficulty, then, is not one of getting the community and legal authorities to accept the mentally ill but of getting them to accept formerly hospitalized patients as people and to judge and react to them accordingly. This is no small task.

Follow-through and Follow-up

Aside from working with various key laymen and appropriate agencies in the community, the hospital clinician must provide other services as well. Whatever of benefit the patient learned in the hospital will be in serious danger of dissipation if there is no follow-up of services on the part of the hospital. Most important, it is essential that patients not feel abandoned once they leave the hospital, that the relationships they developed with staff and fellow patients be maintained, and that the hospital treatment staff be available to help them if the occasion arises.

In our own work, we have found it necessary to provide a twenty-four hour per day, seven days per week crisis service to all discharged patients. For many patients, it is a great relief to know that they can always contact someone at the hospital or at home who knows them. Although this responsibility generally falls under the aegis of the ward social worker, there is no reason why this burden cannot be shared among all the staff. If the problem cannot be resolved over the phone, it may be desirable for the patient to visit the hospital and talk with any available staff. Also, if patients are feeling lonely on weekends, they should feel free to visit the ward for several hours in order to socialize both with the staff and patients.

There are many times when patients either do not recognize the signs of impending psychological danger or are reluctant to reach out for help. In these instances, the philosophy we have adopted is that "If the mountain (i.e., the patient) won't come to Mohammed (i.e., the clinician), then Mohammed must go to the mountain." Translating this philosophy into practice means that hospital clinicians must follow up on the functioning of patients in the community and not necessarily assume that no news is good news. To maintain close contact with patients, aside from evaluating them at regularly scheduled interviews or meetings, clinicians must work closely with employers, landlords, families, etc. and be prepared to intervene therapeutically whenever indicated, especially if the aftercare agencies are not prepared to deal with patient's difficulties. We have come to feel that the twenty-four hour availability of services, combined with this type of aggressive follow-up and follow-through crisis intervention, can eliminate the necessity for innumerable rehospitalizations.

No discussion of rehabilitation programs can be complete without mentioning the innovative work of Fairweather and co-workers (1970). Although their studies involve better integrated chronic schizophrenics, as well as patients of other diagnostic categories, the results are impressive enough to warrant an evaluation of the applicability of their rehabilitation model to more seriously handicapped disturbed chronic schizophrenics. Essentially, these investigators demonstrated that patients released to a community lodge in which they functioned together as a family and provided mutual support for one another did much better than a comparable group of patients released to the community with the regularly available aftercare services. During their initial stay at the lodge, patients were followed by professional staff, but as time elapsed this contact was gradually reduced until the lodge group became completely autonomous. It was significant to note that as part of the process of becoming autonomous, lodge patients began to run their own janitorial service. This resulted in the employment of 50 percent of the lodge group over three fourths of the time compared to 3 percent of the control group. Although the number of patients who left the lodge for independent living arrangements was negligible over the thirty-month period, the cost of maintaining a patient in the lodge with employment was $3.90 per day compared to the hospital cost of $14.34.

Although the program of Fairweather and co-workers is certainly one of the most promising on the rehabilitation scene and serves to demonstrate the value of breaking out of the traditional mold of standard discharge practices, it still leaves many vital issues unanswered. Still to be explored are the possibilities of establishing many gradations of sheltered living situations short of mental hospitalization, the development and refinement of techniques for training patients in work and social skills while in the community, the bringing of community helping agencies or professionals into the hospital, the sending of hospital staff into the community in a totally coordinated treatment-rehabilitation program for patients, the development of more efficient methods for reducing social cost and preventing rehospitalization, etc.

A Closing Homily

By now, it should be clear that the comprehensive treatment of hospitalized chronic schizophrenics, which not only encompasses the conversion of patients and staff alike to a new value system diametrically opposed to that embodied in the code of chronicity but also involves the implementation of inpatient behavior modification programs, predischarge activities, and special aftercare services in the community, cannot be undertaken without the expectation of numerous frustrations, aggravations, and hard work. No wonder most psychiatric professionals shirk working in this area and prefer instead to devote their time primarily to patients with the YAVIS syndrome—that is, people who are young, attractive, verbal, intelligent, and, most important, successful (Schofield, 1964). Although the desire to work with generally well-functioning, responsive, neurotic outpatients is understandable (i.e., it is easier to identify with patient, the relationship is less emotionally draining, the fruits of the therapeutic labor more apparent, more lucrative, more prestigious, etc.), it is not necessarily excusable. To have such a large percentage of the psychiatric professional manpower working with minor psychiatric illnesses and to confer academic respectability on this work (in contrast to mental hospital work) makes as much sense as diverting most of the medical research manpower to investigating minor colds while ignoring the more lethal diseases, such as cancer, strokes, or myocardial infarctions. This, unfortunately, represents the current state of psychiatry. The mental hospital has fallen in disfavor and the tranquilizer-resistant chronic schizophrenic has been given up as therapeutically lost.

Although it seems unlikely that this trend will change in the near future, there is no reason to adopt the value system embodied within it as professionally appropriate. It is true that the work with the hard-core chronic schizophrenic is exceedingly demanding and arduous, but this does not mean that the work should not be done or that it is without its compensations. Moreover, the notion that these patients have a hopeless prognosis represents a self-fulfilling prophesy; it not only justifies the apathy of psychiatric professionals toward these patients but also ensures that no new therapeutic approaches will be tried. Mankind would be in a sorry state if medical scientists had adopted a similar attitude toward such now curable or controllable diseases as pneumonia, tuberculosis, and diabetes. In this regard, what must be emphasized is that the designation of these patients as incurable or hopeless represents more the state of mind of the diagnosing clinician than clinical reality. That little has been done for these patients is more a reflection of lack of ingenuity and persistence of clinicians than the inherent incurability of these patients.

Perhaps the major message I have wished to convey in this book is that all is not so bleak as it may first seem. When traditional psychiatric approaches fail, there is still a considerable amount that can be done to improve the behavior of patients within the hospital or even to help them make a relatively adequate social adjustment outside the hospital. In regard to the exploration of different nontraditional treatment models, this seems essential if for no other reason than to offer hope to those patients who have failed to respond to previous innovative treatment programs. In a sense, each new model serves as a therapeutic filter separating out those patients who respond from those who do not. If some patients sift through one or another of these filters, then different ones may have to be devised. There undoubtedly will be a proportion of patients who, like filterable viruses, cannot be entrapped by currently available treatment approaches. This does not mean that they never can be; rather, it simply indicates that other, more sophisticated and refined filters or treatment models will have to be designed and constructed to do the job.

This optimistic note cannot hide the fact that the treatment picture of chronic schizophrenia is far from complete. Although our treatment programs and studies have helped clarify many vital treatment issues and contributed to the improvement of many patients, they also have pointed up vast areas of clinical ignorance. As long as any treatment model for modifying inpatient behavior is less than able to affect all patients and capable of producing maximal improvement in those it does affect, as long as any predischarge program fails to prepare patients for life outside the hospital or to facilitate the transition of patients from the hospital into society, and as long as any community rehabilitation program does not find means for enhancing the coping abilities and social skills of all patients so that they are capable of a relatively independent existence, for reducing social costs so that they are negligible or for preventing rehospitalization on the part of these patients, the treatment task remains unfinished. Although present treatment approaches permit some degree of success in all these areas, there can be no question that they fall far short of meeting all these goals. This very fact argues for more treatment research and clinical work in order to narrow the gap between what is known and what is unknown and between what can now be done and what remains to be done. This, indeed, represents a formidable challenge to psychiatry, but one worthy of acceptance.

Bibliography

American Psychiatric Association, *Diagnostic and Statistical Manual of Mental Disorders,* 2d
    ed. Washington, D.C.: American Psychiatric Association, 1968.
Atthowe, J. M., Jr., and Drasner, L., Preliminary Report on the Application of Contingent
    Reinforcement Procedures (Token Economy) on a "Chronic" Psychiatric Ward. *J.
    Abn. Psychol.,* 73:37-43, 1968.
Ayllon, T., and Azrin, N. H., The Measurement and Reinforcement of Behavior of
    Psychotics. *J. Exper. Anal. Behav.,* 8:357-383, 1965.
Barton, R., *Institutional Neurosis,* 2d ed. Briston: John Wright, 1966.
Braginsky, B. M., Gross, M., and Ring, K., Controlling Outcomes Through Impression-
    Management. *J. Consult. Psychol.,* 30:295-300, 1966.
Brown, G. W., Bone, M., Dalison, B., and Wing, J. D., *Schizophrenia and Social Care.*
    London: Oxford University Press, 1966.
Carnegie, D., *How to Stop Worrying and Start Living.* New York: Pocket Books, 1965.
Coué, E., *Self-Mastery Through Conscious Autosuggestion.* New York: American Library
    Service, 1922.

Ellenberger, H. F., Zoological Garden and Mental Hospital. *Canad. Psychiat. Assoc. J.,* 5:136-149, 1960.

Fairweather, G. W. (ed.), *Social Psychology in Treating Mental Illness: An Experimental Approach.* New York: Wiley, 1964.

Fairweather, G. W., Sanders, D. H., Maynard, H., and Cressler, D. L., *Community Life for the Mentally Ill: An Alternative to Institutional Care.* New York: Aldine, 1970.

Fontana, A. F., et al., Presentation of Self in Mental Illness, mimeographed copy, n.d.

Fontana, F. F., and Klein, E. B., Self-Presentation and the Schizophrenic "Deficit," mimeographed copy, n.d.

Frank, J. D., *Persuasion and Healing.* Baltimore: Johns Hopkins Press, 1961.

Garmezy, N., The Prediction of Performance in Schizophrenia. *In* P. Hoch and J. Zubin (eds.), *Psychopathology of Schizophrenia.* New York: Grune and Stratton, 1966.

Gericke, D. L., Practical Use of Operant Conditioning Procedures in a Mental Hospital. *Psychiat. Stud. Proj.* 3:5, 1965.

Glasser, W., *Reality Therapy.* New York: Harper & Row, 1965.

Goffman, E., *Asylums.* Chicago: Aldine, 1961.

Goldstein, A. P., Heller, F., and Sechrest, L. B., *Psychotherapy and the Psychology of Behavior Change.* New York: Wiley, 1966.

Goldstein, K., *The Organism.* New York: American Book, 1939.

Gordon, H. L., and Groth, L., Mental Patients Wanting To Stay in the Hospital. *Arch. Gen. Psychiat.,* 4:124-130, 1961.

Grad, J., and Sainsbury, P., Evaluating the Community Psychiatric Service in Chichester: Results. *Milbank Mem. Fund Quart.,* 44(1): and pt. 2, January 1966.

Greunberg, E. M., and Zusman, J., The Natural History of Schizophrenia. *Int. Psychiat. Clinics,* 1:699, 1964.

Haley, J., The Art of Being Schizophrenic. *Voices,* 1:133-147, 1965.

Hunter, M., Schooler, C., and Spohn, H. E., The Measurement of Characteristic Patterns of Ward Behavior in Chronic Schizophrenics. *J. Consult. Psychol.,* 26:69-72, 1962.

Issac, D. M., and Lafave, H. G., An Evaluation-Incentive System for Chronic Psychotics. *Psychiat. Quart., Suppl.,* 38:33-47, 1964.

Jacobson, E., *Progressive Relaxation,* Chicago: University of Chicago Press, 1938.

Kantor, D., and Gelineau, V. A., Making Chronic Schizophrenics. *Ment. Hyg.,* 53:54-666, 1969.

Kaufer, F. H., and Phillips, J. S., Behavior Therapy: A Panacea for All Ills or a Passing Fancy? *Arch. Gen. Psychiat.,* 15:114-128, 1966.

Katz, M. M., A Phenomenological Typology of Schizophrenia. *In* M. M. Katz, J. O. Cole, and W. E. Barton (eds.), *The Role and Methodology of Classification in Psychiatry and Psychopathology.* Washington, D.C.: Government Printing Office, 1965.

Kellam, S. G., Goldberg, S. C., and Schooler, N. R., Berman, A., and Shmelzer, J. L., Ward Atmosphere and Outcome of Treatment of Acute Schizophrenia. *J. Psychiat. Res.,* 5:145-163, 1967.

Kiev, A., *Magic, Faith and Healing.* New York: Free Press of Glencoe, 1964.

LaBarre, W., *They Shall Take Up Serpents.* Minneapolis: University of Minnesota Press, 1962.

Lang, P., and Buss, A. H., Psychological Deficit in Schizophrenia: II. Interference and Activation. *J. Abn. Psychol.,* 70:77, 1965.

Lesse, S., Placebo Reactions in Psychotherapy. *Dis. Nerv. Syst.,* 23:313, 1962.

Lucero, R. J., and Vail, D. J., Public Policy and Public Responsibility. *Hosp. Commun. Psychiat.*, 19:232, 1968.

Lucero, R. J., Vail, D. J., and Scherber, J., Regulating Operant-Conditioning Programs. *Hosp. Commun. Psychiat.*, 19:53-54, 1968.

Ludwig, A. M., An Historical Survey of the Early Roots of Mesmerism. *Int. J. Clin. Exp. Hypn.*, 12:205, 1964.

Ludwig, A. M., Altered States of Consciousness. *Arch. Gen. Psychiat.*, 15:225, 1966. (a)

Ludwig, A. M., The Formal Characteristics of Therapeutic Insight. *Amer. J. Psychother.*, 20:305-318, 1966. (b)

Ludwig, A. M., The Influence of Non-specific Healing Techniques with Chronic Schizophrenics. *Amer. J. Psychother.*, 22:382-404, 1968.

Ludwig, A. M., and Farrelly, F., The Code of Chronicity. *Arch. Gen. Psychiat.*, 15:562-568, 1966.

Ludwig, A. M., and Farrelly, F., The Weapons of Insanity. *Amer. J. Psychother.*, 21:737-749, 1967.

Ludwig, A. M., and Marx, A. J., Influencing Techniques of Chronic Schizophrenics. *Arch. Gen. Psych.*, 18:681-688, 1968.

Ludwig, A. M., and Marx, A. J., The Buddy Treatment Model for Chronic Schizophrenics. *J. Nerv. Ment. Dis.*, 148:528-541, 1969.

Ludwig, A. M., and Marx, A. J., The Effects of Attention and Structure in the Treatment of Chronic Schizophrenics. *Brit. J. Psychiat.*, April, 1971.

Ludwig, A. M., Marx, A. J., and Hill, P. A., Chronic Schizophrenics as Behavioral Engineers. *J. Nerv. Ment. Dis.*, 152:31-44, 1971.

Ludwig, A. M., Marx, A. J., Hill, P. A., and Browning, R. M., The Control of Violent Behavior Through Faradic Shock. *J. Nerv. Ment. Dis.*, 148:624-637, 1969.

Ludwig, A. M., Marx, A. J., Hill, P. A., and Hermsmeier, G. I., Forced Small Group Responsibility in the Treatment of Chronic Schizophrenics. *Psychiat. Quart.*, 41:262-280, 1967.

Marx, A. J., and Lontz, B., Who's Angry at Whom? The Chronic Schizophrenic, His Parents, and the "State", mimeographed copy, n.d.

Marx, A. J., and Ludwig, A. M., Resurrection of the Families of Chronic Schizophrenic—Clinical and Ethical Issues. *Amer. J. Psychother.*, 23:37-52, 1969.

May, P. R. A., *Treatment of Schizophrenia: A Comparative Study of Five Treatment Methods.* New York: Science House, 1968.

Mechanic, D., Therapeutic Intervention: Issues in the Care of the Mentally Ill. *Amer. J. Orthopsychiat.*, 37:703-717, 1967.

Miller, D. H., Psycho-social Factors in the Aetiology of Disturbed Behavior. *Brit. J. Med. Psychol.*, 34:43-52, 1961.

Myerson, A., Theory and Principles of Total Push in the Treatment of Chronic Schizophrenia. *Amer. J. Psychiat.*, 95:1197-1204, 1939.

O'Conner, N., and Rawnsley, K., Incentive with Paranoid and Non-Paranoid Schizophrenics in a Workshop. *Brit. J. Med. Psychol.*, 32:133, 1959.

Pace, R. E., Situational Therapy. *J. Personality*, 25:578-588, 1957.

Pasamanick, B., Scarpitti, F. R., and Dinitz, S., *Schizophrenia in the Community.* New York: Appleton-Century-Crofts, 1967.

Peale, N. V., *The Power of Positive Thinking.* New York: Prentice-Hall, 1952.

Powers, M., *Mind Power Records*, 78 rpm, 8721 Sunset Blvd., Hollywood, California, n.d.

Premack, D., Toward Empirical Behavior Laws: I. Positive Reinforcement. *Psychol. Rev.*, 66:219-233, 1959.

Risley, T. R., The Effects and Side Effects of Punishing the Autistic Behaviors of a Deviant Child. *J. Appl. Behav. Anal.*, 1:21-34, 1968.

Rowland, H., Interaction Processes in the State Mental Hospital. *Psychiatry*, 1:323-337, 1938.

Sanders, D. H., MacDonald, W. S., and Maynard, H. M., The Effect of Group Composition on Task Performance and Role Differentiation. *In* G. W. Fairweather (ed.), *Social Psychology in Treating Mental Illness: An Experimental Approach*. New York: Wiley, 1964.

Sanders, R., Weinman, B., Smith, R. S., Smith, A., Kenny, J., and Fitzgerald, B. J., Social Treatment of the Male Chronic Mental Patient. *J. Nerv. Ment. Dis.*, 134:244-255, 1962.

Sargant, W., *Battle for the Mind*. London: Heinemann, 1957.

Scheff, T. J., *Being Mentally Ill*. Chicago: Aldine, 1966.

Schindler, J. A., *How To Live 365 Days a Year*. New York: Prentice-Hall, 1954.

Schofield, W., *Psychotherapy: The Purchase of Friendship*. New York: Prentice-Hall, 1964.

Schooler, C., Affiliation Among Schizophrenics: Preferred Characteristics of the Other. *J. Nerv. Ment. Dis.*, 37:438-446, 1963.

Schooler, C., and Lang, J., Affiliation Among Chronic Schizophrenics: Factors Affecting Acceptance of Responsibility for the Fate of Another. *J. Nerv. Ment. Dis.*, 137:173-179, 1963.

Smith, K., Pumphrey, M. W., and Hall, J. C., The "Last Straw": The Decisive Incident Resulting in the Request for Hospitalization in 100 Schizophrenic Patients. *Amer. J. Psychiat.*, 120:228-233, 1963.

Solomon, P., and Glueck, B. C., Jr. (eds.), *Recent Research in Schizophrenia*, Psychiatric Research Reports, no. 19. Washington, D.C.: American Psychiatric Association, 1964.

Stevens, H. A., Use of Human Subjects for Research, International Copenhagen Congress on the Scientific Study of Mental Retardation, Denmark, August 7-14, 1964.

Stone, A. A., and Eldred, S. H., Delusion Formation During the Activation of Chronic Schizophrenic Patients. *Arch. Gen. Psychiat.*, 1:73-75, 1959.

Talbot, E., and Miller, S. C., The Struggle to Create a Sane Society in a Psychiatric Hospital. *Psychiatry*, 29:165-171, 1966.

Talbot, E., Miller, S. C., and White, R. B., Some Antitherapeutic Side Effects of Hospitalization and Psychotherapy. *Psychiatry*, 27:170-176, 1964.

Ullman, L. P., and Krasner, L. (eds.), *Case Studies in Behavior Modification*. New York: Holt, Rinehart & Winston, 1965.

Vail, D. J., *Dehumanization and the Institutional Career*. Springfield, Ill.: Charles C Thomas, 1966.

Venables, P. H., and O'Conner, W. A., A Short Scale for Rating Paranoid Schizophrenia. *J. Ment. Sci.*, 105:815-818, 1959.

Weinstein, M. R., A Program for the Rehabilitation of Socially Disabled Psychiatric Patients Through Retraining. *Comprehen. Psychiat.*, 8:249-264, 1967.

Wing, J. K., Institutionalism in Mental Hospitals. *Brit. J. Soc. Clin. Psychol.*, 1:38-51, 1962.

Wing, J. K., and Freudenberg, R. K., The Response of Severely Ill Chronic Schizophrenic Patients to Social Stimulation, *Amer. J. Psychiat.*, 118:311-322, 1961.

Woodbury, M. A., Milieux, Symptoms, and Schizophrenia: The Seven-Year History and Evolution of a Psychiatric Ward. *In* P. Solomon and B. C. Glueck, Jr. (eds.), *Recent Research on Schizophrenia*, Psychiatric Research Reports, no. 19. Washington, D.C.: American Psychiatric Association, 1964.

Zarlock, S. P., Social Expectations, Language, and Schizophrenia. *J. Human. Psychol.*, 6:68-74, 1966.

Index

M